Holland on the Hudson

Holland on the Hudson

AN ECONOMIC AND SOCIAL
HISTORY OF DUTCH NEW YORK

Oliver A. Rink

Cornell University Press

ITHACA AND LONDON

New York State Historical Association

COOPERSTOWN, NEW YORK

International Standard Book Number 0-8014-1866-6
Library of Congress Catalog Card Number 86-2317
Printed in the United States of America
*Librarians: Library of Congress cataloging information
appears on the last page of the book.*

*The paper in this book is acid-free and meets the guidelines for
permanence and durability of the Committee on Production
Guidelines for Book Longevity of the Council on Library Resources.*

Epigraph: Fitzgerald, F. Scott, quoted from *The Great Gatsby*. Copyright 1925 Charles Scribner Sons; copyright 1953 Frances Scott Fitzgerald Lanahan. Reprinted with the permission of Charles Scribner's Sons, and reprinted by permission of the Bodley Head from *The Bodley Head Scott Fitzgerald*, vol. 1.

For Marsha, Diane,
David, and Gary

And as the moon rose higher the inessential houses began to melt away until gradually I became aware of the old island here that flowered once for Dutch sailors' eyes—a fresh, green breast of the new world. Its vanished trees, the trees that had made way for Gatsby's house, had once pandered in whispers to the last and greatest of all human dreams; for a transitory enchanted moment man must have held his breath in the presence of this continent, compelled into an aesthetic contemplation he neither understood nor desired, face to face for the last time in history with something commensurate to his capacity for wonder.

—F. Scott Fitzgerald, *The Great Gatsby*

Contents

Maps and Illustrations

Acknowledgments

I have received many kindnesses and incurred many debts during the research and writing of this book. My oldest debts are to John A. Schutz, of the University of Southern California, who supported my decision to study New Netherland and advised me to consider the comparison with English examples of colonialism in New England and Virginia. John E. Wills, Jr., sent me off to find out more about New Netherland when he became intrigued with the paucity of comparative history on Dutch colonialism in Asia and in the Western Hemisphere. He then served as my first tutor in seventeenth-century Dutch. To the late Simon Hart, director of the Gemeentelijke Archief van Amsterdam, whose critical knowledge of Amsterdam's maritime history helped shape my thoughts on the history of Dutch colonialism in America, I owe a special debt. His suggestion that I find what he liked to call the "thread of profit" in the complex business relationships of the Amsterdam merchants led me to reconsider the historiographical perspective that I believe has restricted studies of New Netherland for too long.

Many others have taken time out of their busy careers to help me with a problem of scholarship or simply to discuss the history of New Netherland. Jan Willem Schulte-Nordholt, of Leiden University, graciously discussed his views on New Netherland's tragic history and encouraged me to work toward a larger, "imperial" view of the colony. He also suggested the quotation from F. Scott Fitzgerald's *The Great Gatsby* that serves as an epigraph to the book. Wendell Tripp, editor of *New York History*, has been unfailing in offering advice and assistance in bringing the findings of my research to print. Stefan Bielinski and the staff of the New York History Seminar have extended innumerable courtesies to me during my stays in Albany. Charles Gehring, director of the New Netherland Project, has kindly read most of what I have written about New Netherland, including a draft version of this book. He has been a sound critic and a constant source of encouragement. Robert C. Ritchie has been a good friend whose persistent asking after the manuscript finally chided me into completing it. Milton Klein, my first critic on a paper done some ten years ago, has continued to offer support and counsel. His pathbreaking article on the importance of New York and the middle colonies as a microcosm for early American history has had a profound influence on my approach to the history of New Netherland. I join many other scholars in thanking Professor Klein for making the colonial history of New York an honorable field of study for a historian.

I have enjoyed the support of colleagues and friends at California State College, Bakersfield, who whether they know it or not have contributed in important ways to this book. Philip M. Rice, the academic vice-president, allowed me time to pursue my scholarship by creatively arranging for release time from classes and encouraging my efforts to do research in a teaching institution. John R. Coash, dean of arts and sciences, has been exceedingly generous with travel money and sympathetic when my research took me away from my duties as chair of the department. Special thanks must also go to Victor Lasseter, Ray Geigle, Jeanne Harrie, Gerald Stanley, and Hugh Graham, who were always ready with words of encouragement when I needed them.

I have long realized the importance of librarians and archivists, and I have long imposed upon their goodwill beyond the gratitude I can convey here. Yet special thanks are tendered to the staff of the Huntington Library and Art Gallery of San Marino, California, especially resident scholar Leland H. Carlson, who has been a delightful fountain of knowledge and a good friend for many years. I wish also to thank the staffs of the Algemeen Rijksarchief and the Gemeentelijke Archief van Amsterdam, as well as the staff and librarians of the University of Southern California and California State College, Bakersfield.

My wife, Marsha, and my children, Diane, David, and Gary, have provided a loving home and numerous diversions from the tedium of college teaching and the drudgery of scholarship.

The research for this book was partially funded by grants from

Acknowledgments

the Haynes Foundation, the Office of Research and Sponsored Programs of California State College, Bakersfield, and the Honors and Awards Committee of the School of Arts and Sciences of California State College, Bakersfield. Portions of chapters 4, 5, and 6 have appeared as articles in *New York History* and appear here with the permission of the New York State Historical Association. The staff of the New Netherland Project and the New York State Library and Museum were most courteous in helping me choose the illustrations. James Corsaro assisted in selecting maps from the rich collections, and Craig Williams of the New York State Museum prepared the photographs. Barbara Tisler helped me read page proofs and assisted in the final preparation of the book. I wish to express a special note of thanks to the New York State Historical Association for its selection of *Holland on the Hudson* as the winner of the 1984 manuscript award. And finally, I am especially pleased that Cornell University Press is copublishing this book with the New York State Historical Association.

OLIVER A. RINK

Bakersfield, California

Chronology

1602   Founding of the Dutch East India Company (Vereenigde Oostindische Compagnie, or VOC).

1609   Henry Hudson, sailing for the VOC, discovers the region soon to be named New Netherland.

1614   New Netherland Company chartered by a cartel of Amsterdam merchants to exploit the fur trade.

1621   Founding of the Dutch West India Company (Westindische Compagnie).

1624   About thirty families of French-speaking Walloons arrive as first permanent European settlers in New Netherland.

1626   Manhattan Island purchased by Pieter Minuit for 60 florins.

1628   First Patroonship plan is approved by the West India Company, but it attracts no investors because the fur trade remains a company monopoly.

1629   Second Patroonship plan approved; it allows patroons to engage in the fur and fish trade.

1630   Kiliaen van Rensselaer founds the patroonship of Rensselaerswyck.

1633   Wouter van Twiller arrives as governor-general.

1638   Willem Kieft succeeds van Twiller, who is dismissed amid charges of alcoholism and incompetence.

1639   West India Company abandons the fur trade monopoly and offers new incentives for colonists, including two hundred acres of land for each head of a household.

1641   Heads of families in New Amsterdam choose a Council of Twelve Men to advise the governor-general.

1643–45   Indian wars, caused by Willem Kieft's attempts to tax the Indian fur trade and to exact reprisals for Indian atrocities against European settlers.

[13]

1647   Director-General Pieter Stuyvesant assumes command at New Amsterdam.

1650   Treaty of Hartford establishes boundaries between New Netherland and New England; Dutch lose claim to eastern Long Island and Connecticut River valley. Large numbers of English colonists begin settling in New Netherland, especially on Long Island.

1652   Outbreak of First Anglo-Dutch War.

1653   New Amsterdam receives a municipal charter and government.

1654   New Netherland is threatened with invasion from New England but is saved when word reaches America of the Treaty of Westminster, ending the First Anglo-Dutch War.

1655   Indian War. The so-called Peach Tree War erupts while Stuyvesant is away leading a military expedition against New Sweden on the Delaware River. New Sweden is annexed as New Amstel, and the Indians are put down in a series of bloody battles.

1659–60   Indian War. First Esopus War engulfs central Hudson Valley.

1663   Second Esopus War. Undeclared Anglo-Dutch naval war in the Atlantic.

1664   English fleet under Colonel Richard Nicolls forces the surrender of New Netherland. New Netherland becomes New York.

1665–67   Second Anglo-Dutch War legalizes capture of New Netherland.

1672   Outbreak of Third Anglo-Dutch War.

1673   Dutch recapture New Netherland and hold it for fifteen months. New York is restored to the English in November 1674 by the Second Treaty of Westminster.

Holland on the Hudson

Introduction

Holland in the seventeenth century experienced a rapid growth of wealth, an urbanization of life, and an explosion of mercantile activity unprecedented in a history rich with achievement. The political patchwork of the Union of Utrecht, formulated as a last-ditch effort to assert the Netherlands' independence from Spain, was forged by war into something resembling a nation-state. Nowhere in the United Provinces were the centripetal forces of war and trade more evident than in Holland's commercial capital on the Zuider Zee.

Amsterdam, a city of more than 150,000 people, sprawled along the Amstel, her partially completed canals expanding in concentric half-circles toward the polders of the hinterland. The city was vibrant with activity. In the warehouse district, the treasures of a maritime empire awaited shipment to ports throughout Europe. In the stately homes along the Heerengracht, merchants sat over glasses of French wine contemplating new schemes for profit. The times were exciting, almost intoxicating. A leisurely stroll across the huge square in front of the Stadhuys was sure to excite the imagination of even the dourest burgher. Everywhere people talked of new colonies, great adventures, and the astounding success of Dutch commercial enterprise. Fortunes were being made and lost daily on the exchange, and the fever of speculation infected the city's business life. An era of spectacular national success and prosperity seemed to be unfolding. Under the glorious mantle of rebellion and liberation, the United Provinces fought the Hapsburgs, defied the pope, surpassed all of Europe in trade, and for a brief moment seized a place among the great powers of the Continent.

The glory was intense and the rewards magnificent. For Dutch historians, the age has long been known as *de goude eeuw*, the golden century. Yet the age was not one of gold, but of ships and seas, tar and masts, glory and God, and above all greed and guilders. Ultimately it was the greed of Dutch merchants, coupled with their phenomenal success in devising schemes for profits, that gave to the age the misnomer of gold. And although the expansive Dutch maritime empire supported the merchant princes in their relentless quest of Mammon, the empire never developed the territorial commitment usually associated with the empires of Holland's chief rivals for imperial splendor.

It was an unusual empire by seventeenth-century standards, and its success owed more to the laxity of Dutch imperialism than to a strict adherence to principles of mercantilism. This was truer of the West India Company's operations in North and South America than it was of the far more lucrative operations in Asia under the management of the United East India Company. Company charters notwithstanding, the empire remained a trade network in which private merchants from the fatherland could and did exercise decisive control over the movement of goods and people. The empire thrived largely because the Dutch merchant marine could harvest colonial products more efficiently and at a lower cost than its English, French, and Iberian competitors. The Dutch preeminence in shipping, warehousing, currency exchange, marine insurance, and credit financing was a constant source of envy and irritation for merchants in other countries. Indeed, the mercantilistic legislation that poured forth from the governments of France and England in the last half of the seventeenth century was, in part, a response to the supremacy of the Dutch carrying trade and the aggressiveness of Dutch merchants in pursuing profits in their empires.

In North America the West India Company's colony of New Netherland survived for a half-century, buffeted by recurrent waves of monopoly legislation only to be saved time and again by the inability first of the Company then of the English to enforce the laws and regulations that sought to close the various loopholes in the mercantilist system. More than anything else, it was the ability of Dutch private merchants to circumvent both the Company monopoly and the English laws of trade and navigation which made New Netherland a successful outpost of Dutch capitalism.

Between 1609 and 1664 New Netherland attracted the Amsterdam merchants. Their interest in turn helped focus national attention on the potential profits in furs. At first only small traders were willing to seek out their fortunes along the shores of the distant colony. Their activity represented the first steps in establishing a vast shipping and commercial system that would be developed, nurtured, and ultimately exploited by the powerful merchant syndicates in Amsterdam. In the course of working out the commercial relationship between the colony and the fatherland, as well as the clandestine trade with the English colonies to the north and south of Manhattan Island, New Netherland became home for thousands of Dutch subjects, a surprising percentage of whom were foreigners from all over Europe. Elsewhere in Holland's vast maritime empire much the same pattern prevailed, and with increasing frequency as the seventeenth century gave way to the eighteenth. This unique colonial history was characterized by an initially limited financial commitment, followed by the increasing involvement of private capitalists in the supposedly closed colonial system. Territorial concerns, which eventually came to dominate policy formulation for the empire, became important only after the failure of the company monopolies had prepared the way for the intrusion of private merchants into the colonial trade. The Dutch experience in New Netherland may serve as a case study, constituting both a unique chapter in America's colonial history and a small but significant episode in the history of the Dutch maritime empire. The history of New Netherland thus provides an exceedingly rich variety of issues for the analysis of colonialism in a non-English context. Moreover, because New Netherland's demise marked the beginning of the history of the colony and state of New York, the Dutch antecedents to English colonialism in this important colony must be understood if our portrait of colonial America is to reflect the variety of contending ethnic and linguistic groups that struggled for recognition in the early years of the American melting pot.

This book seeks to tell the history of New Netherland from a unique perspective. The commercial success rather than the political failure of the colony will be the main focus of the analysis. The traditional emphasis on the West India Company's adminstration of New Netherland will receive proportionately less attention than the role of the private merchants of Amsterdam, who, it will be argued, controlled the transoceanic exchange of goods and influenced the colony's history in ways never before revealed. The underlying assumption of this investigation is that the growth and development of New Netherland was largely the product of those forces responsible for the growth and development of Holland's maritime empire as a whole. These forces, furthermore, served to direct the course of New Netherland's fortunes away from the paradigm that historians have come to associate with the evolution of European colonialism in North America. This approach differs from previous scholarship on New Netherland because new sources have provided an opportunity to reinterpret the history of the colony.

The notarial records of the city of Amsterdam offer a treasure of information on the commercial activities of Dutch merchants who traded with New Netherland. Used for the first time here, this information provides answers to new questions about the relative role of trade and commerce in the fifty-four-year history of the colony. Less directly, the notarial records shed light on the nature of immigration to the colony as well as the ratio of men to women, families to single adults, servants to free persons, and farmers to other occupations. When examined in the context of the so-called "new social history" such data permit a reappraisal of New Netherland. More important, the notarial records expose the underside of New Netherland's history, a history that can now be seen as one that had its own dynamic character and unfolded outside and in some cases in opposition to the history of the West India Company's on again–off again administration of the colony.

The focus is necessarily narrow. The aim is to achieve a firmer understanding of New Netherland as an outpost of a peculiar form of European colonialism. Therefore, it is the central thesis of this book that the merchants of Amsterdam exercised an important economic influence in the affairs of New Netherland. Whether serving within the West India Company as directors, principal shareholders, or both, or operating outside the Company's authority, the merchants of Amsterdam held the vital lifelines that connected the colony to the fatherland. From the earliest years of Dutch exploration and trade with the region it was the Amsterdam merchants who recognized the potential for profit. Throughout New Netherland's half-century of existence these merchants, by hook and many times by crook, succeeded in establishing the colony as the most successful colonial entrepôt for the cirvumvention of the Company charter and the much-heralded English laws of trade and navigation. The merchants succeeded where the Company had failed. In fact, the failure of the mighty Company was brought on, at least in part, by the very Amsterdam merchants who would, by 1650 if not before, dominate the relationship between the colony of New Netherland and the United Provinces.

In the colony of New Netherland, the settlers experienced the classic effects of colonialism. Prices for European goods remained high, while the exchange rate for furs, the one easily marketable "cash crop" available to all New Netherlanders, was set by market conditions and transportation costs in Amsterdam. The Amsterdam merchants reaped the profits of this colonial relationship, even when the West India Company teetered on the brink of bankruptcy. The history of New Netherland must, therefore, be interpreted in the light of these conditions.

Such an interpretation requires the abandonment of the traditional preoccupation with the history of the West India Company's adminstration of New Netherland. This preoccupation was the product of nineteenth-century historiography and the prevailing "whig" school of interpretation, which viewed all colonial history as a prelude to the American Revolution. In the case of New Netherland the whig view has had a stifling effect on scholarship. The ignominious fall of the colony to an English fleet in 1664 and the spectacular success of New York served as object lessons to historians searching for clues to the American willingness to defend the cause of liberty against tyranny. Enamored with the astounding history of Anglo-American culture, nineteenth-century historians shied away from studying non-English examples of colonization. Moreover, the period of Dutch rule in New Netherland coincided generally with the heroic first years of colonization in Virginia and New England. When historians finally came to study New Netherland in the late nineteenth century, the moralizing emphasis was strong. John Fiske's summary of New Netherland's shortcomings as a self-governing colony is an example:

> It [the government of New Netherland] was not government of the people, by the people, and for the people; but it was government of the people, by the Director and Council, for the West India Company. The 300 inhabitants of New Amsterdam, in 1628, lived com-

pactly enough to hold town meetings, yet there was nothing of the sort. At that same time the 300 inhabitants of Plymouth made laws for themselves in a primary assembly and elected their governor; while the 4,000 inhabitants of Virginia, distributed in a dozen communities, had their elected house of representatives, without whose consent the governor appointed by the Crown could not raise so much as a penny by taxation.[1]

The pioneers in New Netherland historiography, John Romeyn Brodhead and Edmund B. O'Callaghan, though less vitriolic than Fiske in their denunciation of Dutch rule, were nonetheless equally prone to view the last years of the colony's existence as ones in which the struggle between the forces of liberty and tryanny determined New Netherland's fate. For Brodhead and O'Callaghan, and thus for at least a generation of historians, the surrender of New Netherland symbolized more than a military conquest—it symbolized the triumph of Anglo-American culture. Pieter Stuyvesant and his predecessors became tyrants, their careers examples of the age-old failure of tyranny to overcome the forces of liberty, and the failure of the Dutch colony a moral lesson anticipating the great struggle of the American Revolution.[2]

Even the more recent attempts to come to grips with New Netherland's history have gone no further than a reexamination of existing sources with an eye toward proving or disproving the hypothesis that blames the colony's failure on shortsighted Company management, incompetent leadership, and faulty cost accounting.[3] The vitality of New Netherland's commerce and the ebb and flow of its settlement have been neglected or left to the imaginations of readers who can find the grains of truth embedded in the whimsical tales of Washington Irving. The economic history of New Netherland, as revealed in the notarial records of Amsterdam, suggests a

1. John Fiske, *The Dutch and Quaker Colonies in America*, 2 vols. (Boston, 1899), 1:153.
2. John Romeyn Brodhead, *History of the State of New York*, 2 vols. (New York, 1853–71); Edmund B. O'Callaghan, *The History of New Netherland; or, New York under the Dutch*, 2 vols. (New York, 1845–48).
3. Thomas J. Condon, *New York Beginnings: The Commercial Origins of New Netherland* (New York, 1968); Van Cleaf Bachman, *Peltries or Plantations: The Economic Policies of the Dutch West India Company in New Netherland, 1623–1639* (Baltimore, 1969).

more vital portrait of the colony. Throughout its brief history, the Dutch colony depended on a relatively few Amsterdam merchants to conduct its trade and wage its political battles in the chambers of the West India Company and in the halls of government at The Hague. The Amsterdam merchants controlled the transoceanic trade, set prices for European goods in the colony, and recruited colonists for New Netherland. They also garnered the profits from a colonial relationship that was essentially exploitive of the colonists, who bore most of the financial burdens of settlement. The financial weakness of the West India Company was a constant throughout the colony's history, and this weakness contributed to the rise of the Amsterdam merchants. Thus New Netherland may be considered a successful experiment in private colonialism under the auspices of a chartered monopoly. It is the contrast between the success of New Netherland as an outpost of Dutch private capitalism and its failure as a company monopoly that makes the history of the colony a unique chapter in America's colonial past.

[1]

Businessmen, Seafarers, and Fur Traders

The land is the finest for cultivation that I have ever in my life set foot upon, and it also abounds in trees of every description. The natives are a very good people; for when they saw that I would not remain, they supposed that I was afraid of their bows, and taking the arrows, they broke them in pieces, and threw them into the fire.

—Johannes de Laet, *Nieuwe Wereldt,* 1625

So wrote Henry Hudson of an encounter with the Indians in the river valley that would bear his name. The year was 1609, and the stretch of North American coastline soon to be called New Netherland was an unexplored wilderness teeming with fur-bearing animals. The English explorer had arrived in the new land as much by accident as by design. His battered vessel, the *Halve Maen,* flew the flag of the Dutch East India Company. He was five thousand miles off course.

Hudson was already famous as an explorer of the Arctic before he hired on with the Vereenigde Oostindische Compagnie (usually referred to as the VOC) to make his third attempt to find a northeast, all-water route to Asia. Little information of his early life has survived the ravages of time. A Henry Hudson was listed as an alderman in London in the last half of the sixteenth century. Scholars have generally agreed that he was the grandfather of the navigator. The Hudson family, probably the grandfather and father, were involved in the activities of the Muscovy Company, which had been chartered in 1555 to trade with Russia. It is highly probable that the younger Henry received his seamanship training in the employ of the same company, in the course of which he became an expert sailor and navigator in northern waters. Later evidence suggests that Henry Hudson was an avid student of exploration. He was certainly familiar with the voyages of John and Sebastian Cabot, as well as those of the Dutchman Willem Barents, whose route to the Arctic in quest of the northeast passage he would attempt to retrace. In 1607 he made his first voyage of exploration.[1]

Hudson skippered a small ship of the English Muscovy Company on a harrowing voyage into the northern waters of the Arctic. His purpose was revealed in the first passage of the ship's log: "to goe to sea . . . for to discover a passage by the North Pole to Japan and China."[2] This bold plan was not the same scheme that would later drive him to seek a northeast passage along the route pioneered by Willem Barents. Indeed, Hudson was not seeking a northeast passage in 1607 because he believed that the Orient could be reached by a direct polar crossing. Numerous reports from other expeditions had told of twenty-four-hour days, warm temperatures, and ice-free straits far above the northern cape of Norway, confirming Hudson's belief that an all-water route lay directly across the pole. The theory was dashed when the progress of the ship was halted by a wall of ice near the northern tip of Spitzbergen. The voyage was not without its accomplishments, however, for Hudson and his crew sailed farther north than any previous expedition, and his report of huge whale packs near the southern tip of Spitzbergen sparked interest in the highly lucrative whaling industry. In the following year, he again captained a ship of the Muscovy Company on a voyage in search of the fabled northeast passage. This time the expedition reached Novaya Zemlya before an early Arctic freeze forced him to seek warmer waters.[3] By 1609 the quest for the fabled northeast passage had become an obsession with him. Failing in an effort to solicit financial backers in England, he turned to Holland.

The times were certainly propitious for Hudson. The United Provinces were just completing negotiations with the Spanish Hapsburgs for a twelve-year truce in the half-century-long civil war. Patriotic Dutchmen were excited by the opportunities prom-

1. G. M. Asher, ed., *Henry Hudson the Navigator* (London, 1860), p. lxiii.
2. Ibid., p. 1.
3. Ibid., pp. 23–39.

ised by peace, particularly in the area of maritime commerce. Indeed, Hudson had received an invitation from the principal directors of the VOC, the so-called Heeren XVII, to report on his explorations. Shortly after his arrival in Amsterdam, the directors gathered to listen to Hudson's report but refused to finance another voyage at that time.[4] The directors paid him for his expenses and requested that he return in a year. The Heeren XVII had reason to be skeptical. Although a northeast passage was certainly desirable, if only because of Portuguese opposition along the cape route, its existence was in serious doubt, and its hardships were well known. Hudson's acquaintance with a prominent Dutch theologian and geographer may have been crucial in the decision of the Heeren XVII to rehear his report in the Amsterdam Chamber of the VOC.

The Englishman's reputation had apparently preceded him, for he was welcomed to Amsterdam by Dr. Petrus Plancius, one of the most influential men in Amsterdam and the chief proponent of the existence of an ice-free Arctic passage east of Novaya Zemlya.[5] Years earlier, to prove his theory, Plancius had helped sponsor the third Arctic voyage of Willem Barents. The voyage had ended in tragedy. After a gruesome winter on the ice with the crew near starvation, Barents and his men set out in two open skiffs. Following one of the most famous Arctic voyages in history, the survivors reached Russian territory. They had left behind their ship, crushed in the ice floes of the previous fall, and Captain Barents, dead from exposure and buried at sea in an emotional ceremony from the heaving deck of an open boat. With the death of Barents also died Dutch enthusiasm for a northeast passage.[6] For Petrus Plancius the voyage's failure was a serious blow because his theory had been repudiated. By the end of the first decade of the new century only Henry Hudson continued to risk life and money on the northeast passage, and few other than Petrus Plancius still considered the risk worthwhile. Hudson's arrival in Amsterdam represented the com-

4. Ibid., p. cciii.

5. Ibid., p. cxxxvii; for Petrus Plancius's involvement with the VOC see J. G. van Dillen, *Van Riikdom en Regenten: Handboek tot de Economische en Sociale Geschiedenis van Nederland tiidens de Republiek* (The Hague, 1970), pp. 108–9.

6. Asher, *Henry Hudson*, pp. cxl–cxli; Boies Penrose, *Travel and Discovery in the Renaissance, 1420–1620* (New York, 1962), pp. 216–17.

ing together of possibly the only two knowledgeable men of the day who seriously believed in a northeast passage.

The learned doctor and the English explorer met to discuss the plan even before Hudson had had an opportunity to present his report to the Heeren XVII. The route must have been uppermost in their minds. With so many previous failures arguing against their case, it is conceivable that Hudson or Plancius proposed an alternate route across the North Atlantic in search of the equally famed northwest passage. Hudson was well acquainted with the theories of his contemporary, John Smith, who had recently mapped the North American coast above Virginia, and Plancius may have been aware that Dutch fishing captains had already reached the Grand Banks and were acquainting themselves with the North American coastline below 44 degrees north latitude.[7] In any case, after the cool reception before the Heeren XVII, Hudson and Plancius turned to other sponsors.

Plancius introduced Hudson to the French merchant La Maire, who offered to engage the explorer in the service of the French. Firm plans were never worked out because when rumors began to spread that the famous Englishman was thinking about signing on with the French, a group of merchants in the Amsterdam Chamber of the VOC offered to sponsor Hudson independently if the other chambers refused. Hudson was called back by the Heeren XVII, and it was agreed that he would sail for the company.

Judging from the condition of the *Halve Maen* and its motley crew, the Dutch sponsors were not willing to risk too much on the Englishman's dream. Less than one-third the size of ships that would regularly make the crossing to New Netherland in later years, the vessel was only barely seaworthy, and her crew was to prove a cantankerous lot. She set sail from the Texel on April 6, 1609, plowing through the North Sea on her way to the passage thought to exist just beyond the Barents Sea. Trouble plagued the voyage from the first. The weather deteriorated as the small ship skirted the northern coast of Norway and entered the storm-tossed

---

7. J. Franklin Jameson, ed., *Narratives of New Netherland, 1609–1664* (New York, 1909), p. 6; Michael Kammen, *Colonial New York: A History* (New York, 1975), p. 2.

waters west of Novaya Zemlya. Even before the sighting of the frozen island, the sea had become an impassable wall of ice, and the men were freezing at their stations. The crew threatened mutiny, and Hudson was forced to sail back into the Atlantic. Turning southwest, he headed toward North America.[8]

The North Atlantic crossing was not without its heroics. The crew barely kept the tiny vessel afloat after losing the mainmast in a violent storm off the coast of Iceland, and by the time the expedition reached Newfoundland in July, provisions were low and the makeshift mast was threatening to collapse. Somewhere below 44 degrees, Hudson put ashore for repairs. While the ship's carpenter and crew were felling a tree for a new mast, a small band of local Indians approached the Europeans with the apparent intention of trading. For some reason, trouble erupted. A cryptic account by a Dutch chronicler blamed the crew for behaving "badly towards the people of the country, taking their property by force, out of which there arose quarrels."[9] The account of Robert Juet, crew member on the *Halve Maen*, was clearer: "Then we manned our boat and scute with twelve men and muskets, and two stone pieces or murderers, and drave the savages from their houses, and tooke the spoyle of them, as they would have done of us."[10] Whether this preemptive attack had been provoked by some action on the Indians' part is not known. In any case, circumstances dictated a quick retreat from the area, and when the mast was repaired, Hudson sailed south along the coast. By summer's end the *Halve Maen* had rounded Cape Cod, coming south along the coast to enter Long Island Sound.

It took some time to explore the shores along the sound, sailing into every inlet and river mouth in search of the northwest passage. On September 12, however, the ship turned north into "as fine a river as can be found, wide and deep, with good anchoring ground on both sides." Hudson, convinced that the northwest passage was connected with the river, sailed the *Halve Maen* into the great waterway. Nearly ninety miles upstream, encountering dangerous shallows and no longer able to appease his disgruntled crew, he

8. Asher, *Henry Hudson*, pp. 45–53.
9. Jameson, *Narratives*, p. 7.
10. Asher, *Henry Hudson*, p. 61.

gave up the search. During the voyage upriver, Hudson had had many opportunities to observe the verdant wilderness along the banks. Later accounts in English and Dutch would echo Hudson's description of the land as a virtual paradise with "an abundance of provisions, skins, and furs of martens and foxes, and many other commodities, as birds and fruit, even white and red grapes."[11]

This eventful third voyage is the one for which Hudson is best remembered. Yet it was a bitter failure for the Englishman, who would give his life and that of his son in a voyage in search of the elusive northwest passage in 1610. With Hudson's death the first phase of Arctic exploration ended. The mapmakers would remember him with place names like Hudson's Bay, Hudson's Strait, and perhaps most famous of all the Hudson River. But as with so many great figures in history, Hudson's fame was to come long after his passing. His Dutch employers failed to grasp the significance of his discovery, and the English government confiscated his ship upon its arrival in Dartmouth. He was imprisoned for a short time, and His Majesty's government filed a formal protest with the Dutch ambassador.

Hudson's arrival in England in the waning months of 1609 touched off a storm of controversy. News of his discoveries reached Amsterdam with members of the Dutch crew. The Heeren XVII ordered Hudson to report directly to them and lodged a counterprotest with the English government, petitioning for the release of the ship and her captain under the laws of the sea.[12] The government of James I viewed Hudson's voyage as a betrayal of the national interest and a violation of an established colonial claim to North America.

The English claim to the area of Hudson's discovery was a point of debate. Although England was never to admit it, the basis for the argument for English sovereignty was that English joint-stock companies had taken advantage of the excessive grants of land in their royal charters to claim an area of the North American coastline that

11. Jameson, *Narratives*, p. 7.

12. The claims and counterclaims have been described in various sources. For Dutch claims see Edmund B. O'Callaghan, *History of New Netherland; or, New York under the Dutch*, 2 vols. (New York, 1845–48), 1:143–54. For English claims see Dorothy Dening, *The Settlement of the Connecticut Towns* (New Haven, 1933), pp. 2–3.

had received virtually no exploration since the voyage of Giovanni da Verrazzano in 1524. Both the London Company in its charter of 1606 and the Plymouth Company in its charter of the same year claimed sovereignty over the unexplored coast between 38 and 42 degrees north latitude. The overlapping claims were to ensure that not a foot of the North American coast from the Chesapeake Bay to the St. Lawrence River could be colonized by any other country. The cogency of such claims, however, was lost on England's rivals. The Dutch and the Swedes, not to mention the Spanish, continued to contest English claims throughout the seventeenth century, and France never fully acquiesced to the English argument until the force of arms in the Seven Years' War crushed the French dream of a North American empire. The English government, moreover, was to demonstrate an amazing flexibility in its claims, as long as the presence of the Dutch on the Hudson did not seriously threaten the English colonies to the north and south and the support of the United Provinces was needed to maintain the Protestant front against popery in Europe. When the Dutch began to replace the Spanish as the chief competitors in the race for empire, English governments from Oliver Cromwell to Charles II would find in the old company charters the justification for wars of colonial conquest. Indeed, the charters would eventually serve to make legitimate the armed seizure of New Netherland in 1664. In 1609, however, Hudson's voyage for the VOC established the Dutch claim to New Netherland. There were many people in the fatherland waiting for such good news. It was, after all, the golden age.

Dutch publicists lost little time in exploiting Hudson's voyage. Johannes de Laet, one of the most widely read popular writers at the time and the author of the immensely popular Dutch adventure-travel series *Nieuwe Wereldt ofte beschrijvinghe van West-Indien* (New World or Descriptions of the West Indies), informed his readers that the land found by Hudson was "a pleasant and fruitful country" well suited in climate and resources "for our people to inhabit." Even the savages seemed tractable: "The natives are well disposed, if they are only well treated; although they are very changeable, and of the same general character as all the savages of the north . . . with mild and proper treatment, and especially by intercourse with Christians, this people might be civilized and brought under better regulation, particularly if a sober and discreet population were brought over and good order preserved."[13] De Laet waxed exuberant when describing the superiority of New Netherland's flora to that of Europe. He noted, for example, that trees, shrubs, and plants that grew "spontaneously" in New Netherland needed but the touch of an experienced hand to yield a "prolific return." Everywhere in this new land grew "various kinds of pulse, especially beans, which have an admirable variety of colors; pumpkins of the finest species, melons, and similar fruits of a useful character; so that nothing is wanting but human industry."[14]

De Laet's description of New Netherland, especially in the later editions of the *Nieuwe Wereldt*, became both a source of accurate information and a compendium of falsehoods. De Laet, a dabbler in botany and pharmacology, received various plant specimens from throughout the Dutch empire. In Leiden University's famed botanical garden he tried without success to raise pumpkins with seeds from New Netherland. The failure of the seeds to germinate only convinced de Laet that New Netherland had a tropical climate, despite persistent complaints from returning sailors and skippers that its winters were more severe than those of Holland. Other writers repeated de Laet's exaggerations verbatim and added nuances of their own until the image of New Netherland came to reflect every Dutchman's midwinter longing for warm weather and clear skies.[15]

Still, the mendacity of the publicists did not excite a mad rush of

---

13. Jameson, *Narratives*, pp. 49–50. In the 1630 edition of *Nieuwe Wereldt*, de Laet inserted a sentence in this paragraph suggesting that the Indians of New Netherland were devil worshipers: "They have no religion whatever, nor any divine worship, but serve the Devil, yet not with such ceremonies as the Africans." These observations were undoubtedly gleaned from disgruntled and angry settlers who were returning to the fatherland in the late 1620s and whose bloody confrontations with the Indians had rendered them less than objective.

14. Ibid., pp. 54–55.

15. Ibid., p. 55. De Laet was less guilty in this respect than other writers, but his constant comparisons of the flora of New Netherland with that of tropical Africa are surprising in light of his well-deserved reputation as a plant specialist. The exaggerations of Dutch writers seemed to increase with time. By the 1660s New Netherland had become a land of milk and honey with a tropical climate that rivaled Jamaica and Barbados. See among other works the anonymous pamphlet *Kort Verhael van Nieuw-Nederlants Gelegenheit, Deughden, Natuurlijke Voorrechten, en bijzondere bequaemheidt . . .* (Amsterdam, 1662).

Dutch citizens to immigrate to the distant colony. Indeed, if the later demographic record of New Netherland is any reflection of the degree to which Dutchmen were convinced by the writers of travel accounts, the work of de Laet and others was wasted. Hudson's northwesterly route across the North Atlantic had to be recovered by later sailors, and it is probable that a Dutch ship's captain named Hendrick Christiaensen actually sailed to the area of Hudson's discovery in 1610 or 1611 by the southern West Indies route.[16] The flurry of excitement which followed immediately upon Hudson's return to England failed to interest the Heeren XVII, who were convinced by Hudson's detention in England and the alarming sounds coming from the English ambassador at The Hague that Hudson's discovery was of little profit to the company. When news of the discovery reached the ears of Amsterdam's merchant community, however, the reaction was much more positive.

The process by which the news of Hudson's third voyage filtered down from the boardroom of the East India Company is not clear. Good news, in any case, traveled on wings of rumor. One can imagine a casual remark being dropped over steaming cups of soup in one of the small cafés bordering the two narrow streets leading to the exchange near the Dam. Hudson's feat would undoubtedly have raised a few eyebrows, especially since he had been in the service of the East India Company. Amsterdam had buzzed with the news of the VOC's recent dividend of 329 percent just months before Hudson's return. News of a possible second opportunity to benefit from the business of colonialism must surely have pricked the interest of merchants seeking new schemes for profit. One of these was the recently arrived Lutheran merchant Arnout Vogels.

Vogels's first attempt to exploit the Hudson River area may have taken place in 1611. In May of that year he chartered the *St. Pieter* in partnership with the Pelgrom brothers, Leonard and Francoys. In the charter contract filed before an Amsterdam notary the ship's destination was listed simply as Terra Nova. The *St. Pieter* was twice the size of Hudson's diminutive *Halve Maen*, and she carried a complement of thirteen men besides her skipper, Cornelis Rijser, and the three supercargoes sent along on behalf of the merchants to

16. Simon Hart, *The Prehistory of the New Netherland Company: Amsterdam Notarial Records of the First Dutch Voyages to the Hudson* (Amsterdam, 1959), p. 19.

supervise trading activities. On board were victuals for a seven-month voyage, but it is only Vogels's prominent participation in numerous later voyages to New Netherland that suggests the 1611 voyage of the *St. Pieter* was the first trading expedition to the area of Hudson's discovery.[17]

Arnout Vogels was simultaneously involved in a scheme to exploit the fur resources of New France as a partner in a French company. Supplying the capital for the outfitting of ships and the purchase of trade goods, Vogels entered into an agreement with two merchants from Rouen. The agreement limited the partnership to an exploitation of the fur trade in the St. Lawrence River region. The terms of the contract specified that all ships were to sail from and return to French ports. Like a gambler hedging his bets, Vogels invested his money in the French venture in the hope that one or the other of his voyages to the New World would turn a guilder. The practice of spreading the financial liabilities of the risky Atlantic trade across a number of enterprises would become characteristic of the Dutch merchants who traded with North America in the seventeenth century. The arrangement with the French was to last five years, but Vogels sold out to his partners long before. By 1613 the New Netherland trade was demanding his time and resources.[18]

In 1612, while still an active partner in the French company, Vogels financed another all-Dutch voyage to the Hudson River area. Nothing is known of this voyage, but it must have been something of a success because no sooner had the *Fortuyn* returned to Amsterdam than she was outfitted immediately for a return crossing in midwinter. The second voyage of the *Fortuyn* proved that secrets could not be kept from competitors. The ship's skipper, Captain Adriaen Block, was on his third voyage to the area. Having sailed with Christiaensen in 1611 as a supercargo, he had earned his own command the following year when he skippered the *Fortuyn* on her maiden voyage in 1612. In the two months before the arrival of competition, Block and his crew conducted a successful trade with groups of Indians who came daily to the riverbanks with their bounty of beaver and otter pelts. In exchange for trinkets, liquor,

17. Ibid., p. 20.
18. Ibid., pp. 15–16.

cloth goods, and firearms, Block obtained a full cargo of furs and
hides. In addition, he dispatched a sloop to explore the coast, perhaps to search for a site suitable for a permanent trading post.
Captain and crew were contemplating a spring crossing to Amsterdam when sails were sighted on the river. The ship was the *Jonge
Tobias*, out of Monnikendam.[19]

The captain of the *Jonge Tobias* was Thijs Volckertsz Mossel. His
arrival on the river signaled the end of the brief period of exclusive
trade enjoyed by Vogels and his partners. No sooner had Mossel
dropped anchor than he sent his supercargo ashore to "spoil" the
trade by offering the Indians twice the price per pelt they had been
offered by Block. Moreover, a crewman aboard the *Jonge Tobias*, a
mulatto from the West Indies identified as Juan Rodrigues, jumped
ship (allegedly with the connivance of Captain Mossel) and fled into
the forest with trade goods consisting of eighty hatchets, some
knives, a musket, and a sword. The dispute among the merchants
sponsoring the two voyages raged for months following the safe
return of both vessels in the fall of 1612. The months spent wrangling with Mossel and his employers forced Vogels and his partners
to reconsider the risks of the trade.

The 1612 expedition had been a financial success for the Vogels
partnership. In a letter written by Francoys Pelgrom shortly after
the *Fortuyn*'s return to Amsterdam, Vogels's chief partner informed
his wife that their investment had paid off: "Further, dearest love, I
cannot help telling you in this letter about the successful arrival of
our ship under master Adriaen Block and our nephew Jan Kin for
which God be praised. Both are in good health and made a good
voyage, yes, a better voyage even than last year."[20]

What Pelgrom failed to tell his wife was that the dispute between
Mossel's and Block's backers was making the rumor mills work
overtime. Soon everyone on the Dam knew that two ships had
traded profitably in America with no opposition from the French or
English. The threat of competition was enough to frighten away
some investors and an invitation to join in the trade for others. For

19. Ibid., pp. 21, 73. The dispute arising from the 1612 confrontation on the
Hudson produced a series of notarial documents in the form of sworn testimony
for use in civil suits. These have been translated and printed by Hart (ibid., pp.
74–77).
20. Ibid., p. 74.

all merchants interested in the fur trade, however, the fear of unrestrained competition was the one overriding concern that demanded a solution if the profits were to keep pace with the high costs of conducting the transatlantic trade.

Competition was particularly worrisome to the first generation of Dutch merchants trading with North America. Long-distance trade in general and the fur trade in particular were high-risk undertakings. As a credit venture with much of the potential profits committed to lenders even before the ships sailed from Amsterdam, the Dutch fur trade was a gamble from its very outset.[21] Competition only made the situation worse by driving up fur prices in New Netherland and flooding the as yet undeveloped market in Europe for New Netherland pelts. The Indians initially benefited from the competition by obtaining higher prices for their pelts. But even this apparent success of the law of supply and demand did not last. Increased competition among Dutchmen led to increased competition among the Indian tribes of the lower Hudson, exacerbating blood feuds already existing, while the trade itself resulted in an armed Indian population increasingly dependent upon the white invader for liquor, cooking utensils, firearms, ammunition, powder, and cloth goods.

To minimize such risks most merchants who traded with New Netherland spread their commercial activities among different trades, as Vogels had done with his French partnership in 1612. Other, more direct methods were employed as well. After 1613 merchants sought to eliminate competition in the trade by merging with competitors in a series of cartel arrangements. In these new associations other merchants emerged to capture Vogels's hitherto unassailed position as the chief trader to New Netherland. One of these was Lambert van Tweenhuysen.

Lambert van Tweenhuysen was a member of the small group of Lutheran merchants of Amsterdam who between 1612 and 1614 came to dominate the trade between the fatherland and the area of Hudson's discovery. Van Tweenhuysen's commercial activities serve as an excellent example of the diversification that was to characterize the affairs of the New Netherland traders. Besides his investment in trading voyages to New Netherland, van

---

21. See Chapter 7.

Tweenhuysen's business included interests in the overland trade with Germany, a soap manufacturing operation in Haarlem, a partnership with some French merchants for the exploitation of the Canadian fur trade, whaling expeditions to Spitzbergen, and a sizable financial investment in the Levant trade.[22] His political connections were no less impressive. He served as a munitions procurer for the States General and as an international arms merchant for foreign governments.[23] He may have been brought into the fur trade by his friend Arnout Vogels, also a Lutheran and a member of the same congregation in Amsterdam. Whatever the circumstances of his initiation into the New Netherland trade, after 1613 he became its leading promoter and most influential merchant. Along with Vogels and the Pelgrom brothers, van Tweenhuysen and his small coterie of traders formed a powerful cartel whose combined wealth and political clout ensured them a dominant role in the trade.

The merchants were held together by more than simply the fear of competition. Each member of the cartel was a successful merchant in his own right. Some were related by blood or marriage to the commercial magnates of Dutch society. The Pelgrom brothers were especially well connected. Francoys's wife, Barbara Springer, was the daughter of one of the most important merchants in Amsterdam. Leonard Pelgrom had succeeded in amassing a sizable fortune in trading schemes to Antwerp, Breslau, Danzig, Seville, San Sebastian, Lisbon, and Constantinople. Hans Hunger, one of the smaller merchants in the cartel, conducted business simultaneously in Germany, France, Sweden, and North Africa.[24]

The members of the cartel had other common interests and backgrounds. They were all exiles from the southern Netherlands, and they were all Lutherans. Their social and religious roots were nearly identical, and their associations formed a series of concentric circles, a web of kinship ties cemented by a common faith and

---

22. Hart, *Prehistory*, pp. 39–41.

23. On May 20, 1620, the States General issued Lambert van Tweenhuysen a passport to enter into the service of the city of Hamburg as an agent for weapons. He was permitted to transport there one hundred thousand fuses and five hundred muskets with bayonets. A month later he received the States General's permission to transport one thousand muskets and four hundred corselet jackets to Hamburg (Algemeen Rijksarchief, De eerste serie registers van ordinaris net-resolutiën van de Staten-Generaal, 3179:247–247v).

24. Hart, *Prehistory*, pp. 41–48.

history. Their common world was that of the Amsterdam *particuliere kooplieden* (private merchant-traders), a world populated by constellations of religious refugees, ethnic and linguistic minorities, and political exiles. In the Amsterdam of the seventeenth century they formed an important thread in the fabric of commercial life.

The role of exiles in the mercantile life of the United Provinces was decisive.[25] Many of the exiles were already successful merchants before they arrived in the north. They brought with them their talents for business and their intricate circles of friends, business associates, and relatives. Frequently, they arrived with large sums of gold and silver because the liberal terms offered by the Duke of Parma to induce the surrender of recalcitrant towns often enabled the refugees to escape to Amsterdam with enough money to set up new businesses or to invest in any of a host of joint-stock ventures available in the city.[26] Like immigrants in all times, they tended to crowd together in their new home with old friends and relatives who had made the trek before. Hence Lutherans from Germany and Flanders, French-speaking Walloons from the border provinces, and Brownists from England were members of socially exclusive congregations. Their children married, and their commercial undertakings were often organized in partnership with friends and relatives of similar origins and interest.

The resulting Dutch merchant community had few ties to a nationalistic conception of the "fatherland." In their dealings with the far-flung Dutch seaborne empire the merchant-traders of Amsterdam would demonstrate precious little respect for the charter rights of joint-stock companies, even those founded as national monopolies. Loyalties existed, to be sure, but they tended to crystallize on the province, town, church, and family. The concept of social mobility was powerfully influenced by the local circumstances in which the merchant-trader found himself. The desire for gain and social standing within the tight circle of one's peers frequently obscured the emerging sense of loyalty to the United Provinces. Colonial trade, even when conducted under the auspices

25. J. G. van Dillen, *Bronnen tot de Geschiedenis van het Bedrijfsleven en het Gildewezen van Amsterdam, 1512–1611* (The Hague, 1929). Van Dillen's monumental study must still serve as the major source for any discussion of the economic life of Amsterdam in the sixteenth century.

26. Violet Barbour, *Capitalism in Amsterdam in the 17th Century* (rpt. Ann Arbor, 1966), p. 23.

of a national joint-stock company, was generally plied in partnership with one's friends and relatives. The New Netherland trade showed this tendency early, and throughout the half-century in which Dutchmen controlled the colony, the merchants who maintained the trade displayed an astounding homogeneity. Hence the New Netherland trade encouraged the consolidation of activities among merchants already tied together by bonds of marriage, religion, and common loyalties.

The van Tweenhuysen cartel moved quickly after Block's return to eliminate competition in the New Netherland trade. Legally the cartel's position was indefensible. Hudson's voyage had established the rights of the East India Company. Van Tweenhuysen and his partners had no better claim to the Hudson River trade than Thijs Mossel's sponsors. The cartel's main hope lay in a plan to deceive the merchant community of Amsterdam into believing the New Netherland trade was unprofitable and risky. Adriaen Block set about spreading the rumor that the recent voyage had been a bust. Simon Willemsz Nooms, an influential merchant interested in the fur trade, met Block outside the exchange in August 1613. He asked the captain about his latest voyage, inquiring whether there was much profit in the new trade. Block answered that it "did not amount to much and was poor work." Nooms feigned surprise that such poor work was being continued, for he was well aware that the cartel was preparing another ship for the trade. Nooms pointed out that other merchants were interested in the trade and that the claim to exclusive rights to the area was by no means unchallenged because "there were still some other countries which wanted to go there." Block became angry and threatened to break off the discussion when Nooms remarked that only a patent from the States General could grant exclusive trade privileges. Block, seizing the opportunity, boasted that his sponsors had already acquired a patent to the area and, if need be, were willing to defend their rights with arms. The discussion ended with Block marching off. News quickly spread across the exchange that the van Tweenhuysen partners had obtained a patent of exclusive trade to the area of Hudson's discovery.[27]

The directors of the VOC were strangely quiet. No attempt was

27. Hart, *Prehistory*, pp. 91–92.

made to pursue the company's rights to the area, and not a single voice was raised to protest the scramble for New Netherland which was taking place among the private merchants of the city. Perhaps the directors had been scared off by the English protests that followed Hudson's return. Certainly a confrontation with England threatened the VOC's operations elsewhere. The grand company's silence contributed to the belief that the North American trade was open to all and encouraged van Tweenhuysen and his partners to pursue their interests by any means available. Block's claim of a patent was one means, but he had overplayed his hand.

The patent held by the van Tweenhuysen cartel was no patent at all. Instead, it was a trade passport issued by the stadholder, Prince Maurice. Such documents had ceased to have any legal validity once the Union of Utrecht had established the States General as the voice of the republic. Stadholder patents were simple documents stating that the enterprise was in accordance with the laws of the United Provinces and that the patentee was authorized to present papers of identification specifying to all strangers he might encounter that he was a citizen of the fatherland. No rights of exclusive trade were implied. Nooms had been correct in stating that only the States General could issue the patent Block was trying to convince him he had. Since the consent of the towns and provinces was needed in the States General, Block's sponsors had little hope of obtaining such a patent.[28]

News of the conversation between Nooms and Block soon reached the ears of Hans Claesz, the principal partner behind the Thijs Mossel voyage. Claesz's partners included several important Amsterdam merchants among whom were Barent Sweers, Arnout van Liebergen, Wessel Schenck, Jan Holscher, and Jacob Bontenos. Like their counterparts in the van Tweenhuysen cartel they had important political connections which they were willing to use when their rights were threatened. Sweers and Bontenos, for example, managed a large marine insurance firm that had dealings with some of the most important overseas traders in the city. They were probably the source of Nooms's information about the van Tweenhuysen cartel's impending voyage to New Netherland. Information was a valuable commodity, and insurance agents were well

28. Ibid., p. 24.

placed to learn about ship outfittings, especially exotic voyages to newly discovered regions. In any case, Block had made no effort to deny that his sponsors were preparing a ship to make the crossing. Hans Claesz and his partners hastened their own plans.[29]

Claesz was not overly concerned with the stadholder patent, but he did realize that such a device, implying government recognition of the van Tweenhuysen cartel's prior rights, could be used later for obtaining the legally binding patent of the States General. A protest was lodged with the stadholder himself, requesting that he reexamine the claims. He did, and after some deliberation, revoked the patent. Both sides now scrambled for lawyers and braced themselves for a court battle.[30] Prince Maurice intervened by directing the quarreling merchants to negotiate their differences for the good of the fatherland. To this end he appointed Dr. Petrus Plancius as arbitrator.

The hearings before Plancius were not amiable. The notarial record of the charges and countercharges extends for pages in the archives, and even the stilted legalese of the Amsterdam notary cannot disguise the rancor both sides brought to the proceedings. The van Tweenhuysen cartel seemed to hold the trump cards. Its members claimed to have been the first to sail to the Hudson River after its discovery; apparently they considered Arnout Vogels's independent undertaking in 1611 part of the cartel's history. As first exploiters of the trade, they claimed to be entitled to a free hand in the trade as a fair return for their investments. The Hans Claesz partners pleaded their case on the basis of fairness and the need to ensure free access to newly discovered lands. They did not wish a monopoly for themselves, only a fair share of the trade. They proposed three possible solutions.

The first proposal merely called for open trade and a pledge of harmony. The van Tweenhuysen partners would have none of it. They demanded that their prior rights of exploitation be recognized. The second proposal offered to share the risks and profits of the trade by the establishment of joint trading posts. Claesz even offered to share the costs of outfitting ships and paying their crews. Van Tweenhuysen refused, for he had plenty of partners already.

29. Ibid., p. 23.
30. Ibid., pp. 23–24.

Finally, Claesz and his partners submitted a third proposal offering to give up the trade altogether, providing that van Tweenhuysen purchase Thijs Mossel's ship and cargo at cost. Claesz also asked for 6,000 fl. in damages, that being the estimated losses incurred in the last voyage as a result of Block's actions.[31]

Plancius could not persuade the two sides to continue their negotiations. The van Tweenhuysen company had rejected the last offer (a generous one considering the shaky claim upon which the van Tweenhuysen case was based) on the grounds that buying out the Hans Claesz partnership would not ensure them against future claims by other competitors. Thus in the fall of 1613 three ships prepared to sail to New Netherland: two for the van Tweenhuysen group and one for Hans Claesz and partners. Shortly before the departure of the *Fortuyn* under the command of Hendrick Christiaensen, the van Tweenhuysen company offered its competitors one-third of the trade in the Hudson River. Christiaensen was to have two-thirds of the trade with one-third going to Thijs Mossel, now commanding the *Nachtegael* for the Claesz partners. The offer did not include Adriaen Block's ship, the *Tijger*, which was scheduled to depart Amsterdam some weeks after the *Fortuyn*. The Claesz company refused to be drawn into the arrangement, preferring to take its chances in New Netherland.[32]

Claesz notified the van Tweenhuysen partners that he would hold them responsible for any injuries or damages resulting from the use of arms in New Netherland. In the meantime, the van Tweenhuysen company filed an affidavit asserting its rights to the fur trade and threatening to sue the Claesz company for any losses that might arise from illegal interference. Both sides appeared to be preparing for a long legal battle, and each group wanted to establish a notarized record of its position before events in New Netherland provided the basis for suits.[33] The van Tweenhuysen company must have expected trouble in New Netherland because in September 1613 Adriaen Block requested naval guns from the Admiralty to arm the *Tijger*. Lambert van Tweenhuysen and Arnout

31. Ibid., p. 78.
32. Ibid., p. 25.
33. Isaac Newton Phelps Stokes, *The Iconography of Manhattan Island, 1498–1909*, 6 vols. (New York, 1928), 6:4–5.

Vogels appeared before an Amsterdam notary to acknowledge receipt of the weapons; their presence left little doubt that Block's warning to Nooms had been no idle threat.[34]

Hendrick Christiaensen arrived first in the Hudson River. He encountered Juan Rodrigues, the alleged runaway from the *Jonge Tobias* from the year before. Rodrigues had been busy making himself welcome among the local Indian tribes. He had acquired a working familiarity with the local tongue and displayed little loyalty to his previous employers, quickly agreeing to sign on with Christiaensen as an interpreter and trader. When Mossel dropped anchor in the river a few weeks later, he was furious to find his deserter working for his competitors.[35]

When Block arrived in the *Tijger* shortly thereafter, Christiaensen and Mossel were deadlocked in their efforts to outbid each other for furs. Block, as commander of the van Tweenhuysen operations, recognized a disastrous situation emerging. Neither ship had a full cargo, and the cost of the trade was rising daily as the Indians allowed the Dutchmen to bid up the price. Block suggested a compromise. He offered to divide the trade with Mossel receiving two-fifths and Christiaensen three-fifths. Block was later to claim that the agreement was meant to apply only to the Hudson River trade. Block had other plans for himself, for he intended to explore the region in search of other promising fur-trading sites. Before he could weigh anchor, however, the agreements began to break down.[36]

Thijs Mossel, perhaps operating under a misunderstanding, prepared to send his supercargo, Hans Hontom, in a sloop through the Hellgat (East River) in March with a cargo of trade goods. His intention was to pursue the fur trade elsewhere while the *Nachtegael* stayed in the Hudson. When news of the expedition reached Jan Kin, Block's supercargo aboard the *Tijger*, Block lodged a protest with Mossel, claiming a violation of the compromise and threatening to scrap the agreement. Negotiations continued as fall lapsed into winter. Neither side seemed willing to concede or compromise. Then, as ice appeared in the Hudson, a fire broke out on board the *Tijger*, and she burned to the waterline.[37]

34. Hart, *Prehistory*, p. 76.
35. Ibid., pp. 26–27.
36. Ibid., p. 27.
37. Ibid., pp. 28, 84.

This loss weakened Block's position, and Mossel naturally pressed hard for concessions. Mossel offered to divide the crews of the two remaining ships, to pay the wages of all those who transferred to the *Nachtegael*, and to accept for this generosity only one-half of the winter's fur trade. Block not only refused Mossel's offer but forbade his crew to board Mossel's ship. Mossel offered to take on the entire crew of the *Tijger* for a proportionately larger share of the trade. Meanwhile, the crews aboard both vessels planned a mutiny.[38]

The mutiny was hatched by members of Block's crew, who were no doubt weary of their captain's endless negotiations. Block was spending much of his time ashore supervising the construction of a ship to replace the lost *Tijger*. The mutineers took advantage of Block's absence by forcing their way aboard the *Nachtegael*, where they quickly seized muskets and forced Mossel and his few remaining loyal crewmen ashore. What followed thereafter remains unclear. Mossel and his backers, the Hans Claesz company, later claimed that Block was involved in the mutiny because most of the mutineers had come from the *Tijger*. Testimony taken in 1615 from a reluctant member of the mutinous crew suggested a different scenario.

The crewman was a twenty-five-year-old seaman named Claes Woutersen, who claimed to have been kidnapped by the mutineers when he tried to assist a wounded member of Mossel's crew to get ashore after an exchange of gunfire aboard the *Nachtegael*. He testified before an Amsterdam notary at the request of Adriaen Block, who was desperately trying to clear his name of the charge leveled by Hans Claesz, Thijs Mossel, and company. Woutersen claimed that the mutineers acted on their own without any help from Adriaen Block. Indeed, Woutersen noted that the mutiny had "happened to the regret, against the will and to the great dissatisfaction of . . . Block, and that the said Block also did his best and used all possible diligence to restore the ship." The mutineers then weighed anchor in the *Nachtegael* and, leaving the others to an uncertain fate, set sail for the West Indies. After a few months in the West Indies the *Nachtegael* returned to the Hudson River, but by that time Block, Mossel, and Christiaensen had found a way to return to Amsterdam. The mutineers then set sail for New-

38. Ibid., p. 28.

foundland, became lost, headed for Spain, and eventually reached Ireland, where they abandoned their ship and, with the exception of Woutersen, disappeared from the pages of history.[39]

The situation the mutineers left behind on the Hudson was desperate. Only Christiaensen's *Fortuyn*, the two sloops from the *Nachtegael*, and the just completed *Onrust* were left. The sloops and the *Onrust* were too small for an ocean crossing, and the *Fortuyn* had little enough room for her own crew. The situation was saved by the arrival of two new competitors from the fatherland.

The newcomers were the ships *Vos* and *Fortuyn*, the former from Amsterdam and the latter from Hoorn. The Amsterdam sponsors of the *Vos* were Jonas Witssen, an influential merchant in the whaling industry, and Block's old antagonist, Simon Willemsz Nooms.[40] The Hoorn company sponsoring the *Fortuyn* included among its shareholders Pieter Clementsz Brouwer, Jan Clementsz Kies, and Cornelis Volckertsen.[41] These two new entrants into the race for the Hudson River fur trade arrived in time to prevent a tragedy, but they exacted a price for their willingness to transport Block and his stranded crew back home.

They demanded and received an equal share in all furs. Block was hardly in a position to argue. The agreement reached stipulated that each company receive one-quarter of the total, even though the majority of the furs had been purchased by Block and his supercargo. In early summer 1614, with full cargoes, the two *Fortuyns* and the *Vos* set sail for Holland, where they arrived after an uneventful crossing in July.[42]

While all of these events were transpiring in New Netherland, van Tweenhuysen and his partners were busy consolidating their position and seeking political support for their exclusive rights. Even before the ships had set sail for Holland, the provincial States of Holland and West Friesland had in March 1614 passed a resolu-

39. Ibid., pp. 97–98.

40. For some time scholars could not confirm that the *Vos* had ever reached New Netherland. Evidence brought to light, however, by S. Muller Fz and Simon Hart not only affirms the presence of the *Vos* in the Hudson, but also presents significant details about the events that took place there in the spring of 1614. See Fz, *De reis van Jan Cornelisz May naar de IJszee en de Amerikaansche kust, 1611–1612* (The Hague, 1909), and Hart, *Prehistory*, p. 31n.

41. Hart, *Prehistory*, p. 31.

42. Fz, *De reis van Jan Cornelisz May*, p. liii.

tion granting to "diverse merchants wishing to discover New Unknown Rivers, Countries, and Places not sought for (nor resorted to) heretofore from these parts," the privilege to make four voyages "to such lands and places from these Countries, exclusive of every other person."[43]

This resolution was, in actuality, no more than a favorable committee report on a petition that had been submitted to the States General three years before.[44] The "diverse merchants" cannot be easily identified, but circumstantial evidence points to the van Tweenhuysen partners. The partners' intentions had always been clear—to acquire a legally binding monopoly ensuring their exclusive rights to the fur trade of New Netherland. That the petition took nearly three years to wind its way through the provincial States of Holland and West Friesland is not surprising considering the byzantine structure of Dutch politics in this period. The first political skirmishes usually took place in the provincial States, and Holland and West Friesland were frequently the first battleground of partisan politics before the sides took up their cudgels for the wars in the national States General. In this case van Tweenhuysen and his partners won the war before the petition reached the States General. A week after the States of Holland and West Friesland had issued their report, the States General approved their actions and issued its own "Resolution of the States General respecting newly discovered Countries."[45]

The States General resolution followed that of Holland and West Friesland in all significant respects. Originally the diverse merchants had asked for the exclusive right to make six voyages after the discovery of new territories. The States General tempered this privilege by permitting only four voyages, "on condition that the Petitioners having completed the first voyage, shall render a pertinent report to their High Mightinesses of their progress and discovery, in order that their High Mightinesses may then adjudge and declare in what time the four voyages shall be made."[46]

Not all delegates in the States General were pleased with the

---

43. John Romeyn Brodhead, comp., Edmund B. O'Callaghan and Berthold Fernow, eds. and trans., *Documents Relative to the Colonial History of the State of New York*, 15 vols. (New York, 1856–87), 1:4; hereafter cited as *DCHNY*.

44. Ibid.

45. Ibid., p. 5.

46. Ibid.

action. The most vocal opposition came from the representatives of Zeeland, who suspected a political maneuver by Amsterdam's merchants to capture the North American fur trade. They argued that such charters could prejudice previous concessions, and they demanded that the resolution be rewritten to protect enterprises already undertaken. The States General responded with a weakly worded line stating that the grant of exclusive trade privileges "shall not prejudice other their High Mightinesses' previous charters and concessions." This provision did not satisfy the suspicious Zeelanders, who requested and received another limitation on the monopoly privileges. The final version provided that "in case two or more Companies shall find out such land or passages in one year, they shall then enjoy this benefit and privilege in common." The Zeelanders remained dissatisfied with the resolution and refused to vote for it, vowing instead "to refer this matter to their principals."[47]

Zeeland's opposition to the resolution in the States General is the most convincing proof that the diverse merchants were Amsterdamers. The traditional rivalry between the towns and provinces was always reflected in the stormy proceedings of the States General, but the rivalry between Zeeland and Holland was by the seventeenth century no longer one of equals. In political power and economic influence the merchants of Amsterdam held the trump in almost every confrontation with the merchants of Middleburg. They dominated the province of Holland and decisively influenced the political direction of the States General on most matters. Zeeland's strategy consisted largely of forming alliances with the other provinces by proclaiming the sinister intentions of the Amsterdam merchant princes. Although Zeeland won few victories in these years, the Middleburgers could always be relied upon to curb the power of the Amsterdam patriciate.

Zeeland's spirited opposition notwithstanding, the action of the States General had the force of law. Less than seven months after the passing of the resolution, there appeared before their High Mightinesses "deputies from the united company of merchants" requesting exclusive trade privileges for four voyages to a region on the North American coast. The united company of merchants sub-

47. Ibid.

mitted with their petition a report justifying their claim and a "figurative map" indicating the geographical limits of their discovery. The report and map were convincing, and that same day the States General issued a "Grant of Exclusive trade." The grant was the first official document to refer to the region as New Netherland. Consequently, once operations commenced in 1615 the united company of merchants began calling themselves the New Netherland Company.[48]

The united company of merchants represented a wide spectrum of Amsterdam's merchant community. The charter listed Gerrit Jacobsz Witssen, former burgomaster of the city, and Jonas Witssen, his brother and legal counsel to the city, first. Simon Morrissen, merchant and owner of a small fleet of merchant vessels, appears to have been a partner of the Witssen brothers for he was listed next. This small group represented financial interests in ships, warehouses, and marine insurance. The Witssen brothers' political connections were undoubtedly used to pilot the initial resolution through the provincial States of Holland and West Friesland. That they occupied a more prominent position on the charter document than Lambert van Tweenhuysen suggests that the once dominant trading partnership had had to pay a price for the Witssen political connection. Also on the charter were the names of Hans Claesz, Barent Sweers, Paulus Pelgrom, and Wessel Schenck. The New Netherland Company thus represented a new coalition of merchants organized to exploit the fur trade of the Hudson River region. This new group included a large segment of the Amsterdam merchant community, even though the Hoorn merchants, Pieter Brouwer, Jan Kies, and Cornelis Volckertssen, were listed as minor partners. Political connections were becoming increasingly important.[49]

The New Netherland Company could not silence all opposition, however. Shortly after the States General had issued the charter to the united company of merchants, Albert Gerritz Ruyl challenged the claim to exclusive trade privileges, arguing that the "newly-discovered land" of New Netherland was known to many. Ruyl

---

48. Ibid., opposite p. 13. For a scholarly discussion of the "figurative map" that appears in *DCHNY*, see F. C. Wieder, *Onderzoek naar de oudste kaarten van de omgeving van New York* (Leiden: E. J. Brill, 1918).

49. Hart, *Prehistory*, pp. 39–69.

had had finanical interests in an expedition to North Amreica before 1614, and he could claim that his rights had been violated in
the exclusive charter issued to the New Netherland Company.
Ruyl's interest in New Netherland dated from his participation in
an expedition of 1612–13 in which he was a nonvoting investor. He
had been excluded from the list of merchants founding the New
Netherland Company, and in 1614 he sought to break the monopoly before the company could begin operations.[50]

The threat posed by Ruyl roused the directors of the New
Netherland Company to action. Within days of Ruyl's public announcement, papers were served on his skipper, Erasmus Pietersz,
forbidding the equipping of his ship for trade in New Netherland.
Ruyl protested this action and filed a notarized statement claiming
that he had equipped his ship before the charter was issued. The
New Netherland Company was bound by the provisions of its
charter to recognize prior concessions (Zeeland's demand) and thus
was forced to buy Ruyl's rights for a cash indemnity.[51]

The New Netherland Company was a modest success in its three
years of operation. The company organized the fur trade through
annual spring voyages and erected a few trading posts in the area.
In addition, numerous voyages of exploration were undertaken,
and geographical knowledge continued to accumulate. Company
agents surveyed and mapped the Delaware coast, Long Island
Sound, the Jersey shore, and the North American coastline as far
south as the Carolinas. In 1616, the Company petitioned for an
exclusive charter to the area around the mouth of the Delaware
River. The States General considered the petition but at the request of the delegates from Zeeland refused to grant the charter.
Meanwhile, plans were afoot to establish a national chartered company to exploit the Western Hemisphere. Modeled after the immensely successful VOC, the West India Company was to super-
sede all previous charters and grants of exclusive trade. When the
New Netherland Company's charter expired in 1618, the directors
made only a halfhearted effort to continue their operations. Between 1618 and 1621 the company sponsored annual voyages but
gave up any effort to exploit the region by establishing permanent

50. Ibid., p. 35 n 2.
51. Stokes, *Iconography*, 4:42.

trading posts. Other merchants entered the trade in these years as the once dominant company broke up into ad hoc partnerships and informal cartels.[52]

The demise of the New Netherland Company did not result in open competition. The former partners continued their dominance of the fur trade. Better financed than other groups of merchants, they had also the advantage of experience. In the numerous charter contracts that were notarized before Amsterdam notaries in these years the familiar names of Lambert van Tweenhuysen, Gerrit Witssen, and Hans Claesz continue to appear with astonishing frequency. Newcomers to the trade seldom embarked upon trading ventures without the backing of members of the former company. Indeed, the united company of merchants would continue to trade successfully in the Hudson until the establishment of the West India Company in the 1620s.[53]

52. Hart, *Prehistory*, pp. 35–38.
53. Ibid.

[2]

The West India Company: An Enfeebled Giant

Among all the wonderous virtues that have been performed in our time by the state of these United Provinces . . . I thought to be very noteworthy the achievement of the chartered West India Company.

—Johannes de Laet, *Iaerlijk Verhael*, 1644

For citizens of the United Provinces, the founding of the Dutch West India Company marked the formal end of private trade in the Western Hemisphere. Nationalists such as Johannes de Laet praised the achievement as a triumph over the incessant political squabbling that had characterized the republic since its inception. More ominously, the founding of the Company signaled the termination of twelve years of peace and a return to the eighty years' war with Hapsburg Spain. Great expectations accompanied the establishment of the national joint-stock company; more money was pledged for its initial capitalization than for the VOC in 1602. Yet much of the optimism was based upon the dream, perhaps crusade, of smiting the Spaniard "beyond the line." If any generalization can be made about an organization as complex as the West India Company, it is that the Company was conceived and designed as an instrument of war.

The charter, which eventually survived the political battles of the States General, was issued in 1621. It reflected the war conditions of the time, and it would serve as a blueprint for military operations in Brazil, West Africa, and the Caribbean in the years ahead. It was a far cry from the original plan, however. One man in particular—Willem Usselinx—had reason to be disappointed, for his twenty-year effort to create a national joint-stock company with jurisdiction over the Western Hemisphere had been disregarded when the delegates sat down in The Hague to draw up the charter. Usselinx had cause to feel betrayed by his countrymen.

Willem Usselinx spent his youth as a trader's apprentice in the great ports of Europe.[1] By his twenty-fourth birthday he had witnessed the arrival of treasure fleets in Seville, watched the offloading of Brazilian sugar in Oporto, chatted with merchants in the Azores, and generally mastered the thousand and one details necessary for success in the expanding trade with the New World. He also spent these years observing the increasing brutality of Spain's efforts to crush the Protestant rebellion in his homeland.

The rebellion of the United Provinces exerted a powerful influence on young Usselinx. Having adopted the new Calvinism sweeping the Netherlands and the cause of the republic against the centralizing tendencies of the expanding Hapsburg monarchy, he was unwelcomed in his native Antwerp. Forced to find a new home, Usselinx fled like many others to Amsterdam. Sketchy accounts of his first years in the city confirm that he prospered more than most. He had immigrated with enough money to permit successful investment in a series of mercantile ventures involving the thriving carrying trade between southern and northern Europe. His knowledge of trade and business and his fluency in the languages of commerce (Spanish, Portuguese, and Italian) undoubtedly assisted him in acquiring contacts and vital information so necessary for success in the wide-open atmosphere of Amsterdam. He was also something of an intellectual, and he quickly entered the small circle surrounding the famed geographer and promoter of Dutch overseas adventures, Petrus Plancius. In the stimulating conversation that must have been commonplace in this group, Usselinx became a firebrand of colonial expansion. He told his listeners that Spain's dominant position on the Continent was the result of her empire, its riches the sustaining force behind her war against the Dutch. The United Provinces were on the brink of greatness that could result not only in the defeat of the popish

---

1. Willem Usselinx's life is chronicled in two works. In English, see J. Franklin Jameson, "Willem Usselinx, Founder of the Dutch and Swedish West India Companies," *Papers of the American Historical Association* 2 (1887). In Dutch, see Catharina Ligtenberg, *Willem Usselinx* (Utrecht, 1914).

Iberians but also in the establishment of a Protestant Dutch empire in the New World. In 1600, encouraged by England's founding of the East India Company and privy to the discussions then under way for the establishing of its Dutch counterpart, Usselinx set his thoughts to paper.

His plan called for a national joint-stock company, subsidized by government subscriptions and private investment, that would challenge the Iberians in the New World.[2] The Iberian would be defeated in his own empire by an ambitious scheme that emphasized colonization by free Dutch citizens and an intense program of Christian education for the American Indians. On farms sturdy Dutch burghers would oversee voluntary Indian workers trained in advanced techniques of European agronomy. Plantings would include the valuable cash crops of the New World such as sugar, but the main thrust of the plan would be toward the creation of a European-style staple agriculture that could support the colonies' population while simultaneously establishing the cultural milieu for the conversion of the savages. In marked contrast to the Iberians, whose empire rested solely on the sword, the Dutch empire would rest on the foundation of goodwill and the irresistible example of Christian virtue. Slavery was to have no place in Usselinx's empire, for it encouraged laziness and debauchery among the masters. Profits from gold and silver were discounted because Usselinx believed America's greatest wealth to be her soil and climate. His dream was of a utopian empire, an agrarian Christian extension of all that was best in Dutch society. This vision would sustain Usselinx's struggle for two decades, which he spent in the attempt to convince merchants, politicians, and a generation of Dutch adventurers that the best hope for success in the race for empire lay in long-term investment in agriculture and a kind, if noblesse oblige, attitude toward the native inhabitants.

Usselinx's plan became the center of a political debate in 1606, when he presented it before the States of Holland. The States appointed a subcommittee to consider the plan and to draft a charter for examination by the entire body. In an unusual move, Usselinx was made an ex-officio member of the subcommittee. Nevertheless, Usselinx's influence was limited. He failed, for ex-

2. Ligtenberg, *Willem Usselinx*, p. 38.

ample, to convince the committee of the need for peaceful, long-term settlement in the New World. The charter that emerged from the committee was markedly different from Usselinx's proposals. The grandiose scheme for Indian conversion and agricultural exploitation was notably absent from the charter, as was the hope of creating an empire based on Christian virtue and voluntary labor. Instead, it called for a national joint-stock company with exclusive rights to trade, colonize, and above all make war in the New World. Disappointed, Usselinx protested the wording of the draft charter and disclaimed responsibility.[3]

Meanwhile, the government at The Hague was negotiating a truce with Spain. The driving force behind the peace initiative was the *raad-pensionaris* (chief advocate) of the province of Holland and the grand old man of Dutch politics, Johan van Oldenbarnevelt. As the leader of the peace party in the States General and spokesman for the most powerful province, van Oldenbarnevelt wielded tremendous political power. His support of the peace initiative doomed any hope of establishing a West India Company in 1606, for such a company was rightly seen as a provocation to Spain.

Spain, exhausted by nearly thirty years of war with her obstinate Dutch subjects, was willing to make concessions in the first decade of the seventeenth century which would have been unthinkable just a few years earlier. Even before the subcommittee of the States of Holland had completed its revision of Usselinx's plan, Spain had taken the first step toward recognizing the independence of the United Provinces. In agreeing to negotiate with the United Provinces "in the capacity of, and as taking [them] for, free lands, provinces, and towns" Spain had virtually guaranteed the birth of a new nation.[4] Van Oldenbarnevelt soothed the arch-Calvinists, bullied the obstinate politicians from the border provinces, and mustered the public opinion of Amsterdam to support his peace plan. In this atmosphere of impending peace and independence, the subcommittee's draft charter for a bellicose West India Company was easily defeated in the States General.

The "hawks" remained determined. Defeated in the States General, they took their case to the people and exploited that soon-to-be

3. Ibid., pp. 20ff.
4. Pieter Geyl, *The Revolt of the Netherlands, 1555–1609* (London, 1958), p. 250.

genre of Dutch popular literature, the political pamphlet. In pamphlet after angry pamphlet the peace party and its leader were attacked by a motley collection of political bedfellows unusual even for Dutch politics. Calvinist ministers, xenophobic provincial politicians, university professors at Leiden, greedy merchants with an eye to the profits of war, and many ordinary folk who had grown up hating the popish enemy were told that peace promised a dark future. Van Oldenbarnevelt was accused of treason for negotiating with Spain while the king's troops still occupied the southern provinces. In this poisoned atmosphere of invective and character assassination, Usselinx's scheme for a West India Company became a weapon of partisan politics.

Willem Usselinx soon became one of the most important voices of the war party. This group saw in the West India Company both a powerful tool for attacking Spain's New World empire and a highly useful political device for attracting the merchant princes of Amsterdam, Rotterdam, and Middleburg to their cause. Usselinx saw the opportunity to resurrect his idea before a national forum of public opinion. He was apparently not averse to using the circumstances to promote his plan, even though he must have known that he was placing his services at the command of a political faction that wanted a war with Spain. His plan for a less bellicose national joint-stock company was clearly not what his new-found allies wanted to hear. Still he persisted, taking up his pen to demonstrate "how necessary, useful and profitable it was for the United Netherlands to maintain freedom of trade with the West Indies."[5] Freedom of trade was already a well-known euphemism that suggested a policy of no peace beyond the line, a policy that not only supported the hawks' cause but could always be turned in debate to suggest a just demand for Dutch rights to overseas trade. Usselinx was careful in his writings not to attack the doves directly. Instead, he couched his ideas in the political jargon of the day and called for a limited truce that would permit the establishment of his beloved West India Company. His efforts were in vain, but the association of the plan for a West India Company with the war party was an

5. Willem Usselinx, *Vertoogh, hoe nootwendich, nut ende profijtelick het sij voor de Vereenichde Nederlanden te behouden de Vryheyt van het handelen op West-Indien, In den vrede met den Coninck van Spanien* (Amsterdam, 1608). The quotation comes from the title.

irreversible consequence of the pamphlet war of 1606–9.[6] Under van Oldenbarnevelt's leadership all plans for a West India Company were shelved. In March 1609, a twelve-year truce was concluded between Spain and the Netherlands.

The truce represented a magnificent victory for the United Provinces. Spain, the most powerful nation in Europe, had admitted its inability to dominate the diminutive Dutch provinces. The provisions of the truce also recognized the United Provinces as a colonial power by granting the Dutch the rights of trade and navigation in the East Indies, where the VOC was involved in staking out its colonial claims at the expense of Spain's ally, Portugal. Even the Spanish Main was open to Dutch merchants who wished to conduct their trade through Iberian middlemen. On every count it seemed that the Dutch had won a stunning victory. The golden century had dawned.[7]

Freed from the financial burdens of war, the Dutch merchant community poured profits into expanding the overseas trade. In every area of maritime commerce the Dutch emerged as Europe's preeminent carriers. In the Baltic, where the Dutch merchant fleet dominated the grain, wine, cloth, and fish trades, ships from the United Provinces constituted about 83 percent of all vessels sailing east and over 60 percent of those sailing west through the Danish Sound between 1610 and 1619. In Asia, the truce gave the VOC a free hand in eclipsing the once dominant Portuguese. One year after the truce was announced, the company declared a dividend of 162 percent, and stocks on the exchange began a decade-long upward spiral.[8]

The impact of peace was evident everywhere. Increased capital expenditures, made possible by the reduced cost of shipping in peacetime, and a series of technological improvements in ship design enabled the United Provinces to outstrip the competition. The heightened prosperity of the truce years provided many Dutch merchants with the opportunity to expand their field of activity. As capital accumulated, the costs of loans declined, and trades once thought too risky were taken up with a vengeance. The activities of

6. Ibid., pp. 26–40.

7. Geyl, *Revolt of the Netherlands*, p. 254.

8. J. G. van Dillen, *Van Rijkdom en Regenten: Handboek tot de Economische en Sociale Geschiedenis van Nederland tijdens de Republiek* (The Hague, 1970), pp. 19, 125.

the early New Netherland traders took place in the first years of the truce, and the optimism surrounding the period is one explanation for the fierce competition among these traders that was described in the previous chapter. Elsewhere in the Western Hemisphere much the same pattern prevailed. During the truce, for example, Dutch trade to Brazil (ostensibly through Portuguese middlemen, but much of it in fact direct) increased from fewer than forty thousand chests of raw sugar to more than one hundred thousand chests annually. The sugar trade gave rise to the secondary industry of refining. In Amsterdam, Rotterdam, and Dordrecht the raw sugar was refined for transshipment throughout Europe. By the middle of the century most sugar consumed in Europe had been refined in the United Provinces.[9]

Most Dutch were happy to hear the clink of coins in the silence of peace, but for some only the din of war could bring relief from the stifling effects of the truce. In the war party's schemes to prevent the renewal of the truce, Willem Usselinx's plans for a West India Company became a pawn in the nation's power struggles.

Usselinx was not idle during the truce years. Imbued with patriotic fervor and encouraged rather than daunted by his past failures, he continued to promote his dream. In 1614 he appeared before the provincial States of Holland to argue once more for a West India Company. The timing could not have been worse. Trade was booming, private companies (including the New Netherland Company) were acquiring charters to regions of the Western Hemisphere, and van Oldenbarnevelt's popularity was at its apogee. Usselinx was politely refused. Two years later he was at work again. This time he submitted a written argument in numbered paragraphs pleading for the need to establish a West India Company before the expiration of the truce in 1621. So persistent was Usselinx that the States of Holland referred the matter to The Hague. There a haggard States General agreed to have a special committee review the proposal once more. At this point, van Oldenbarnevelt stepped in to block the hearing.[10] The fate of the West India Company hinged on the ability of the war party to discredit or defeat van Oldenbarnevelt.

9. Ibid., pp. 138, 35, 551–53.

10. O. van Rees, *Geschiedenis der staathuishoudkunde in Nederland tot het einde der achttiende eeuw*, 2 vols. (Utrecht, 1868), 2:102ff.

Ironically, an academic debate between two professors at Leiden University proved to be the old man's undoing.

The dispute rested upon the question of free will. Professor Jacobus Arminius maintained that man possessed free will, thus suggesting that the individual had control over his own salvation and that good works were effective in attaining grace. His opponent, Professor Franciscus Gomarus, took a staunchly Calvinist approach to the question, denying free will while glorying in the doctrine of predestination. To Gomarus and his ardent followers the position maintained by Arminius was a denial of the Reformation and smacked of popery. More was at stake than an issue of theology. The Arminians threatened the very foundations of Christian fellowship. If individuals possessed free will and the power to determine their own salvation, what would happen to the system of church polity so meticulously built by John Calvin in Geneva and shaped on a smaller scale by his zealous followers in the United Provinces? Here indeed was a heresy that touched the lives of all Dutch Protestants. It also touched politics.

Into the midst of this controversy strode the towering figure of van Oldenbarnevelt. He supported the Arminians publicly, thereby antagonizing their opponents and adding political fuel to what was then becoming a national conflagration. Van Oldenbarnevelt's position was that of a moderate among extremists. A worldly man with a keen eye for practical matters, he could not condone the self-righteous Gomarians, who were willing to proclaim themselves saints and the rest of society sinners. He was vulnerable, however, to charges of popery, and his worldly attitude was seen by his opponents as his greatest weakness. His leadership of the peace party in the truce negotiations had already created formidable political opposition among powerful merchant syndicates and die-hard refugees from the southern provinces. His public support of Arminius sealed his fate with the conservative Calvinist ministry. The grand old man's support of the Arminians, which was characteristic of a life spent walking the middle road among radicals, succeeded in uniting his enemies as never before.

The controversy raged on throughout 1616 and 1617, while van Oldenbarnevelt's political position deteriorated. As long as van Oldenbarnevelt remained in power, the Arminians maintained their hold on the national Reformed church, and the Gomarians fumed and condemned while they desperately looked for a political ally. The Gomarians found such an ally in Prince Maurice, stadholder of Orange. The struggle between the House of Orange and the regent-oligarchs represented by van Oldenbarnevelt was the driving force in Dutch politics and eventually determined the unique brand of Dutch republicanism which would emerge in the latter half of the seventeenth century. Prince Maurice had few victories over van Oldenbarneveld in the early years of the century, but the religious dispute promised great rewards. When he received a petition from more than half of the nation's clergy to intervene in the dispute, he decided to act, calling for a national synod to meet in 1618 to decide the issue.[11]

In 1618 the Dutch Reformed church held one of the most important synods in the history of Protestantism. The Synod of Dordrecht opened on November 13, 1618, to great fanfare and expectation. From the first session it was clear that the Arminians were in trouble. The president of the synod was Johan Bogerman, a fierce advocate of the Gomarian position and a predatory inquisitor whenever orthodoxy seemed threatened. The Arminians had submitted a five-point Remonstrance defending the doctrine of free will. Short work was made of the Remonstrance once Bogerman established the "theological proof" of the Gomarian position. All that remained was to institutionalize the Gomarian view as the official orthodoxy of the Reformed church. More than 180 sessions were held before a final draft statement was completed and submitted to the States General in May 1619. Yet the outcome was never in doubt. The Synod of Dordrecht condemned the Arminians as heretics, schismatics, and teachers of false doctrines. Ministers and theologians who refused to accept the new orthodoxy were barred from any academic or clerical post. They were forbidden to teach children, give public lectures, hold public office, or conduct prayer. Meanwhile, van Oldenbarnevelt had been imprisoned (along with others, including the great codifier of international law, Hugo Grotius) on a charge of high treason.[12]

11. Pieter Geyl, *The Netherlands in the Seventeenth Century: Part One, 1609–1648* (New York, 1961), pp. 42–63.

12. Several sources are available in English on the Synod of Dordrecht (called Dort in English). The most readily available analysis of religion and politics in this era of Dutch history is Jan den Tex, *Oldenbarnevelt*, 2 vols. (Cambridge, 1973),

Technically, the treason trial and the Synod of Dordrecht were not connected, but few believed that fiction. The trial was postponed several times until the synod could complete its work of condemning the Arminians. Thus van Oldenbarneveld sat day after day in the small apartment in the Binnenhof at The Hague awaiting his fate. In March 1619 the trial began with the nation looking on and the forces ominously arrayed behind the stadholder.

Prince Maurice had been busy organizing hard-line Calvinist ministers and other disgruntled groups into a powerful nationalist movement aimed at establishing not only theological orthodoxy but political orthodoxy as well. The prince's goal was nothing less than the restructuring of Dutch political life. While the old man was awaiting his fate in the Binnenhof, Prince Maurice wrought a revolution in local politics by winning the support of municipalities in the States General, appointing sympathetic magistrates, and isolating the powerful province of Holland and the city of Amsterdam. In this work the prince found many willing cohorts, including the province of Zeeland, which harbored an age-old grudge against Holland. By the time van Oldenbarnevelt was brought to trial, the verdict had been assured.

The charges against van Oldenbarnevelt consisted of a potpourri of accusations tailored to satisfy the formidable coalition of angry Dutchmen who stood behind Prince Maurice. For the jealous merchants who chafed under Amsterdam's hegemony the old man was accused of promoting Holland's welfare at the expense of the other provinces. For the Gomarians, still working on the final draft of the Synod of Dordrecht's catechism, van Oldenbarnevelt was accused of "attempts at novelty through changes in religion, in justice and in the fundamental laws of all orders of polity." His crime was part of a wide conspiracy that included almost anybody who could be accused of liberalism. After a months-long show trial in which the old advocate displayed an enormous grasp of the issues and as-

2:654–98. For a superb analysis of Dutch and English Calvinism—how they differed and at which points they converged—see Keith L. Sprunger, *Dutch Puritanism: A History of English and Scottish Churches of the Netherlands in the Sixteenth and Seventeenth Centuries* (Lieden, 1982), pp. 354–68. For an exhaustive account of Arminianism, see the classic A. W. Harrison, *The Beginnings of Arminianism to the Synod of Dort* (London, 1926), esp. chaps. 9 and 10.

tounded everyone with his dispassionate defense of republicanism, the tribunal convicted him of high treason and ordered his execution. On May 13, 1619, the seventy-two-year-old statesman was beheaded before a crowd estimated at five thousand in the Binnenhof at The Hague. Less than three weeks later the Synod of Dordrecht finished its work.[13]

The hawks were delirious, and the plans for a West India Company once more found a receptive audience. Even before the trial had ended, a proposal for the founding of such a company was winding its way through the cumbersome committee network of the States General. In November, a draft charter was ready for submission to the States. The draft charter was, upon the request of a number of representatives, given to Prince Maurice asking for his views. The reply was favorable, and within a week the charter, accompanied by several pages of arguments, accumulated reports, maps, and resolutions, was placed in the hands of a select committee charged with writing a final draft for publication.[14]

In June 1621 the committee's task was complete, and a copy of the charter was sent to the printer. Meanwhile, the States General issued a resolution outlining the general points of the charter and warning all private merchants who were engaged in trade with the New World to cease and desist. A one-year grace period was established to give the merchants time to close down their operations. On July 7 the official charter was published, and a resolution of the States General backdated it to June 3.[15]

Willem Usselinx had been involved in almost every phase of the work on the charter. Still, he was disappointed by the final product of the committee's labor because the charter was a more elaborate version of the bellicose draft issued by the States of Holland in 1606. The colonization plans, which Usselinx had hoped would be the centerpiece of a Dutch empire, were given little attention, and hardly any mention was made of Indian conversion. Angry, disappointed, discredited, and offended, Usselinx refused repeated offers of employment in the company. He continued to write and

13. John Lothrop Motley, *The Life and Death of John of Barneveld*, 2 vols. (New York, 1874), 2:306, 385–89.
14. Algemeen Rijksarchief, De eerste serie registers van ordinaris net-resolutiën van de Staten-Generaal, 3179, pp. 303v, 329v–30, 369.
15. Ibid., 3180, p. 316v.

speak out against the war operations undertaken by the company, but his pen had lost its magic. And although he was to find a receptive audience in Sweden where he helped found the Swedish West India Company, he died in 1647, a broken man, at the age of eighty.[16]

The Dutch West India Company displayed a grandiose illusion of strength. Article One of the charter announced the intention to cordon off the Western Hemisphere for company trade: "For the period of twenty-four years no native or inhabitant of these provinces shall be permitted, to sail or trade with the coasts and countries of Africa, from the Tropic of Cancer to the Cape of Good Hope, to or with the countries of America or the West Indies . . . nor to or with any islands situated on either side or between both, not even to or with Australian or South Lands . . . except in the name of this United Company."[17]

The proud language ignored the realities of geography, politics, and the Company's financial resources. Stretching across the chartered territories lay the immense Spanish-Portuguese empire. Areas still untouched by Iberian settlement promised little in profits. The gold mines, sugar plantations, and dyewood supplies were controlled by the hated papists, and the struggling tobacco plantations of North America had yet to prove their profitability. War and piracy held out the only real hope for quick returns, and the Company's first operations would be directed to that end, a policy Usselinx had condemned but which would characterize the Company throughout its colorful history.

Colonization was clearly a secondary goal of the Company, and it was not to be undertaken lightly. Since the Company could hardly afford a hemispheric campaign of conquest in territories already occupied by the Iberians, the directors were forced to choose sites largely on the basis of fiscal pragmatism. Financial considerations thus came to dictate Company policy in matters of colonization, and it was plagued by financial problems from its inception.

At the beginning of operations in 1623 the company had only

16. Cornelis Ch. Goslinga, *The Dutch in the Caribbean and on the Wild Coast, 1580–1680* (Gainesville, 1971), p. 41. See also Ligtenberg, *Willem Usselinx*, p. 236.

17. Arnold J. F. van Laer, ed. and trans., *The Van Rensselaer–Bowier Manuscripts* (Albany, 1908), p. 88; my translation.

twenty ships of its own and a promise of twenty more from the States General. Consequently, the grand monopoly had to borrow from private shipowners and financiers before commencing its operations. Some areas of the chartered territories such as New Netherland were considered good risks and had attracted private capital before the establishment of the Company. They would continue to be centers of operations largely because the Company could obtain ships and financial backing from private merchants. Other areas, which offered greater risks, could be expoited directly only at Company expense, and these areas would become the foci of Company management decisions, leaving the other areas languishing in a vacuum of disinterest.

Brazil absorbed the Company's resources for twenty-five years. The abortive attempt at long-term occupation of Pernambuco, or New Holland as it was wistfully christened, eventually impoverished the Company's treasury and damaged public confidence. The slave trade held less risk and more potential profits, so the Company turned its attention to West Africa in the late 1630s, hoping to profit from the insatiable demand for labor in the New World. In its last years the Company became the most important slave trader in the Western Hemisphere. Elsewhere in the chartered territories the presence of the Company was less visible. New Netherland, in particular, would benefit from this early benign neglect. Later, after repeated failures in South America and after the Company had long ceased to maintain its chartered monopoly, New Netherland would become the center of the Company's last-ditch effort to hold on to its "empire." That empire had been lost long before 1664, however. From its very beginning the West India Company was an enfeebled giant.

The corporate structure of the huge joint-stock company appears byzantine to the modern observer, although in actuality it was purely Dutch. The Company's administration was divided into five chambers, each representing not only a specified amount of the subscribed capital but also the political influence wielded by the chamber in national politics. The five chambers, each with widespread decision-making powers, met separately in Amsterdam, Middleburg, Rotterdam (alternately in Dordrecht and Delft), Enkhuizen (alternately in Hoorn), and Groningen. The chambers represented not only the cities in which the meetings were held but the surrounding countryside as well. Their territories were divided into districts corresponding to medieval tradition as well as seventeenth-century commercial development. Hence the capital of investors in and around Amsterdam was managed by the Amsterdam chamber; investors from any of the Maas cities (Rotterdam, Delft, and Dordrecht) looked to the Maze chamber to represent their interests; those from Zeeland trusted their accounts to directors in Middleburg; and so it went with chambers representing the Noorderkwartier (Northern Quarter or North Holland), Groningen, and Friesland.

To make matters more complicated, the charter stipulated that the central administration of the Company was to be organized in the College of Nineteen, or simply the Nineteen, as it came to be called. Members of the Nineteen, in turn, were elected by the chambers with representation based on the percentage of subscribed capital controlled by the chambers. The Amsterdam chamber was the most powerful and sent eight delegates. Zeeland sent four representatives, and each of the remaining chambers was authorized to send two. The nineteenth delegate represented the States General and theoretically was responsible for overseeing the proper use of the huge government subsidies which their High Mightinesses had pledged in 1621. Even the meeting place of the Nineteen reflected the internecine particularism of Dutch politics. By charter, the Nineteen was obligated to meet six years in Amsterdam and two years in Middleburg. Each chamber, moreover, was authorized to keep its own books, outfit its own fleets and trading expeditions, establish its own colonies, and compete with every other chamber.[18]

The chamber system reflected the provincial animosities that had long characterized Dutch political life. Modeled after the VOC, the charter of the West India Company was intended to inspire investor confidence, and the chamber system (also found in the VOC) was an important factor in ensuring that confidence. Since the

18. The chamber system is described in articles 18–24 of the charter (ibid., pp. 100–103). The best concise analysis of the administrative peculiarities of the company can be found in van Dillen, *Van Rijkdom en Regenten*, pp. 146ff. Van Cleaf Bachman discusses the charter in *Peltries or Plantations: The Economic Policies of the Dutch West India Company in New Netherland, 1623–1639* (Baltimore, 1969), pp. 25–43.

system kept provincial contributions separate and based power on the percentage of the total capital invested by each chamber, stockholders could be assured that their risks were limited and their capital looked after by men from their own areas. The decentralized administration was effective in blunting the power of the Amsterdam chamber, but it did not produce a tidal wave of investment.

Indeed, the much-heralded West India Company was dangerously dependent on government subsidies to maintain its operations in the first five years. Article Thirty-nine of the charter provided a government commitment of 1 million guilders—500,000 in purchased shares and 500,000 as an outright subsidy. The initial capitalization was not reached until 1623. In the meantime, the only hedge against insolvency was the government subsidy. When the initial capitalization was reached, it was in excess of 7 million guilders, a sum nearly 1 million guilders greater than that which established the VOC in 1602. Such figures are misleading, however. In 1602 the city of Amsterdam provided 3,674,915 guilders to the VOC and in 1621 only 2,846,582 guilders to the West India Company. Given the astounding growth of the city in the intervening years and the increased availablity of capital following the truce, Amsterdam's reduced level of support for the West India Company suggests that the citizens of the city were much less enthusiastic about the new monopoly than were their magistrates.[19]

Amsterdamers were not the only ones skeptical about the West India Company. The merchants of Hoorn and Enkhuizen had reluctantly agreed to its establishment provided that the crucial salt trade to Punto del Rey remained outside the monopoly. The salt trade was vital to the herring industries in the Noorderkwartier, and a special clause had been inserted in the charter at the request of the Noorderkwartier merchants to keep it open. What was good for the Noorderkwartier merchants, however, was not good for others. A year after the publication of the charter, powerful forces in the States General moved to include the salt trade in the monopoly. The reason was clear: the bellicose language of the charter had frightened away many investors, and the salt trade promised one of

19. Van Dillen, *Van Rijkdom en Regenten*, pp. 177, 150.

the few peaceful and steady enterprises within the Company's domain (the fur trade of New Netherland was another). Thus in June 1622 an amendment passed the States General which extended the Company monopoly to the salt trade. The delegates from Hoorn and Enkhuizen protested vehemently and thereafter complained that the monopoly had ruined the herring industry. Still, the amendment had little effect among investors, who remained apathetic. A controversy then raging between the directors and principal shareholders of the VOC had chilled enthusiasm for the West India Company. In 1622 its charter was amended again.[20]

Shareholders of the VOC had long complained that they had too little voice in the election of company directors. In 1622 their dissatisfaction had become public when a number of principal shareholders petitioned the States General to intervene on their behalf. Since it was widely thought that the West India Company charter contained similar weaknesses, the challenge posed by the shareholders of the older company encouraged several shareholders in the West India Company to request a reorganization of the directorship. The States General responded by appointing a committee to arbitrate the dispute in the West India Company. An "agreement" was reached within a month, and it was to have a profound effect on Company administration in the years ahead.[21]

The revised organization enlarged the powers of the principal shareholders of the chambers; those who owned a minimum of 6,000 fl. of chamber stock were to elect delegates to the Nineteen from among themselves. In addition, principal shareholders could "audit" the directors, limit their appointments, and generally circumscribe their actions. The new scheme gave these men control over the directorate while increasing the power of the chambers. This complex system of shared governance, originally designed to prevent the Nineteen from making reckless decisions, paralyzed decision making in the Company.

The complexity only began with the chamber system. Each chamber acquired its own internal structure, and sometimes important decisions for the Company reflected hard-fought compromises and concessions won in discussions involving one or two investors.

20. Van Rees, *Geschiedenis der staatshuishoudkunde*, 2:134.
21. Van Laer, *Van Rensselaer–Bowier Manuscripts*, pp. 126–35.

An example may be found in the decision to establish patroonships in New Netherland. The Amsterdam chamber, to whose hands the fate of New Netherland had been entrusted, developed its own system for making decisions. In the 1620s a series of commissions (*commissie*) was established to provide advice and consultation on special matters. The commissions soon evolved into permanent in-house lobbies that reflected the internal jockeying for finanical position among the principal shareholders of the chamber. The chamber eventually established eleven commissions with memberships ranging from three to seven. One of the largest was the New Netherland Commission on which Kiliaen van Rensselaer, Michael Pauw, and other patroons sat. The decision to abandon the Company's monopoly of the fur trade in New Netherland in favor of a vainglorious attempt to establish feudal estates on the Hudson River may be viewed as the logical consequence of a power struggle in the New Netherland Commission in the years 1628–29. Similarly, decisions made for Brazil and the West Indies all too often reflected the internal workings of these commissions.

The amendments to the charter had their desired effect. West India Company shares became the hottest stock on the exchange in the fall of 1622, and by October 31, 1623, more than 7 million guilders lined Company coffers. Almost immediately the Nineteen began preparing war fleets.

The first theater of operations was Brazil, where the rich sugar plantations and close access to supplies of dyewood seemed to hold out the best chance of profit. A fleet was outfitted in 1624 to attack All Saints Bay as a preliminary to an assault on northern Brazil. After an initial success the expedition collapsed, and the fleet limped home. For the next ten years the Nineteen continued to outfit fleets to prey on shipping in the Spanish Main. Some of these fleets, notably that commanded by Piet Heyn in 1628, brought home fabulous riches from captured silver fleets. Most, however, failed to repay their outfitting costs. So expensive were the war operations that before the decade had ended the once mighty Company was in debt.[22] The stock exchange reflected the Company's declining fortunes.

During the term of the first charter, West India Company stock

---

22. Van Dillen, *Van Rijkdom en Regenten*, pp. 151–52.

was one of the most volatile on the exchange. In the 1620s the initial enthusiasm of the company's founding sustained stock prices at 20 percent above the original price of 1621. In 1628, Piet Heyn's capture of a silver fleet sent Company stock soaring. By the 1630s, however, prices were on the decline. And in the last two decades of the 1640s and 1650s, when the Company was forced to abandon Brazil and the first in a series of disastrous Anglo-Dutch wars shattered the Protestant alliance, Company stock prices plunged. In 1645, Amsterdam chamber stock (the most valued of Company stock) sold for less than 44 percent of its original price. In 1653, a share of Amsterdam chamber stock was worth less than 13 percent of its original value.[23] In 1648, the financial condition of the Company had deteriorated to the point that the directors could no longer acquire bottomry loans on Company ships. The city of Amsterdam had to guarantee a loan of 100,000 fl. to outfit ships for the Guinea trade. Pamphleteers made much of this loan, although the Company had been virtually bankrupt for years.[24]

For the territories within the chartered domain, the West India Company's insolvency had mixed blessings. For New Netherland, it usually meant that funds for defense and development had to be acquired elsewhere. It also meant that the Company played a much smaller role in the colony's development than tradition has led us to believe. The Nineteen could not devote enough time and money to develop New Netherland as a major colony. Given the war policies of the early years and the later fiscal disasters, New Netherland's problems must have seemed relatively insignificant to the men sitting in Amsterdam and Middleburg. Faced with catastrophes over the length and breadth of the chartered territory, the Nineteen left the colony's fate in the hands of the Amsterdam chamber, in which a small group of principal shareholders waged a twenty-year battle for control of the New Netherland Commission. When conditions in New Netherland did demand action, the problems were seldom analyzed. The bizarre Company administration prevented reasoned analysis, especially when interchamber rivalry and intrachamber factionalism determined the outcome. Quick and forceful

23. Simon Hart, "The Dutch and North America in the First Half of the Seventeenth Century: Some Aspects," *Mededelingen van de Nederlandse vereniging voor zeegeschiedenis* 20 (March 1970): 11–12.

24. van Dillen, *Van Rijkdom en Regenten*, p. 169n.

actions were seldom forthcoming, and the decentralized administration accentuated provincial antagonisms while fostering a pervading sense of distrust among the chambers.

New Netherland benefited from Company neglect and suffered
in the later years from Company interference. The colony's main
asset was the fur trade, but even this activity was risky when
competition drove up on-station prices. In the first years of Company administration the Amsterdam chamber took its cue from the
precompany traders and attempted to enforce a strict monopoly on
the fur trade. After 1629, however, the chamber abandoned the fur
trade monopoly for an agricultural colony with limited settlement
in large baronial estates called patroonships. Within ten years the
patroonship plan had failed, and the Company opened up the colony to free settlement, while it tried to regulate the fur trade as a
monopsony. This policy came to nought when unscrupulous settlers and incompetent Company officials precipitated an Indian war
that nearly wiped out the colony. By the 1650s the Company was
bankrupt, the English were clamoring for their rights to the Hudson, and the colony was thriving as an outpost of private trade and a
smugglers' paradise.

Still, the role of the West India Company was crucial in New
Netherland's history because it was the Company that undertook
the first small-scale settlement of Europeans in the colony. The
initial effort was only partially successful, but once the decision had
been made to turn New Netherland into an outpost of European
culture, the Company found itself harnessed to the colony for years
to come. Once settled, the colony could not be abandoned. Reluctantly and always grudgingly, the Nineteen, under the relentless
urging of the Amsterdam chamber, siphoned off scarce capital from
its other operations to sustain the colony on the Hudson. These
efforts were almost always made too late and with too little financial backing. From a Company viewpoint, the colony was a commercial failure. As the costs of maintaining the colony mounted,
the Company abandoned nearly all of its authority. Private merchants from Amsterdam filled the gap and prospered where the
Company had failed. New Netherland's fate hung in the balance
between the Company's efforts to hold on to its authority and the
efforts of Amsterdam's private merchants to exploit the colony for
profit.

[3]

The Territorial Commitment Established, 1623–1628

Subjects of the English Lords to their honor and quality have, for a long time past, been in possession of the precincts of Virginia and have planted there their habitation, and [also] in certain new quarters of Nova Anglica, desired by their Majesty . . . for the advancement of Religion and enlargement of commerce. The King's government has lately been informed that the Hollanders have planted a colony in these regions, and renamed the ports and harbors, as is their fashion, and are of the intention to continue trafficking there.
— Sir Dudley Carleton to the States General, 1622

Sir Dudley Carleton, English ambassador to The Hague, began his protest of West India Company activities in New Netherland with a defense of English rights to the entire North American seaboard. Years would pass before the legal issues were arbitrated, and a war would eventually settle the matter in favor of the English. But in February 1622, when the English ambassador registered his government's displeasure, the rival claims to the area of the Hudson River had yet to be studied, and the activities of the newly founded West India Company in the region would soon establish a territorial commitment that the United Provinces could not easily abandon.[1]

The first Company-sponsored voyage to New Netherland occurred as part of a fifteen-ship expedition to various regions in the Western Hemisphere in the late summer and early fall of 1623.

1. Algemeen Rijksarchief, De eerste serie registers van ordinaris net-resolutiën van de Staten Generaal, 3181:54–54v.

Nicolaes van Wassenaer, a popular chronicler of Dutch overseas adventures, briefly noted the voyage of a sixty-ton yacht, the *Mackereel*, to New Netherland. The yacht had accompanied another ship, the *Pigeon*, as far as the coast of Guiana before sailing off alone along the North American coast. On December 12, 1623, she dropped anchor off the island of Manhattan, remaining in the area to trade along the coast of Long Island and far up the Hudson River throughout the unusually warm winter of 1624. She was anchored in the roadstead of the East River in the spring when the 260-ton *Nieu Nederlandt* arrived with the first European colonists.[2]

The arrival of thirty Walloon families marked the beginning of New Netherland as a Dutch colony. The decision to settle the families in the remote region had not come easily and might not have come at all had not England and France challenged the Dutch claim to New Netherland.

The English ambassador's protest of February 1622 was not the only ominous sign of foreign competition facing the West India Company in its efforts to exploit the fur trade of New Netherland. The French were also concerned about the Company's operations in North America. In 1624, while preparations were under way to transport the first settlers to New Netherland, Company agents acting on information received from the Noorderkwartier chamber, seized a ship at Hoorn before she could weigh anchor for a voyage to the chartered territories. The ship was under French sponsorship and apparently outfitted for a fur trading voyage to North America. The Company agents informed the Nineteen "of evil intentions and designs maliciously intended by a certain skipper there and other persons more directly contrary to the favorable charter and amplifications."[3] The Nineteen turned to the States General for help, requesting that the sails and equipment of the

2. J. Franklin Jameson, ed., *Narratives of New Netherland, 1609–1664* (New York, 1909), p. 76.

3. Algemeen Rijksarchief, Staten-Generaal Liassen: De liassen West-Indische Compagnie, 5751: April 2, 1624 [in loose packet]; hereafter cited as De liassen West-Indische Compagnie. A translation also appears in John Romeyn Brodhead, comp., Edmund B. O'Callaghan and Berthold Fernow, eds. and trans., *Documents Relative to the Colonial History of the State of New York*, 15 vols. (New York, 1856–87), 1:30; hereafter cited as *DCHNY*. Quotations are from my translations of the original.

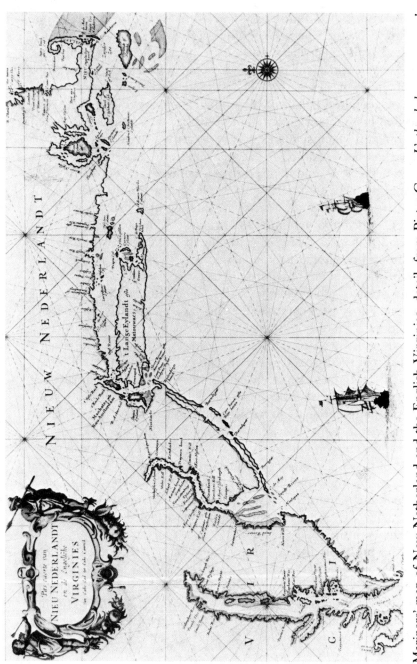

Mariners' map of New Netherland and the English Virginias, detail, from Pieter Goos, *L'atlas de la mer, ou monde aquaticque, representant toutes les costes maritimes de l'univers descouvertes & cogneues* (Amsterdam, 1667). Courtesy of the New Netherland Project, New York State Library, Albany.

ship be impounded and her captain prosecuted. An investigation, authorized by the States General, revealed that the ship had been outfitted by French merchants for a voyage to the "Virginnes."

In the meantime, the issue had become more delicate. The skipper of the sequestered ship, David Pieters, sent a petition to the States General on behalf of his French sponsors. Pieters was convinced of his rights and confident of his backing. When questioned by Company agents he responded angrily, "as if the crown of France had been insulted."[4] His petition to the States General was no less belligerent, and their High Mightinesses reacted with diplomatic caution. In an official letter to the Nineteen, the States General advised the Company to avoid "coming into disputes with the subjects of neighboring kings and princes."[5] The letter further recommended that the directors settle the matter either by purchasing the ship or by negotiating a notarized bond with Captain Pieters to prevent the violation of charter rights.

The cautious advice of the States General reflected an ongoing discussion in The Hague about the possibility of a commercial alliance with English and French joint-stock companies to further the war with Spain in the New World. A resolution had recommended that the States General investigate the possibility of merging the West India Company with a French or English company for joint war operations and commercial activities. The idea of establishing an international joint-stock company to prey on the Iberian empire in the New World was unique in this age of emerging nationalism. In conjunction with the investigation, a special committee of the States General requested the Nineteen to draw up a report listing their objections, if any, to the establishment of a multinational company. The Nineteen responded within two weeks with a twenty-nine-paragraph report that dashed any hope of such a venture.

In the preamble the Nineteen stated that "it is judged neither advisable nor in any sense practical to make any combination of companies, compromise, or trade, with the French or English." Joint war operations against Spain were possible and to be encouraged, but the companies "should maintain their capital, trade, and

4. Ibid.
5. *DCHNY*, 1:32.

accounts separate."[6] The report went on to define the Company's position on colonies, specifically stating the legal guidelines for determining ownership. Since the Dutch were relative newcomers in the race for colonies, claims based on first discovery could not support a Dutch empire. In opting for a different definition of legal ownership, the Company helped establish an argument for its colonizing expedition to New Netherland.

The report made it clear that the simple fact of discovery did not grant the rights of ownership. Occupation and effective use of disputed territories were the only bases for colonial claims: "Any nation who for itself possesses such places, harbors, and rivers . . . and already occupies the same with colonists, cities or forts, containing at least 50 persons from the respective kingdoms and countries sent there, does possess and therefore has exclusive rights to said districts."[7]

The Company's directors were especially concerned that occupation be permanent. Each colony had to be continuously occupied to maintain possession, and only continuous occupation would confer perpetual title to a region. The Company would not recognize claims to perpetual title acquired by papal decrees, first discovery, or other means not involving the actual settlement of people.

The report was nothing less than a denial of every European claim to unoccupied land in the New World. Nothing came of the proposed multinational company, but the report which the proposal provoked sheds light on the first colonization attempt in New Netherland of the same year and may partly explain the rapidity of the decision to colonize. The threat of a possible merger with an English or French company may have influenced the Company's decision to colonize New Netherland in 1624. Prompted by their own definition of legal ownership, the Nineteen took action on a petition received from a group of Walloon families who had requested permission to settle in the chartered territories. The decision to settle Walloon refugees in New Netherland was made with amazing speed, especially in light of the delays that had plagued the efforts of earlier colonists to settle in New Netherland. Before

---

6. De liassen West-Indische Compagnie, 5751: April 22, 1624. The resolution had passed on April 9, 1624.

7. Ibid.

1624, at least two opportunities to colonize the area had been passed up.

The first opportunity antedated the founding of the West India Company. In 1620, the van Tweenhuysen partnership (a remnant of the defunct New Netherland Company) requested the Admiralty to supply two warships as an escort for a small fleet carrying four hundred families from Leiden and England to New Netherland. The families were part of the flock of English separatists living in scattered groups around Rotterdam, Leiden, and the south of England.[8] The van Tweenhuysen partnership had consulted with some influential members of the States General after receiving a petition from the English exiles for transportation, livestock, and land in New Netherland. Apparently encouraged by the response, Lambert van Tweenhuysen contacted the Admiralty as a preliminary to outfitting the fleet. The Admiralty, no doubt acting upon the advice of the stadholder and a majority of the States General, refused the request, blocking an action that might have placed an unbearable strain on the alliance with England just at the time when renewed war with Spain was a certainty.[9]

The second opportunity had come just months before the final amendments to the Company charter had passed the States General. In 1622, "diverse families of all manner of manufacture" petitioned the provincial States of Holland and West Friesland "to be employed by the West India Company."[10] The States refused to discuss the petition until it had been reviewed by the Company, and it was turned over to the Amsterdam chamber for consideration and advice. The directors of the chamber enthusiastically re-

8. William Bradford noted that the Pilgrims were well liked by their Dutch hosts at Leiden. The city magistrates stated publicly that "these English have lived among us these twelve years, and yet we never had any suit or accusation against them." The opinion of the magistrates was somewhat different toward the French-speaking Walloons, whose "strifes and quarrels are continual" (William Bradford, *The History of Plymouth Plantation, 1608–1650*, ed. Harold Paget [New York, 1920], p. 17).

9. *DCHNY*, 1:22–23; Simon Hart, *The Prehistory of the New Netherland Company: Amsterdam Notarial Records of the First Dutch Voyages to the Hudson* (Amsterdam, 1959), p. 37; and, Isaac Newton Phelps Stokes, *The Iconography of Manhattan Island, 1498–1909*, 6 vols. (New York, 1928), 4:45.

10. Algemeen Rijksarchief, Resolutiën van de Staten van Holland en West Friesland, 55:72.

ported that the request appeared to be "very serviceable to the company." Meanwhile, the newly established New Netherland Commission within the chamber set to work devising a plan "to bring the same to hand, with promises that they will be employed."[11] The plan was temporarily shelved because the discussions in the States General over the reorganization of the Company directorate prevented the Nineteen from acting on the petition. Not until 1623 could the Company review the Amsterdam chamber's plan to settle the families in New Netherland.

The identity of the "diverse families" has remained a mystery. The terse report of the States of Holland and West Friesland noted that the petitioners had "solicited the English to be transported to Virginia,"[12] suggesting that they were the little group of Walloons assembled by Jesse de Forest in early 1621 for emigration to North America. It is known, for example, that de Forest had sought the permission of James I to take his group of refugees to Virginia. Permission was never granted, probably because the Virginia Company was facing bankruptcy and the loss of its charter at the time. If the cryptic reference is accurate, de Forest must have followed up his request to James I with the petition to the provincial States of Holland and West Friesland.[13]

After the controversy over the reorganized directorate had subsided, in the early months of 1624 the directors authorized the

11. Ibid., p. 73; *DCHNY*, 1:28. Brodhead apparently missed the previous document. That he did so is difficult to explain because the resolution of April 20 faces directly opposite the one he transcribed for April 21. Together the two form an integral whole, as is evident in the first line of the April 21 resolution, which states *de voorschreve directeurs* (the forescribed directors). Edmund B. O'Callaghan compounded the mistake by mistranslating the phrase, "directors of the West India Company." One possible explanation for Brodhead's omission is that it was a mistake of one of his transcribers, in this case, J. A. Blom. Brodhead, contrary to traditional belief, did not perform all of the transcription work himself during his sojourn in The Hague. At least three separate hands, in addition to Brodhead's, appear on the margins of the original documents housed in the Algemeen Rijksarchief. J. A. Blom, the most frequently used transcriber, is the only one, however, whose name is on a document.

12. Algemeen Rijksarchief, Resolutiën van de Staten van Holland en West Friesland, 55:72.

13. Mrs. Robert de Forest, *A Walloon Family in America: Lockwood de Forest and His Forebears, 1500–1848; together with A Voyage to Guiana, Being the Journal of Jesse de Forest and His Colonists, 1623–1625*, 2 vols. (Boston, 1914), 1:34–35.

Amsterdam chamber to transport "five or six families" to New Netherland. Once again the families were not identified; they were merely described as having "presented themselves" for emigration.[14] If they were the same little group who had petitioned the States of Holland and West Friesland the previous year, they may have already sailed to New Netherland aboard the yacht the *Mackereel* as a vanguard colony for the larger contingent aboard the *Nieu Nederlandt*. In any case, they were soon followed by several other families in a well-organized colonizing expedition.

The Amsterdam chamber, acting through the New Netherland Commission, took the first step toward establishing a colony when it approved a set of "Provisional Orders" for governing the settlement and establishing the obligations and privileges of the settlers. The directors of the chamber went far beyond a simple listing of Company rules and regulations. Indeed, the Provisional Orders may have been one of the best planned colonization schemes in early American history.

The Provisional Orders remains one of the most neglected documents in American colonial history. As a statement outlining the rights and obligations of colonists in New Netherland, it should rank with the Mayflower Compact and John Winthrop's "Model of Christian Charity." Yet it has seldom been studied or analyzed, even though it has been available in English translation since 1924. Moreover, the Provisional Orders represent more than simply the views of the company's leaders, for there is reason to suspect that they were hammered out in meetings between Company officials and colonists before the official public reading and signing on March 29, 1624, when the thirty families boarded the *Nieu Nederlandt* for the Atlantic crossing.

The Provisional Orders suggest a well-conceived set of compromises reached after serious bargaining. Weighing Company authority against personal incentives, the orders appear to have provided some important concessions to the colonists in return for a pledge of permanent settlement. Given the sense of urgency pervading the negotiations in 1624 and the Company's stated position on continuous occupation as the only viable basis for imperial claims, it seems

---

14. G. J. van Grol, *De grondpolitiek in het West-Indische domein der generaliteit; een historische studie*, 3 vols. (The Hague, 1934–47), 2:30–31.

reasonable to assume that the Walloons exacted a price for their settlement in New Netherland. It is difficult to imagine that the Walloons, inured to the folly of good intentions in war-torn Europe, would have easily bargained away their rights before sailing to the colony. The Provisional Orders may, therefore, be examined as a prism separating Company motives from colonists' incentives.

Article One of the orders obligated the colonists to observe "the respective articles and instructions, during the voyage and their residence, and in changing their location, be bound to obey and to carry out without any contradiction the orders of the company." All Company regulations in matters of administration and justice were likewise to be obeyed faithfully and without contradiction. At first glance this article appears uncompromising and severe, and indeed its language did serve to blunt the generous impact of the articles that followed. But the vagueness of the terms is important. Matters involving criminal offenses and violations of persons were subject to the laws of the United Provinces, as were all Company regulations.[15] The colony's commander was appointed by the Company, but he was required to rule with a council drawn from among the settlers. His responsibilities were extensive: to enforce Company regulations in matters of trade, to conclude treaties with local Indian tribes, and to allocate food and tools. He had the authority to enforce religious conformity and to restrict certain types of manufacturing, notably weaving. The Provisional Orders said nothing about internal administration, leaving a great deal of authority to the commander.

In religion, the Company permitted freedom of conscience in private matters but required public worship to be in keeping with the catechism of the Synod of Dordrecht. In theory, therefore, this provision established the hard-line Gomarian position adopted in 1618. In practice, however, indifference characterized the Company's attitude toward religion. Years would elapse before an ordained minister settled in New Netherland, and in the meantime the Walloons were left alone to worship as they wished. Even the commander's responsibility to punish "any one among them or

15. The Provisional Orders, complete with English translation and Dutch facsimiles, may be found in Arnold J. F. van Laer, ed. and trans., *Documents Relating to New Netherland, 1624–1626, in the Henry E. Huntington Library* (San Marino, Calif., 1924); hereafter cited as *Huntington Documents*.

within their jurisdiction [who] should wantonly revile or blaspheme the name of God or of our Savior Jesus Christ" was, considering the religious atmosphere of the times, hardly unusual.[16]

The right of the commander to "make alliances and treaties with foreign princes and potentates" could, if handled irresponsibly, be a threat to the colony's existence. The colonists were bound to observe such alliances, even though "by so doing they should be involved in war with others, their neighbors, and even be obliged to take the field."[17] In the early years of New Netherland's settlement, the Dutch were very careful to appease the Indians of the region and to avoid conflict. But the Company's assumption of the power to make alliances and treaties with the Indians would cause the colony much grief in the future.

The Company also reserved the right to allot land, select crops, and choose settlement sites, although some general rules were to be applied. The commander was instructed to allot land solely on the basis of family size, the largest families receiving the largest allotments. Crops were to be selected on the basis of what was best for the entire colony. And sites for settlement were to be determined by the strategic necessities of defense and the needs of the fur trade.

The fur trade received special consideration in the Provisional Orders. The colonists were encouraged to engage in the trade either as trappers or middlemen between the Company and the Indians. The Company was to be the sole purchaser of furs in the colony, and although prices were to be "reasonable," they were not required to be competitive with those offered by the English. In other potentially lucrative colonial trades the colonists were given a somewhat freer hand.

The Walloons were encouraged to search for "mines of gold, silver, copper or any other metals, as well as of precious stones, such as diamonds, rubies and the like, together with pearl fisheries."[18] The discoverer of any treasure was permitted 10 percent of the net profit after transportation expenses for the first six years. The Company retained ownership of all mines, pearl fisheries, and the like.

Taken as a whole, the Provisional Orders were what one might

16. Ibid., Article 2.
17. Ibid., Article 3.
18. Ibid., Articles 10 and 11.

expect of a joint-stock company founded on the strict principle of monopoly. Yet the colonists received several generous incentives to settle in New Netherland. All colonists received free passage, free land, and livestock at "reasonable prices" or on credit without interest. Profits were expected in the fur trade, and the colonists were invited to share in them. Implicit in the orders was the expectation that the Walloons would prosper and raise children, thus providing the fledgling colony with a permanent population upon which the company could stake its imperial claim. In view of the circumstances surrounding the first colonization effort in New Netherland, the West India Company appears to have been exceedingly flexible in its interpretation of its monopoly privileges and at least as generous as the Virginia Company in providing its settlers with the rudiments of freedom and protection in the wilderness.[19]

After the Provisional Orders were agreed to, the thirty families set sail under the command of Cornelis Jacobsz May for a spring crossing to their new homes. May was one of the most experienced New Netherland sailors available. He had sailed to the Hudson as captain of the *Fortuyn* in the first expedition undertaken by the New Netherland Company in 1614. Along with Adriaen Block, Hendrick Christiaensen, and Thijs Volckertsz Mossel, he had explored and traded along the North American coast for a decade. He had been the first to explore the Delaware River area in the last attempt by the van Tweenhuysen partnership to acquire trading rights before the takeover by the West India Company, and he had a well-deserved reputation for courage and reliability. Interestingly, he was the only one of the early skippers to receive employment by the West India Company after 1623.[20]

After an uneventful crossing the *Nieu Nederlandt* reached the Hudson in late spring 1624, coming upon the *Mackereel*, which had

---

19. Thomas J. Condon in *New York Beginnings: The Commercial Origins of New Netherland* (New York, 1968), pp. 73–74, has dismissed the Provisional Orders as a permanent colonization plan. He views them as a scheme to plant "a company establishment, or colony of resident traders, supported by bookkeepers, clerks, artisans, soldiers, and farmers," all designed to protect the Company monopoly on furs. This judgment is too severe in my opinion because it fails to take into consideration the established Company position on the need for permanent colonists as a basis for colonial claims.

20. Hart, *Prehistory*, pp. 30–31, 37, 38n, 65, 81–82, 91.

been there since the previous winter. Anchoring somewhere north of Manhattan Island, May dispatched a coastal sloop with a few families to the Delaware River to set up a garrison as the colony's southern line of defense against attack by sea. It was the clear intent of the directors to make the Delaware garrison on High Island the center of Company operations and authority for New Netherland. Weighing anchor, Commander May sailed east along Long Island Sound, perhaps stopping at the mouth of the Connecticut River to settle more families. This settlement may have been intended to establish the eastern border of the colony in anticipation of possible disputes with the English at New Plymouth. Returning to the mouth of the Hudson, he anchored at Governor's Island to disembark another contingent of families. Finally, he pushed up the Hudson River to a spot just south of present-day Albany to discharge the final group of colonists. There, May commanded the ship's carpenter to construct a small redoubt, which was immediately christened Fort Orange, after the stadholder's family. Leaving the colonists behind, May set sail for the United Provinces to pick up supplies and perhaps more settlers for a return passage the following spring.[21]

The unusual pattern of settlement may have been inspired by the realization on the part of the Nineteen that the entire area was under jurisdictional dispute.[22] The English settlements at New Plymouth and Jamestown had established England's claim to a substantial portion of the North American seaboard. Moreover, the presence of English colonists to the north and south of New Netherland threatened the Dutch colony with encirclement and provided the English with easy access to the important waterways of the region. Thus May's settlement of the Walloons at the mouths of all the principal rivers may have been an effort to provide defense against a sea-launched attack, while simultaneously acquiring con-

---

21. Van Cleaf Bachman, *Peltries or Plantations: The Economic Policies of the Dutch West India Company in New Netherland, 1623–1639* (Baltimore, 1969), pp. 81–82.

22. Sir Dudley Carleton's protest of Dutch settlement in North America had ended with the omnious request that the States General "prohibit not only those ships already equipped, but also cease the continued existence of this plantation" (Algemeen Rijksarchief, De eerste serie registers van ordinaris net-resolutiën van de Staten Generaal, 3181:54v).

trol of the water-dependent fur trade that was vital to the financial success of the colony.

The doctrine of effective occupation proposed in the Company's report to the States General in 1622 may have influenced the settlement pattern as well because the decision to spread the colonists from the Delaware to the Connecticut was foolish in view of the threat of Indian attack. The settlement pattern established in 1624 also suggests the company's territorial goals, staking out the limits of the colony of New Netherland to include a large part of the future English colony of Connecticut and virtually all of Delaware. This settlement pattern was not to last, however. In the very next year, a relief expedition under the command of Willem Verhulst would bring more colonists to New Netherland, and the need for a more centralized settlement on Manhattan Island would become evident.

The relief expedition was the largest fleet yet to make the eight-week crossing to New Netherland. A total of six ships ferried hundreds of colonists and ample provisions and livestock. The lead vessel, the 150-ton *Oranje Boom*, sailed from Amsterdam in January 1625 but nearly foundered in heavy seas in the English Channel. Forced to put in at Plymouth, she was immediately seized by English customs agents when news of her destination became known after discovery of farming tools, seeds, and live plants aboard the ship. Explanations were demanded, and the captain and crew had to negotiate their release with promises they had no intention of keeping. In the meantime, the crew and several passengers contracted a plague (perhaps typhus), and a few died. The disease must have frightened the English authorities because they released the ship immediately. The *Oranje Boom* then completed the crossing without another mishap, and the plague subsided.[23]

While the *Oranje Boom* languished at Plymouth, the main body of the expedition sailed from the Zuider Zee in a four-ship squadron under the command of Willem Verhulst. Verhulst's instructions have survived, and they confirm the Company's intention to establish a permanent agricultural colony in New Netherland. The commander was under orders to transport to New Netherland "divers

23. Bachman, *Peltries or Plantations*, p. 84n.

trees, vines, and all sorts of seeds" and to have them "planted and sown in their proper season."[24] Livestock was also an important part of the cargo. To provide the necessary space aboard ship for cattle, horses, sheep, and hogs, special transports were chartered and refurbished at the Company's expense. Stalls were constructed aboard two large ships, the 280-ton *Griffoen* and the slightly smaller *Swarte Paert*. While construction was still under way, Company agents attended livestock auctions all over the United Provinces buying 103 horses and at least twice that number of milch cows, hogs, and sheep. Some of the animals were purchased through a livestock agent in Hoorn, whose lucrative contract with the Company guaranteed him 125 fl. for each "horse or horned beast" that survived the voyage. The livestock wholesaler was one of many merchants willing to gamble on the new colony in return for a Company contract. Others supplied the expedition with farm implements, flour, blacksmithing tools, firearms, liquor, cloth goods, and tons of cheap goods for the fur trade. The other ships in the squadron, the 200-ton *Schaep* and the armed yacht *Mackereel*, carried Verhulst and an undisclosed number of Company employees and settlers.[25]

The crossing was not without incident. Near the entrance to the English Channel, the *Mackereel* engaged a pirate ship operating out of Dunkirk. The yacht was captured, but the rest of the squadron was able to escape to open sea. In the North Atlantic, a storm dispersed the ships for a few days, but good luck smiled on the expedition because all three of the remaining ships arrived unscathed in New Netherland in the early summer of 1625.[26]

Another ship, the 260-ton livestock transport *Ruijter*, which had been chartered by four influential members of the Amsterdam chamber as a private trader, sailed shortly after the departure of the

24. Van Laer, *Huntington Documents*, pp. 39, 44, 47, 48, 56, 59, 60, 63, 67.

25. Nicolaes van Wassenaer, *Historisch verhael alder ghedenck-weerdichste geschiedenissen die hier en daer in Europa, als in Duijtschlant, Vranckrijck, Enghelant, (Denemarcken) Hungarijen, Polen, (Sweden, Moscovien) Sevenbergen, Wallachien, Moldavien, Turckijen, (Zwitserland) en Nederlant, (in Asia . . .; in Africa . . . ;) van den beginne des jaers 1621: (tot Octobri 1629), voorgevallen sijn,* 17 vols. (Amsterdam, 1622–30), 9:40. The reference to the livestock and their numbers is in Gemeentelijke Archief van Amsterdam, Notarial no. 226, May 27, 1625, p. 64v.

26. Stokes, *Iconography*, 4:60.

squadron. Her voyage was not as fortunate. Her cargo included "sheep, hogs, wagons, ploughs, and other implements of husbandry," all apparently shipped on consignment by the four principal shareholders and destined to be sold to the colonists for furs. The four shareholders were Samuel Godijn, Cors Bicker, Gomer Sprangers, and Kiliaen van Rensselaer. Godijn and van Rensselaer were fated to play a dominant role in New Netherland's history as patroons and leading members of the New Netherland Commission within the Amsterdam chamber. The voyage of the *Ruijter* was their first involvement as private traders with the colony.

On her outward voyage the *Ruijter* avoided the North Atlantic passage for the better-known South Atlantic route, which would have taken her to the West Indies and then up the North American coast to New Netherland. The choice was unfortunate. Becalmed off the coast of Africa, she fell prey to Moorish pirates and was lost, although her backers were able to recover most of their losses through a marine insurance policy. The voyage of the *Ruijter* is important if only because it represented the first violation of the myth of the Company monopoly and demonstrated how easy it was for well-placed shareholders to take advantage of their privileges. Kiliaen van Rensselaer and Samuel Godijn would continue to use their influence to profit from the trade with New Netherland. Van Rensselaer would become the strongest advocate of free trade and private enterprise as the remedy for the colony's many ills. The loss of the *Ruijter* simply delayed the profits from private trade.[27]

The next two years were busy ones for the settlers of New Netherland. The threat of Indian war at Fort Orange and the need for a more centrally located seat of authority forced Peter Minuit, Verhulst's successor, to vacate the scattered settlements on the Delaware and Connecticut rivers as well as the one on Governor's Island. At Fort Orange, women and children were evacuated to Manhattan Island, where the Company would eventually build a large fort for their protection. For the time being, most of the colonists had to find shelter where they could, and many lived with their hogs and sheep in makeshift stables without access to fresh water and dangerously exposed to the elements. Minuit may have decided to concentrate settlement on Manhattan because the settle-

27. Gemeentelijke Archief van Amsterdam, Notarial no. 652, June 17, 1625, p. 11v.

ments on the Delaware and Connecticut were indefensible against Indian attack, and wind conditions on Long Island Sound and along the Jersey coast often delayed the coastal sloops for days as they tried to resupply the outposts of European settlement. Forced to such measures when he assumed command of the colony in the spring of 1626, Peter Minuit saved the colony by forcefully grasping authority in the wake of Verhulst's dismissal by the council. Indeed, Minuit's coup would be the first of several untidy administrative changes in New Netherland.[28]

Verhulst had angered many of the settlers by his authoritarian attitude toward their efforts to enrich themselves in the fur trade. He had berated many of the colonists for their failure to work on the Company farms. In a letter written some years after the fact, Jonas Michaëlius, a preacher (*predikant*), alluded to the conditions that had evolved under Verhulst's leadership: "Some Directors and Heads, by bad management, have rather kept back than helped the people and the country, and many among the common people would have liked to make a living, and even to get rich, in idleness rather than in hard work, saying they had not come to work; that as far as working is concerned they might as well have stayed at home."[29]

Verhulst had also been responsible for a number of irregularities in the Company's accounts. Isaac de Rasiere, the Company secretary, informed his superiors that the commander had had a heated confrontation with the council, during which a unanimous vote had called for his resignation. He had apparently doctored some of the Company invoices for his own personal benefit, and the bookkeeping procedures had been so sloppy that large stores of trade goods were missing and unaccounted for.[30]

The root cause of Verhulst's problems with the council may have been an overzealous exercise of his power to inflict punishment on recalcitrant colonists. The secretary complained in his report that "owing to bad government hitherto prevailing, it is necessary to

28. Dingman Versteeg, *Manhattan in 1628 as Described in the Recently Discovered Autograph Letter of Jonas Michaëlius Written from the Settlement on the 18th of August of That Year, and Now First Published; with a Review of the Letter and an Historical Sketch of New Netherland to 1628* (New York, 1904), pp. 70–71.

29. Ibid.

30. Van Laer, *Huntington Documents*, pp. 180–83.

administer some punishment with kindness . . . as they [the set-tlers] have heretofore been very harshly ruled by Verhulst."[31]

Matters had reached a crisis in the spring of 1626 when the council requested Verhulst's resignation. The commander refused to step down, vowing to take his services elsewhere, even threatening to sign on with the English or French. The council took a vote and agreed to banish Verhulst "now and forever from the limits of your Honor's charter."[32] The council placed the commander under house arrest, where he remained until the arrival of a ship from the fatherland. The final humiliation came when he was deported with his wife aboard the *Wapen van Amsterdam*, the same ship that had transported Peter Minuit to the colony the previous May.

Peter Minuit had been dispatched to the colony to assist Verhulst in surveying New Netherland's rivers for possible new settlements.[33] When he arrived to discover Verhulst under house arrest and colonists scattered the length and breadth of New Netherland, many living in deplorable conditions in the Company compound, he declared himself the commander and set about dealing with the most immediate problem of consolidating settlement on Manhattan Island and finding shelter for the colonists before the onset of winter.

Fortunately, Minuit had the means at hand to deal with the housing shortage. The Company engineer, Cryn Fredericksz, had been dispatched to the colony to begin construction on the much needed Fort New Amsterdam at the tip of Manhattan Island.[34] That work had commenced before Minuit could officially purchase the island seems doubtful. Hence the earliest the fort could have been started was in the early summer of 1626, and construction had probably barely begun when Minuit ordered work stopped and

31. Ibid., p. 187.
32. Ibid.
33. This may have been Minuit's second voyage to New Netherland. Fragmentary evidence suggests that he may have accompanied Verhulst to the colony on the *Oranje Boom* as *ondercommis* in 1625. See ibid., p. 258 n 1.
34. Cryn Fredericksz had accompanied Verhulst to New Netherland in 1625. The West India Company employed him specifically to build a central fort and Company facilities in the colony. His "special instructions" outlining precisely the dimensions of Fort New Amsterdam arrived via a second ship (perhaps the *Mackereel*, assuming she eventually escaped her Dunkirk captors) a few months after Fredericksz's own arrival on the ill-fated *Oranje Boom*. See ibid., p. xxi.

drafted Fredericksz and his small band of carpenters to build houses for the colonists. Some of the materials originally intended for the fort were used for the houses, forcing the engineer to scale down his plans for the fort. Instead of a fortress with a masonry palisade and houses for the commander and colonial administration, the people of New Netherland had to be satisfied with a spartan blockhouse surrounded by palisades of red cedar and sod, a most unimpressive structure as many visitors would remark. But thanks to Minuit, the colonists had shelter for the winter, and a tragedy had been averted.

Other problems faced Minuit, too. At Fort Orange the Indians were becoming disenchanted with the white invader. Complaining of mistreatment by Company employees, several local sachems had threatened to remove the Dutchmen by force. Moreover, intertribal war between the Mahicans and the Mohawks, exacerbated by Dutch intervention on the side of the Mahicans, threatened to suspend the trade altogether.[35] The Company's accounts were a mess. Goods had disappeared from the Company store, furs had been purchased only to discover that they were moldly and worthless, and secretary de Rasiere was pestering the new commander with complaints about dishonest Company employees.[36] Sometime in the midst of all these concerns Minuit purchased Manhattan Island.

Logic rather than evidence suggests that Verhulst had failed to buy Manhattan Island as per Company instructions and policy.[37]

---

35. The Indian troubles of 1625 were to have a positive effect from a Dutch perspective. Kiliaen van Rensselaer, in his "Account of the jurisdictions, management and condition of the territories named Rensselaerswyck," reported that the intertribal wars of that year had so exhausted the Indians around Fort Orange that they gladly sold their land to his agents in 1630 and 1631 (Arnold J. F. van Laer, ed. and trans., *The Van Rensselaer–Bowier Manuscripts* [Albany, 1908], p. 306). For the role the Mohawk-Mahican war may have played in the decision to make Manhattan Island the center of colonial administration, see the nice little piece of historical detective work by Charles Gehring, "Peter Minuit's Purchase of Manhattan Island—New Evidence," *De Halve Maen* 55 (Spring 1980): 6ff.

36. Van Laer, *Huntington Documents*, pp. 175–77.

37. It may be surprising that scholars are still divided over the question of who purchased Manhattan and when. I have been persuaded (mostly by the logic of the tale) to accept the traditional interpretation, which assigns the honor to Peter Minuit, rather than the revisionist position, which credits Willem Verhulst. For

This mistake could have been costly because the deteriorating relations with the Indians had already threatened Dutch settlements elsewhere. Thus Minuit purchased the little island, probably sometime between May 4 and June 26, 1626, for a trifle (60 fl.) paid in standard trade goods. Later he would secure Manhattan's defense perimeter with the purchase of Staten Island.

By September 1626, New Netherland was beginning to look like a colony. Secretary de Rasiere could report that Manhattan Island now boasted thirty log houses, a new fort, a countinghouse with walls of solid stone, and a mill with two stories and an upper loft so large that it could be used for church services.[38] When the *Wapen van Amsterdam* arrived in the fatherland, the Nineteen were overjoyed to discover that she carried grain from the colony's first harvest, samples of exotic plants, strings of wampum, huge oak and hickory timbers, and furs. Nicolaes van Wassenaer recorded the ship's arrival and noted that her cargo included 7,246 beaver skins, 675 otter skins, 48 mink, and 36 wildcat. The colonists were prospering, according to van Wassenaer. In terms his readers could appreciate, the chronicler described the colony as a happy society where each person could pursue his own fortunes: "Men work there as in Holland; one trades, upwards, southwards and northwards; another builds houses, the third farms."[39]

Unknowingly, van Wassenaer had described one of New Netherland's persistent problems. The Walloons trading "upwards, southwards and northwards" were not assisting the colony to get on its feet. Verhulst had clashed with the colonists and been sent back in chains. Minuit, largely through the force of his personality and the perilous conditions he had discovered on arrival, had managed to exact work from the colonists, but only with the impending threat of winter. Secretary de Rasiere's report contained some sobering descriptions that must have made the directors reconsider their decision to undertake colonization. The secretary

---

the controversy, see C. A. Weslager, "Did Minuit Buy Manhattan Island from the Indians," *De Halve Maen* 43 (October 1968): 5–6, and Gehring, "Peter Minuit's Purchase" Michael Kammen in his *Colonial New York: A History* (New York, 1975), accepts the revisionist view (p. 30n).

38. Van Laer, *Huntington Documents*, pp. 175ff.

39. Jameson, *Narratives*, pp. 83–84.

noted that the colonists were consumed with the fur trade. In September, the Company warehouse had run out of trading truck, prompting some colonists to barter victuals for furs at a time when provisions were being set aside for the winter months. De Rasiere described one incident as an example of the settlers' truculence in matters of trade: "It happened one day that the wife of Wolfert Gerritsz came to me with two otters, for which I offered her three guilders, ten stuivers. She refused this and asked for five guilders, whereupon I let her go, this being too much. The wife of Jacob Laurissz, the smith, knowing this, went to her and offered her five guilders. . . . Thereupon to prevent the otters from being purloined, I was obliged to give her five guilders."[40]

The Company was also suffering from inexperience. The warehouse at Fort New Amsterdam had stocks of unusable trade goods. Secretary de Rasiere, who had already reported the dangerous practice of colonists trading victuals for furs, was dismayed to discover copper kettles in the warehouse. He informed his employers that these kettles, sent out by the Amsterdam chamber, were virtually useless in the Indian trade because the Indians "would not give more for them than for other [kettles], which would not make good the cost."[41] Even the iron kettles, which had quickly sold out in the first months of the trade, were of little value to tribes living at great distances from the trading posts. They were too heavy to carry, and the Indians around Fort Orange were beginning to refuse them. De Rasiere thought he had a solution that promised great profits in the future. He recommended that the Company set up a secondary trade in wampum by trading "duffels" (a coarse, diagonally woven cloth) for the polished shells. The best wampum supplies were available on the shores of Long Island Sound and near the mouth of the Connecticut River valley. By trading duffels for the wampum, the Company could acquire the highly valued shells for shipment to the wampum-poor areas around Fort Orange. Wampum might draw the "French Indians" south to trade with the Dutch, thus assuring the Company of access to the thick furs of the far North. The Company could also spoil the fur trade

40. Van Laer, *Huntington Documents*, pp. 216–19.
41. Ibid., p. 223.

Table 3.1. Cost estimates of the colonizing expeditions of 1624–1625 (florins)

Freightage (chartering fees calculated per ton)	18,620
Insurance premiums (at 5 percent value of vessels)	14,994
Wages (ship crews: average 15 per ship)	19,320
Wages (dock workers: Amsterdam day laborer rates)	8,000
Passage for colonists (company rate = 50 fl. one way)	15,000
Livestock (Hoorn wholesale prices = 125 fl. average)	12,625
Trade goods (calculated per ton)	14,000
TOTAL	100,559

of the "Brownists at New Plymouth" by enabling its agents to outbid "them with duffels or hatchets."[42]

De Rasiere's recommendations required new expenditures by the Company. For the wampum trade alone, the secretary estimated that two or three large sloops would have to be stationed permanently in the sound. The directors of the Amsterdam chamber viewed these suggestions warily. From the chamber's viewpoint, and certainly from that of the Company as a whole, New Netherland had already consumed an inordinate amount of capital.

The costs of the colonizing expeditions of 1624–25 were high. Although the absence of reliable Company records makes any estimate of expenditures necessarily rough, some general sense of the financial outlay entailed in settling the Walloons in New Netherland may be obtained by calculating freightage fees, marine insurance premiums, passenger transportation costs, livestock prices, and wages for ship crews, dock workers, and Company employees in New Netherland. The breakdown of costs is shown in Table 3.1.[43] Even these estimates are probably lower than the actual costs

42. Ibid., p. 224.

43. Various sources were used to calculate the figures in Table 3.1. Much of the information was obtained from the notarial archives of the Gemeentelijke Archief van Amsterdam. The standard sources for the history of New Netherland were also consulted, and the *Van Rensselaer–Bowier Manuscripts* were especially useful. The article by Simon Hart, "The Dutch and North America in the First Half of the Seventeenth Century: Some Aspects," *Mededelingen van de Nederlandse vereniging voor zeegeschiedenis* 20 (March 1970): 3–9, served as a check for some of the estimates on freightage costs and marine insurance premiums.

because the establishment of colonists in New Netherland demanded several nonrecoverable expenditures such as the building of houses on Manhattan Island. Trouble with the Indians would eventually require stationing soldiers in the colony, and the scaleddown Fort New Amsterdam would require constant repair and a complete rebuilding in 1633.

Despite the optimism following the return of the *Wapen van Amsterdam*, New Netherland's future was cloudy. Receipts from the fur trade were promising, but the costs were rising. Furthermore, smuggling was already a serious problem as the numerous suits filed by Company agents against former employees and colonists attest.[44] The sixty-three thousand pelts purchased by the Company between 1626 and 1632, although worth approximately 454,000 fl., may not have covered the Company's expenses in this period.[45]

Other worries plagued the directors in these years. Investments in North America after 1626 were hindered by the rising costs of maintaining the fur trade in New Netherland and the Company's financial losses in Brazil. The latter may have been decisive in New Netherland's history, for the disasters in South America pushed the Company to the brink of bankruptcy from which it never was to recover fully.

The catastrophe in Brazil had its beginnings in 1624. While the first colonists were boarding ships for New Netherland, across the harbor plans were afoot to assemble the largest war fleet ever financed by a joint-stock company. The fleet's objective was the capture of the Brazilian stronghold of Sao Salvador de Bahia de Todos os Santos. The Nineteen had decided to make a bold thrust into the heart of the Iberian empire in the hopes of achieving a

44. Reports of smuggling among the colonists and Company employees in New Netherland are found throughout the massive notarial archives of Amsterdam. One case from 1630 involved the smuggling of 300 fl. worth of beaver pelts aboard the ship *Eendracht*. Testimony before the Amsterdam notary Nicolaes Rooleeu confirmed that Company employees supplemented their meager salaries regularly by smuggling furs home in their chests. In this case, the Company supercargo, who was responsible for catching such violations of the Company's monopoly, had actually shared in the profits for the smuggled furs (Gemeentelijke Archief van Amsterdam, Notarial no. 758, April 3, 1631, p. 210).

45. Stokes, *Iconography*, 4:72.

quick victory over an enemy thought to be unprepared. The bold thrust turned out to be an unmitigated disaster. The great fleet of twenty-three ships was decimated by a storm in mid-Atlantic, and the attack at Sao Salvador was thrown back into the sea before the Dutch could consolidate their beachhead. For months, remnants of the fleet limped into refuge harbors all over the Spanish Main. When the defeated and disease-ridden flotilla returned to the fatherland, panic swept the exchange. West India Company stock began to fall, and by December 1626 Amsterdam chamber shares were selling for less than their original price in 1621. Undaunted, the Nineteen attempted a three-pronged attack on the Spanish and Portuguese in Africa, Puerto Rico, and, once again, Brazil. This venture, too, miscarried, although the assault on the slave coast convinced some directors that the trade in humans held great potential for profits. The reports from New Netherland arrived in an atmosphere of despair and amid clamorings from stockholders for the ouster of the Nineteen.[46]

The result might have been anticipated. The Nineteen pulled back from their commitment to New Netherland. Leaving the colony in the hands of the Amsterdam chamber, where a fierce debate on colonial policy was already heating up, the West India Company, as a whole, abandoned the colony after 1626. Ships continued to make the crossing, but profits remained elusive. Four ships arrived in New Netherland in 1627, but none returned with a full cargo of furs. The year's total receipts showed a net loss of over 43,000 fl. In 1628 only two ships were sent, but even the 50 percent drop in shipping failed to produce a profit for the company.[47]

Reports coming back to the fatherland from the colony were increasingly distressing. The colonizing expeditions of 1624–25 had settled about 300 colonists in New Netherland, 270 at New Amsterdam, and about 30 at Fort Orange. Many were returning

---

46. Cornelis Ch. Goslinga, *The Dutch in the Caribbean and on the Wild Coast, 1580–1680* (Gainesville, 1971), pp. 148–66. Information about Amsterdam chamber stock prices is drawn from Hart, "Dutch and North America," p. 11.

47. Gemeentlijke Archief van Amsterdam, Notarial nos. 443, January 15, 1629, p. 16; 767, January 9, 1629, p. 172. The ships mentioned as "sailing to the Virginias" (*vaerde nae de Verginnes*) were the *Naerden* and the *Eendracht*. The latter vessel made repeated voyages to New Netherland, and there is little doubt that both were in the colony in 1628.

home in the years 1627–28. Indeed, the returning ships were filled with former colonists, many of whom would file suit against the company in later years for personal losses. Those settlers who remained in New Netherland were a motley lot. In 1628 the Classis of Amsterdam, after repeated requests from Company officials to dispatch a preacher to New Netherland, finally responded by sending Jonas Michaëlius to the colony. His observations confirmed the Company's worst suspicions.

Confronting a colonial congregation that was thinly dispersed and almost evenly divided culturally and linguistically between Dutch and Walloon, Michaëlius endured many difficulties in establishing the first permanent church in New Netherland. The lack of a common religious and cultural tradition frustrated the preacher's efforts to set up a functioning church at New Amsterdam. The once dominant Walloons and their families were leaving annually.[48] And the employees of the Company were single men with little interest in religion. The language barrier was especially troublesome because so few Company employees had fluency in French, and the Walloons clung to their language as a mark of identity. Michaëlius, whose French was poor at best, noted that the Walloons' lack of fluency in Dutch was thwarting his efforts to spread the Word: "We administer the Holy Sacrament of the Lord once in four months, provisionally until a larger number of people shall otherwise require. The Walloons and French have no service on Sundays, otherwise than in the Dutch language, of which they understand very little."[49]

Michaëlius's complaints would be echoed by many others in the years to follow, for New Netherland would remain a patchwork of nationalities, languages, and races. The diversity of the colony's population would always stand as a stark contrast to the religious, linguistic, and cultural homogeneity of New England. It was, perhaps, the inevitable extension of the diversity of the United Provinces to the colony on the Hudson that rendered any attempt at the creation of a loyal and thriving Dutch colony impossible. Like the

48. "A portion of the Walloons are going back to the fatherland, either because their years here are expired or also because some were not serviceable to the Company" (Letter from Dominie Jonas Michaëlius to Classis of Amsterdam in Samuel Purple, ed., *Index to the Marriage Records of the Dutch Reformed Church in New Amsterdam and New York* [New York, 1890], p. v).

49. Ibid.

fatherland, New Netherland would always be a haven for foreigners. The West India Company had assured as much by the decision to settle the French-speaking and clannish Walloons in 1624–25. The directors would discover that their decision was irreversible. Try as they might, the colony could not be abandoned, the settlers could not be repatriated, and the expenses of maintaining the Company presence could not be reduced. In the Amsterdam chamber, voices were already being raised in defense of the colony's continued existence. These men were not willing to abandon the experiment so soon. They were convinced that a new plan for settling even more colonists in New Netherland could turn the red ink into black. They hoped also to become rich in the process.

[4]

The Patroonships

There are many people in this country, among them some of large means, who would like to invest their capital in New Netherland if the Company would admit other colonies, in refusing which it makes a great mistake in my opinion, for instead of many poor beggars whom it now gets, it would find people of means who with their money could send all sorts of men and the patroons who stayed here would secure the Company against loss and offense in that country.

—Kiliaen van Rensselaer, 1628

The controversy concerning the nature of the struggle over the patroonship plan for New Netherland has raged for more than a century. John Romeyn Brodhead and Edmund B. O'Callaghan, the two pioneers in Dutch New York history, writing in the second half of the nineteenth century, concluded that the struggle between the Dutch West India Company and the group of wealthy principal shareholders of the Amsterdam chamber was essentially the age-old conflict between capitalism and monopoly. The investors who sought ducal grants in New Netherland were aristocrats attempting to stem the tide of democracy. The Company was a passive giant aiding these power-grabbing men by abandoning its responsibilities to its colonists. The conflict was, therefore, between democracy and aristocracy, between the forces for individual freedom and those for personal aggrandizement.[1]

Although this whig theory of the patroonship system has been

1. John Romeyn Brodhead, *History of the State of New York*, 2 vols. (New York, 1853–71); Edmund B. O'Callaghan, *The History of New Netherland; or, New York under the Dutch*, 2 vols. (New York, 1845–48).

seriously challenged, few scholars have seen fit to dust off the old documents and reexamine the motives and intentions behind the two patroonship plans for New Netherland.[2] Historians interested in the origins of the patroonship system have been dismayed to discover that the all-important first plan, approved by the Amsterdam chamber on March 10, 1628, has been lost for at least a century and a half. The original document disappeared with the rest of the West India Company papers in 1813, when they were released by a government agency to a scrap paper merchant. No other copy was thought to have survived. Kiliaen van Rensselaer's private correspondence mentioned its existence, and a Dutch antiquarian in the nineteenth century reported having seen it in the national archives before 1813.[3] Without the original plan, historians have been forced to draw their conclusions from the later scheme of June 7, 1629, which significantly expanded the patroons' privileges. The chronology of the intense struggle for the patroonship system as well as many of its salient features have been lost.

Fortunately, a copy of the 1628 plan has survived, and it sheds considerable light on the obscure period between January 1628 and June 1629.[4] This period witnessed a bitter struggle between two factions within the Amsterdam chamber, the outcome of which

2. The first two scholars to challenge the Brodhead-O'Callaghan thesis were Arnold J. F. van Laer, in *Van Rensselaer–Bowier Manuscripts* (Albany, 1908), and S. G. Nissenson, in *The Patroon's Domain* (New York, 1937). Van Cleaf Bachman has attempted to reconstruct the events surrounding the development of the first patroonship plan by reference to a similar plan drawn up for the colonization of Guiana. The effort is ingenious, but the result is more speculation than history and far off the mark in many respects. See *Peltries or Plantations: The Economic Policies of the Dutch West India Company in New Netherland, 1623–1639* (Baltimore, 1969), pp. 95–107.

3. For a discussion of the mystery surrounding the disappearance of the March 10, 1628, patroonship plan, see Bachman, *Peltries or Plantations*, p. 103n.

4. There are many examples of historical puzzles solved or new insights presented by the rediscovery of lost documents. While doing research in the Algemeen Rijksarchief in The Hague, I came across a reference in the printed catalog of the *Aanwinsten* (acquisitions) to *"een kopie van de Vrijheden en Exemptieen voor 10 maart 1628."* My examination of the document revealed it to be a third (possibly fourth) copy of the long-lost "Freedoms and Exemptions." For unknown reasons, the copy had been preserved in the private family archives of a former West India Company director. The Rijksarchief had acquired the document in 1891, and there the document remained until I accidentally found it in 1974.

influenced the Company's policies for New Netherland for more than a decade.

The struggle within the Amsterdam chamber can be examined only by careful comparison of the two patroonship plans of March 10, 1628, and June 7, 1629. The issues focused on the important question of whether the Company's economic policies, hitherto aimed at the establishment of a permanent settlement in New Netherland, should abandon the concept of Company monopoly of the fur trade and permit certain privileged shareholders to participate in the trade under Company license. At the heart of the debate lay two distinct visions of New Netherland's future—the "Company view," which reflected a strict constructionist interpretation of the charter and its monopolistic grant of exclusive authority over colonial trade, and the "patroons' view," which reflected a loose interpretation of the charter and sought to open up the colony to private enterprise, albeit limited in scope.

By 1627 the Company view was gaining converts within the chamber. The disappointing returns from New Netherland and the disastrous losses incurred in the attempts to gain a foothold in South America had convinced several principal shareholders that the colonization of New Netherland was a profitless undertaking. A possible solution to the Company's plight, and one that had a great deal of appeal to a sizable majority of the chamber's principal shareholders, was to close off colonial immigration to New Netherland. With few colonists the Company would be spared the expenses of defense and supply, and smuggling would decrease. The Company could then put its energies into improving the efficiency of the fur trade, which had proven to be potentially lucrative if only the competition from the colonists could be eliminated. The trade would be confined to a few trading posts staffed by Company agents and supplied from Holland. This "factory system," modeled after the examples established in West Africa and elsewhere, would permit the Company to maintain a commercial presence in the region for a minimum expenditure of capital. The chamber could dispatch vessels from the fatherland to pick up the year's furs that were gathered during the winter months at the trading posts, thus assuring the Company of full cargoes. Perhaps the most attractive feature of the factory system was the increased control over on-station prices for furs. Strategically located "factories" would eliminate the troublesome colonists, who had already demonstrated a tendency to bid up prices. The Company's agents could deal directly with the Indians, thereby keeping prices down and profits up.

The declining fortunes of the Company as a whole undoubtedly also influenced the chamber's directors. As we have seen, the once mighty Company had fallen on hard times in the late 1620s. Stock prices had dropped, the provinces were withholding their subsidies, and debts were rising.[5] Faced with mounting financial problems, the Amsterdam chamber was under some pressure to reduce expenses. Hoping to cut their losses, the dominant faction on the New Netherland Commission favored a policy of retrenchment in New Netherland.

Some of the chamber's principal shareholders opposed this policy, however. The faction led by Kiliaen van Rensselaer wanted to colonize New Netherland with private capital. He and his associates placed the cause of failure in New Netherland upon the Company's shortsighted policy of restricted trade. The colonists had been denied the right to improve their lot by the Company's intransigence regarding the fur trade. Van Rensselaer complained that Company management had been incompetent, and the reports of secretary de Rasiere confirmed, as many had already suspected, that the colonists had rebelled against Verhulst because they had been treated miserably and in violation of the Provisional Orders. Moreover, the colonization expeditions of 1624–25 had failed to create enough interest in the colony to attract investors, and the colony would continue to languish until sufficient incentives were made available to attract men of means and competence.

A weak compromise was reached in the spring of 1628, when the first patroonship plan for New Netherland was endorsed by the New Netherland Commission and approved by the chamber's directors. The plan was entitled "Freedoms and Exemptions for the

---

5. On October 24, 1628, the Nineteen submitted a report to the States General which listed the subsidies by province and chamber. Every chamber was in arrears. Holland was 382,845 fl. behind and Zeeland 125,256 fl. The total debt of the Company was 869,379 fl., or almost one-seventh of the total capitalization (Algemeen Rijksarchief, De liassen West-Indische Compagnie, 5752, October 24, 1628).

Patroons and Masters or Private Persons who would plant a colony and cattle in New Netherland."⁶ The plan envisioned the use of private capital to colonize New Netherland, and, as such, it reversed Company policy and blunted the attempt to pull back from the territorial commitment established with the settlement of the Walloons. The essential features of the plan were its reopening of the colony to private traders and abandoning of the Company's effort to restrict further settlement in the region. To carry out these objectives, private entrepreneurs were permited to ferry colonists to New Netherland aboard Company ships. In return, they received large tracts of land in exchange for assurances that they were willing to bear the expense of colonization. The "Freedoms and Exemptions" thus established a precedent for the return of private capital to the colony. By tapping the enormous pool of private wealth in the United Provinces, the directors hoped to shift the financial burden to the individual merchants and at the same time stimulate a migration of permanent colonists whose presence in the colony would serve to establish the Company's claim to the region.

Prospective patroons were invited to send "three or four persons to examine the opportunities" in the colony, paying their transportation at a fixed rate of six stuivers per day for regular fare and twelve stuivers per day for cabin accommodations. After having thus acquired data for future colonization, the entrepreneurs were allowed to petition the appropriate chamber of the West India Company for a patroonship.⁷ Grants would be made on a first-come-first-served basis.

Patroons were given three years to settle sixty persons in New Netherland at their own expense. Because the Company wished to

6. The following discussion is based upon Algemeen Rijksarchief, Aanwinsten, "Archief Wassenaer," no. 28 (1891): Kopie van de Vrijheden en Exemptien voor maart 10, 1628, cataloged in *Jaarboek Register voor 1895*.

7. Although the Amsterdam chamber had been charged with the administration of New Netherland, any shareholder in one of the other chambers was entitled to apply for a patroonship through his own chamber. That no one from outside the Amsterdam chamber ever did suggests that the plan was little publicized. In the plan of June 7, 1629, no mention was made of other chambers' rights to patroonships in New Netherland, although by company charter they could not have been excluded.

populate Manhattan Island first, it offered generous concessions to patroons willing to settle just thirty colonists there. These special provisions probably reflected the need to maintain the island as the center of the colony. Since the island was small, fewer colonists were required for the establishment of patroon rights. At least one-third of the total number of colonists had to be transported to the colony in each of the three years.

The land grants given the patroons were generous even by seventeenth-century standards. Each was entitled to "three leagues along the coast or on one side of a river and another half league along two sides of a river." From a river or coastline grants were to extend "as far inland as the situation of the residents shall permit." The size of these holdings was less of a concern to the directors than the size of the river frontage. Because the most efficient means of transportation from farm to market was by water, the directors defined the size of the patroonships by river or coastal frontage. Inland from the river or coast the patroon theoretically could claim lordship over a thin slice of the continent.

The patroonships carried with them substantial rights and privileges in the plan of 1628. Within the patroon's domain he had unlimited right to all "fruits, flora, minerals, rivers, and springs." In addition, each patroon appointed officers and agents who would exercise in his name the rights of "middle and low jurisdiction." In the legal language then prevailing in the United Provinces, this meant that the patroon was to have judicial authority over the punishment of all crimes within his territory, with the exception of capital offenses. Moreover, the patroon could tax his colonists at the maximum rate of 10 percent of their annual income from farming, fishing, and/or mining. These rights were possessed by the patroon as a perpetual fief and could be transferred by will to his heirs for the nominal registration fee of twenty florins.

The patroons were free to sail the entire coast from Newfoundland to Florida and to engage in any trade (except furs) with the colony. The restriction on the fur trade was undoubtedly the most important concession made by those advocating the patroonship plan. Kiliaen van Rensselaer complained later that the failure of the Company to open the fur trade to the patroons was the principal reason why the 1628 Freedoms and Exemptions were never implemented.[8] To those advocating the Company view, however, the Freedoms and Exemptions must have appeared overly generous even without the fur trade. Van Rensselaer and his supporters were unconvinced.

Though the patroons were free to trade anywhere along the North American seaboard, they could not ship the products of their domains directly to the United Provinces. The 1628 plan restricted most colonial trade to Manhattan Island, which was to serve as the staple center for the colony. Every cargo, whether from New Netherland or elsewhere, had to be inventoried by the company secretary at Fort New Amsterdam before shipment home, and every trade voyage departing the colony for other ports along the American coast required prior approval and sanction from the Company commander and council.

The Company faction succeeded also in restricting the use of privately chartered ships in the New Netherland trade. Hoping to derive some profit from freightage fees and wishing to maintain a tight control on the number of ships making the New Netherland crossing, the Company faction required patroons to use Company ships and to pay a fixed fee for cargo space, rated per ton. Van Rensselaer's group, however, was able to obtain a dispensation from this regulation should Company ships be unavailable. In such cases, the patroons were permitted to outfit their own vessels, provided they took aboard a Company supercargo. More important, the patroons obtained a ten-year reprieve from paying the convoy, toll, and excise fees that the Admiralty levied on all Dutch merchant vessels.

The 1628 plan provided opportunities for "private persons" other than patroons who wished to settle in New Netherland. For these people, land grants were limited to "as much . . . as they can comfortably work." Each "free colonist" was likewise given privileges of trade similar to those held by a patroon. A free colonist's land was to be held in perpetuity with rights of testament. The Company faction may have hoped to attract enough free colonists with these provisions to offset the power of the patroons, while creating a sizable colony of people dependent on the Company for supplies. Special clauses in the plan encouraged the establishment

8. Van Laer, *Van Rensselaer–Bowier Manuscripts*, p. 237.

of salt pans and provided substantial rewards for free colonists who discovered precious minerals and other treasures. In this regard the Freedoms and Exemptions of 1628 were more generous than the Provisional Orders of 1624. Free colonists were reckoned as patroons on their property and could keep all the profits from gold mines, pearl fisheries, and the like after paying the Company a percentage of the gross profit. The settlers on the patroonships, however, could not profit from such discoveries beyond receiving a finder's fee to be set by the patroon. Precious minerals and other fortuitous discoveries within the patroon's domain became the property of the patroon, who was obligated only to pay the Company a percentage of the gross profit.

This early plan also provided protection for the patroonships in wartime by requiring the Company to dispatch troops from the fatherland if necessary. The plan also permitted the free colonists a voice in the management of New Netherland through appointed representatives to the commander's council at Fort New Amsterdam. To ensure a law-abiding community, the plan instructed the patroons to care for the intellectual and spiritual well-being of their subjects by providing schoolmasters and preachers at their own expense. The labor shortage, already a chronic problem for New Netherland, required a series of meetings in March 1628, at which it was decided to supplement the labor force with African slaves drawn from other parts of the chartered territory or, if need be, imported directly from the slave coast.[9] The slaves were to be used as farm labor only. European colonists were to work farms, trade, or engage in artisan activities. The development of a colonial-based textile industry (which might conceivably compete with home manufacturing) was expressly forbidden, as was the immigration of skilled textile workers.

The intent of the 1628 plan appears clear. Having decided that it would be unprofitable to continue to colonize New Netherland at Company expense, the Amsterdam chamber had responded to the pressure of a few ambitious directors by modifying its trade monopoly to permit a limited policy of colonization financed by private capital. The salient feature of the first patroonship plan was

9. Agenda of directors' meeting contained in the same packet with the March 10 Freedoms and Exemptions. Algemeen Rijksarchief, Aanwinsten, "Archief Wassenaer," no. 28 (1891), cataloged in *Jaarboek Register voor 1895.*

the provision allowing private enterprise to bear the expense of the colony's development. The adoption of the Freedoms and Exemptions reflected a hard-fought compromise between opposing factions within the Amsterdam chamber. The Company or monopolist faction, termed the "contrary-minded" by Kiliaen van Rensselaer, had failed to halt further colonization of New Netherland. They had succeeded, however, in limiting the plan of the patroons to open up the colony to free trade. The fur trade remained closed to the patroons, and although other important concessions had been wrenched from the Company faction, the lucrative trade in furs continued to be a Company monopoly.

Like most compromises, the Freedoms and Exemptions of 1628 pleased few people and failed to fulfill the essential need of the colony for more settlers. On a policy level the plan achieved much, for it challenged the theory of monopoly and succeeded in opening a small door for the return of private capital to New Netherland. The next step awaited some extraordinary event that could turn the West India Company's finances around and blunt the opposition of the Company faction within the Amsterdam chamber. Such an event occurred shortly after the approval of the 1628 plan.

On November 15, 1628, the yacht *Ouwevaer* dropped anchor at Rotterdam. The vessel brought news that Admiral Piet Heyn had captured a Spanish fleet in the West Indies and was en route home with a load of booty. The news spread across the United Provinces with the fevered pace of rumor and even excited the speculative instincts of the West India Company directors. Company stock on the Amsterdam exchange surged to great heights as principal shareholders scrambled to increase their investments. When Admiral Heyn's fleet arrived carrying gold, silver, hides, dyewood, sugar, and merchandise estimated at 11.5 million fl., the excitement was boundless. The Company gathered into its nearly empty treasury almost 7 million fl. after expenses, a sum almost equal to the entire subscribed capital in 1621. The Nineteen profited handsomely, receiving together some 70,000 fl., and stockholders pocketed a 50 percent dividend, which totaled more than 3.5 million fl.[10]

Piet Heyn became a national hero, and the fate of New Netherland was once again debated in Amsterdam. This time the Com-

10. Cornelis Ch. Goslinga, *The Dutch in the Caribbean and on the Wild Coast, 1580–1680* (Gainesville, 1971), pp. 195–96.

pany faction offered less opposition to van Rensselaer's proposals. The news of Admiral Heyn's triumph affected the general mood in the Amsterdam chamber, and the contrary-minded directors on the New Netherland Commission could not prevent a review of the patroonship plan for the colony.[11] For those supporting the cause of the patroons the joyous atmosphere presented a second opportunity to carve out fiefdoms on the Hudson. Three would-be patroons hired agents to survey areas in New Netherland for patroonships even before the commission had begun its review of the 1628 plan.[12]

Meanwhile, Kiliaen van Rensselaer and others demanded a review of the 1628 plan. The discussions dragged on through the winter months of 1629, while van Rensselaer and his supporters diligently worked behind the scenes drumming up support for a major revision of the Freedoms and Exemptions. The Company faction soon recovered from the heady intoxication that followed the 50 percent dividend and renewed its opposition to the efforts of van Rensselaer to expand the trade and territorial privileges of the patroons. The group was unable this time, however, to carry the votes on the New Netherland Commission, in which van Rensselaer had succeeded in obtaining a majority in support of his position. In April, the commission passed a resolution calling for a general meeting of the directors of the Amsterdam chamber. The purpose of the meeting was clearly stated: "To reconsider all the former articles, freedoms and exemptions granted the respective colonies in several former meetings and the matters connected therewith and to deliberate whether the same might be amplified by the accompanying articles requested by several influential participants and amended as the occasion requires."

The "accompanying articles" were a list of amendments submitted back in February by van Rensselaer's group. These amendments

11. The minutes of the Amsterdam chamber have been lost. Hence it is impossible to reconstruct the exact timetable for the debates on the new Freedoms and Exemptions. Fragmentary evidence suggests, however, that the March 10, 1628, Freedoms and Exemptions were reviewed as early as October of the same year. Their inability to attract sufficient public interest had probably forced the New Netherland Commission and the directors of the chamber to rethink their plans for New Netherland in the months preceding Admiral Heyn's return to the fatherland. See van Laer, *Van Rensselaer–Bowier Manuscripts*, pp. 237–39.

12. Ibid., p. 154.

were immediately reviewed when the April meeting was called to order in the West India Company house in Amsterdam. The Company faction tried to block the proceedings by recommending that the amendments. be examined by a special committee before they were put before the general assembly of chamber directors, thereby postponing a decision until the jubilation over Admiral Heyn's return had had time to subside. Van Rensselaer protested the delay but could not prevent the general assembly from referring the matter to a special committee, which was appointed to consider the amendments in closed session. By the first week in June it had completed its work, and the general assembly voted on the amendments. The vote was favorable, and on June 7, 1629, a revised version of the Freedoms and Exemptions was made public.[13]

The new Freedoms and Exemptions retained much of the wording of the 1628 document. The new plan was longer and more detailed, but the numbered paragraphs were kept in the same sequence.[14] The first change occurred in Article III, which had specified the requirements for obtaining a patroonship. The new plan liberalized the terms, requiring the settlement of only fifty persons in a "colony" and extending the time limit from three to four years. These terms were restricted somewhat by the requirement that all fifty settlers be "upwards of 15 years old." Only one-fourth of the total number had to be transported to New Netherland in any given year instead of the one-third demanded by the 1628 plan. Another change applied to the granting of patroonships on Manhattan Island, which in the new plan was to remain free territory under Company authority and management. This alteration may be considered a minor victory for the Company faction because it aimed at maintaining Company control of the all-important Hudson River estuary. Patroonships established above Manhattan Island on the Hudson were less likely to become hotbeds of smug-

13. The revised Freedoms and Exemptions of 1629 have been printed in various sources. The most readily available copy, complete with Dutch transcriptions and English translations, is in van Laer, *Van Rensselaer–Bowier Manuscripts*, pp. 136–53. The following discussion is drawn from this translation.

14. The numbered paragraph or article format was the standard form employed by the directors of the West India Company throughout its history. From all appearances it seems that the 1628 version of the Freedoms and Exemptions was used as a model for the revision of 1629.

gling because slipping by the Company agents on the island would have been difficult.

Article IV of the new document employed language more positive than the 1628 version to describe the ownership rights to the land. The older plan had granted the patroons the "use and possession of all such lands," whereas the newer plan termed such privileges "free ownership of all lands." The semantic difference between the two versions points to the influence of van Rensselaer and his group, as does the granting of enlarged territories in the 1629 plan.

A patroonship was to extend "four leagues along the coast or one side of a navigable river, or two leagues along both sides of a river," thus increasing the territories of the patroons by nearly 25 percent. The extended size of the patroonships, coupled with the reduced requirements for ownership, clearly demonstrated van Rensselaer's victory. Nevertheless, some precautions were taken against land monopoly. The 1629 Freedoms and Exemptions prohibited contiguous boundaries between patroonships. In Article V, a clause was added to prevent a rival patroon from acquiring land "within seven or eight leagues" of another patroon. The land between the patroonships was retained by the Company, but patroons were granted the use of such land until the Company could decide what use to make of it.

The 1629 document enlarged the patroons' political and legal privileges by giving them jurisdiction not only over minor felonies and misdemeanors (as in the 1628 plan) but also over capital offenses. This grant of the power of life and death over tenants had the effect of making the patroons the most powerful law enforcement officials in New Netherland. Some safeguards were instituted, however, such as the automatic right of appeal to the Company commander for any crime involving more than 50 fl. Despite such legal safeguards, however, the Freedoms and Exemptions of 1629 gave the patroons an almost unrestricted hand in legal affairs involving their tenants. Article VI, for example, gave the patroons the right to appoint all magistrates within their domain and to confer titles upon their subjects. Such privileges were obviously important in political and social relationships and gave the patroons a good deal of power over social mobility within the colony. The West India Company was forced to compete with the patroons for talented administrators, even though theoretically the patroons' privileges were held on Company sufferance.

The most startling differences in the two plans occurred in those articles dealing with trade. In Article X, the Company assessment on freight was lowered from 10 to 5 percent of total value, and no time limit was imposed on the payment, which in the 1628 plan had been assessed on the return voyage. This slight change amounted to a grant of unlimited credit to patroons for the stocking and peopling of their colonies. Livestock was given free passage in Company ships as in the 1628 plan, but the new scheme made the privilege permanent, whereas the earlier document had imposed a time limit of six years. Article XI renewed the right to trade along the entire coast of North America, but no notice had to be given the Company commander at Fort New Amsterdam as in the earlier plan. The Company had apparently abandoned its effort to regulate the day-to-day commercial activities of the patroons. The effect was to permit commerce to develop among private traders of New Netherland, New England, and English Virginia. The Company required the patroons to pay a 5 percent staple tax at Fort New Amsterdam on all goods obtained outside the colony, but without adequate customs control this tax was all but uncollectible. Moreover, private traders prevented "by contrary currents and other things" could sail directly to the fatherland with their cargoes, a privilege specifically prohibited in 1628.

Article XV contained an important concession to private enterprise. It opened the fur trade to all patroons and "free persons" in areas where the Company did not maintain a factor. In practice, this provision opened most of the colony and all of the coastline to private fur traders. Traders were required to carry their furs to Manhattan Island for Company inspection and inventory, where they were to be assessed one florin per pelt. Ships unable to return directly to Manhattan were once again permitted to take their cargoes to the United Provinces—a clause that allowed much smuggling in years to come. Other privileges were also renewed or expanded, but in Article XXIII a new concession granted the patroons the right to transport fish directly to "neutral lands." The fish trade, one of the most jealously guarded monopolies in Dutch maritime commerce, was placed beyond the control of the Company. Even though a Company supercargo was supposed to be aboard all fishing vessels departing for the Mediterranean to enforce the regulations, the sheer size of the potential trade would have required many more super-cargoes than the Company had in New Netherland. Furthermore, honest supercargoes proved hard to find, and bribery and fraud were destined to make the fishing concession an open door for smuggling furs and tobacco to Europe.

The remaining articles affected the welfare of the free colonists, particularly with respect to their newly won privileges of land-ownership. In the 1629 Freedoms and Exemptions free colonists' land titles were no longer perpetual; rather, property was to revert back to the Company upon the death of the titleholder. In effect, this change permitted the Company to retain control of the largest portion of New Netherland, and it may be viewed as a minor point won by the Company faction. Yet the elimination of testament rights for the free colonists may have had an unforeseen result. By prohibiting the free colonists to become perpetual landowners, the 1629 Freedoms and Exemptions left the patroons in an unassailable position as the colony's only permanent landowners. The perpetual fiefs given the patroons far exceeded the land rights held by the Company, which were limited because the charter was due to ex-pire in less than sixteen years from the date of the creation of the patroonship system.

As might be expected, the ratification of the new Freedoms and Exemptions attracted a flurry of attention from would-be patroons. Although Kiliaen van Rensselaer, Samuel Godijn, and Samuel Blommaert had already staked out sites in New Netherland in January 1629, they waited until the new plan had been approved by the chamber directors before submitting their requests for pa-troonships. Michael Pauw, a principal shareholder in the chamber and, one suspects, a strong supporter of the patroons' faction on the New Netherland Commission, filed a claim for a patroonship east of the Connecticut River on the same day that van Rensselaer announced his intention to establish a patroonship on the Hudson River. Samuel Godijn soon followed suit by sending two agents to the Delaware River to survey the area for his estate. Other prospec-tive patroons filed claims in the following months: Albert Burgh sought a patroonship near the mouth of the Delaware River and Samuel Blommaert a colony on the Connecticut. Kiliaen van Re-nsselaer was the best prepared of all. In the last months of the year, he filed all the requisite papers, including field reports, surveys, and maps for his patroonship of Rensselaerswyck.

The requests for patroonships were quickly recommended by the chamber directors and approved by the Nineteen. The new patroons set about purchasing land from the Indians. Van Rensselaer sent out Bastiaen Jansz Krol with instructions "to buy the lands hereafter named for the said Rensselaer, from the Mahijcans, Maguaas or such other nations as have any claim to them." For these lands Krol was to exchange Company merchandise then available in the colony and charge it to the patroon, taking care to obtain a bill of sale from the Indians and registering the transaction with the Company secretary at Fort New Amsterdam. Krol was also under orders to oversee the erection of buildings, the purchase of cattle, and the surveying of farms, and, van Rensselaer added, "to look out that my men work faithfully and diligently and that they do not cheat me or sell any of my goods." The patroon wanted an annual report from Krol in which he was to be especially careful to report "the number of horses, cows, sheep, and hogs . . . and how old they are and how many have died or been born each year."[15]

Despite such planning, the tasks ahead were difficult. Detailed plans had to be drawn up, suitable employees recruited, and sources of supply located for livestock, wooden casks, nails, farm implements, seed, smithing tools, and other necessities. Notwithstanding the expanded privileges won, the risks were monumental. The patroons soon found themselves in competition with one another for the limited sources of supply. Under an agreement, which amounted to a cartel, the patroons of 1629 pledged to share their resources. They collaborated on nearly everything from the chartering of ships to the hiring of employees. To bring down prices and spread the liabilities of colonization, they took out shares in each other's patroonships. Thus, Kiliaen van Rensselaer had shares in the patroonships of Godijn, Burgh, and Blommaert. Godijn and Blommaert also held shares in Rensselaerswyck. Only Michael Pauw acted alone. Each patroonship, however, was to be under the management of a single patroon, and the pooling of liability was not intended to convey joint ownership of the estates. Junior partners

---

15. Van Laer, *Van Rensselaer–Bowier Manuscripts*, p. 160.

in the patroonships were entitled only to a percentage of the estate's net produce.[16]

To be successful, the patroons had to have the cooperation of Company officials on both sides of the Atlantic. Conflict of interest between the patroons and Company officialdom was inevitable. Van Rensselaer complained repeatedly that the directors blocked his plans in Amsterdam and that Company agents sabotaged them in America. He pointed to the lack of shipping space aboard Company vessels as but one example of the Company's conspiracy to effect his ruin.

The Company had pledged to assist the patroons by providing shipping space aboard any Company vessel bound for New Netherland. Van Rensselaer and his partners were quick to demand that this promise be fulfilled. Requests were submitted to the chamber directors in the early months of 1630 for cargo space and passenger accommodations on the first scheduled ships to the colony in the spring. The directors refused, citing war operations in Brazil as the cause of the shortage of ships and space. Van Rensselaer, who had made commitments to suppliers and prospective colonists based on the assumption of adequate space on Company ships, was incensed. He fired off angry letters to his fellow directors and threatened lawsuits. He came to view the shipping problem as symptomatic of a broad-based conspiracy of the contrary-minded to bankrupt him. He was convinced the conspiracy was led by his old nemesis, Marcus de Vogelaer, leader of the Company faction on the New Netherland Commission.[17]

Shortly after the approval of the Freedoms and Exemptions, van Rensselaer and his fellow patroons lost control of the New Netherland Commission. Members of the Company faction, led by de

16. The legal liabilities of such agreements were felt by Kiliaen van Rensselaer's heirs. The patroon's partners tried for years to obtain some of the profits from Rensselaerswyck and took their cases to court. The fascinating history of the legal dispute, only hinted at in the *Van Rensselaer–Bowier Manuscripts*, can be traced in detail in the notarial records of Amsterdam: Gemeentelijke Archief van Amsterdam, Notarial nos. 873, November 2, 1644, p. 360; 1975, November 18, 1645, p. 189; 1078, February 5, 1646, pp. 80–81; 1079, June 26, 1646, pp. 180–180v; 1079, August 18, 1646, pp. 328–328v, 329.

17. Van Laer, *Van Rensselaer–Bowier Manuscripts*, pp. 238–49.

Vogelaer, gained back all their seats on the commission and ousted the patroons from the board of directors in the chamber. With the ink hardly dry on the Freedoms and Exemptions, de Vogelaer began a systematic attack on the patroons, accusing them of having defrauded the Company of the best lands in New Netherland and threatening to review the situation yet again. A chance meeting between van Rensselaer and de Vogelaer on the Dam nearly four years later showed how deep the emotions ran. The heated discussion in front of witnesses nearly erupted into a fist fight, with van Rensselaer reporting that "he went at de Vogelaer in such a way on the crowded Dam that he will not soon forget it."[18]

Van Rensselaer's complaints were not without foundation. Disgruntled members of the opposition had accused him of fraud in the acquisition of his claim to Rensselaerswyck. When these charges passed from rumor to public slander, he drew up a detailed remonstrance denying the charges and arguing that New Netherland remained a virgin colony in which "not a hundredth part of the land has as yet been trodden by Christian foot."[19] The remonstrance did not stop de Vogelaer. Determined to squeeze the patroons out of the fur trade as a preliminary to removing them entirely from the chartered territory, de Vogelaer set in motion an investigation into the manner in which the patroonships had been acquired. To implement his plan, the chamber hired Hans Hunthum to expand the Company's fur trade at Fort Orange in an effort to deny the furs of the upper Hudson to van Rensselaer. Hunthum apparently enjoyed his work because within months after his arrival, the patroon's fur trade collapsed.[20] Although van Rensselaer's financial interest in the fur trade did not assume an overriding proportion of his invested capital at this time, he was convinced that Hunthum's actions were aimed at his ruin. Other patroons experienced even greater difficulties.

Albert Burgh, van Rensselaer's junior partner and longtime member of the patroons' faction in the chamber, was the first to falter. To save himself, after a series of bad investments and mishaps in establishing his patroonship, Burgh withdrew from the patroons' cartel; he gave up his claim to the land and became a

18. Ibid., p. 267.
19. Ibid., p. 239.
20. Nissenson, *Patroon's Domain*, pp. 171–72.

spokesman for the opposition. Burgh's defection caused van Rensselaer much anxiety because his public attacks on the patroons gave credence to the charges of fraud leveled by de Vogelaer and the contrary-minded. The shareholders began to believe that the patroons really had defrauded the Company of the best lands in New Netherland. The patroons' situation had become desperate by 1631. De Vogelaer proposed that the chamber draw up a new set of Freedoms and Exemptions to ensure that the Company's charter rights had not been violated. The proposal sent both sides scrambling for lawyers, and the remaining patroons braced themselves for a legal test.

To clear the air, van Rensselaer proposed that the charters of 1629 be reviewed and the charges of fraud substantiated or denied. Since the feud between de Vogelaer and van Rensselaer had deadlocked the Amsterdam chamber, the States General was forced to intervene. Their High Mightinesses appointed a select committee to review the charges and arbitrate the dispute. Its report accused both sides of exceeding their rights. More important, it chastised the West India Company for obstructing the operations of the patroons and suggested that the Company pay them for any losses.[21]

The select committee's report was a partial victory for the patroons and a blow to the prestige of the contrary-minded. Van Rensselaer was permitted to complete the organization of expeditions to settle colonists in Rensselaerswyck. By the terms of the Freedoms and Exemptions he was obliged to transport colonists to his patroonship before November 19, 1630. Throughout 1629 and 1630, amid the turmoil of the controversy with de Vogelaer, van Rensselaer had recruited colonists, gathered supplies, and made arrangements for the transportation of livestock. These preparations caused him much trouble. Colonists were not easy to find, and he may have had to conscript tenants from his ancestral estate to fill the ships departing in the summer of 1630. Livestock presented special problems because shipping space proved difficult to obtain, and the Company refused to build stalls for cattle below decks. Van Rensselaer eventually solved the problem by establishing a breeding farm on Manhattan Island, by building livestock transports at his own expense, and by buying yearlings from free

21. Ibid., p. 175.

settlers along the Hudson River. Through ingenuity, tenacity, and a good deal of luck, van Renssealer succeeded in launching Rensselaerswyck on a sound footing. The other patroons were not so successful.[22]

Samuel Blommaert promptly abandoned his patroonship when the opposition proved to be too well organized. Michael Pauw held on to his Pavonia for some time, but lacking the capital resources of a partnership for large-scale colonization, he gave up the struggle and sold his claim back to the Company.[23] Samuel Godijn's story was somewhat more complicated.

Godijn, like van Rensselaer, had prepared well for the founding of his patroonship. In 1630, he had asked the well-known ship captain David de Vries to manage his patroonship. De Vries, who was in the employ of the VOC at the time, had to decline the offer but let it be known that he was interested in buying into the patroonship as a partner. Godijn promptly accepted the offer and formed a partnership of investors with van Rensselaer, Blommaert, and that ardent advocate of overseas expansion, Johan de Laet. Four others were soon added to the partnership in an effort to acquire enough working capital to begin colonization. De Vries was angered by Godijn's expansion of the partnership and threatened to withdraw his money unless he could be assured that his liability would cover only the proposed patroonship of Swanendael to be established on the Delaware River. Apparently the assurances were forthcoming because de Vries kept his money in the partnership.[24]

The partnership commissioned an Amsterdam surveyor to visit the Delaware and select a suitable site for an agricultural settlement. The surveyor was accompanied by a whaling employee of Godijn, Captain Pieter Heyes, who was to assist the surveyor in choosing a site that would be suitable not only for farming but also for whaling, since it was Godijn's plan to make his patroonship pay its costs from whaling until his colonists could be established. The two men sailed to the Delaware in 1630. After a preliminary survey revealed that the best whaling sites were along the southwest shore of Delaware Bay on a tract of land running north some twenty-four

22. Ibid., p. 188.
23. Ibid., p. 177.
24. The following account is drawn from Charles McKew Parr, *The Voyages of David de Vries* (New York, 1969), pp. 108–35.

miles from Cape Henlopen, the two men drew up a set of maps and purchased the area from three local Indian sachems. After persuading the three sachems to accompany them to Manhattan Island, the two men appeared at Fort New Amsterdam to register the purchase before departing for the fatherland. Upon his return to Amsterdam, the surveyor transferred the land title to the partnership. Shortly thereafter, Godijn and his partners were awarded the patroonship by the Amsterdam chamber. In the meantime, the partners busied themselves with preparations for the first colonizing expedition to Swanendael. But before the expedition could be outfitted, the partners had a falling out. When Samuel Godijn recommended de Vries as the colony's first commander, the other partners protested that as a partner he was unlikely to look after all of their interests with the same enthusiasm as his own. Godijn relented and appointed Pieter Heyes to be Swanendael's first commander and captain of the expedition.

The expedition, consisting of a converted whaler, the *Walvis*, and a small cargo ship, the *Salm*, sailed forth from the Texel on December 12, 1630. On board the *Walvis* were huge granite blocks, heavy timbers, iron hinges, and braces for the construction of a fort and warehouse. Sharing shipboard with this equipment were sixty Huguenot peasants and their livestock. They were destined to reinforce a colony Godijn had already founded on the island of Tortuga in the West Indies. The *Salm* carried indentured field hands, farm tools, firearms, and trade goods, as well as extra supplies of food and liquor. The outward voyage began badly when the *Salm* was captured by Dunkirk pirates just before she broke into the North Sea. The *Walvis*, sailing behind the faster *Salm*, escaped capture and set a course for the West Indies by the now-familiar South Atlantic route. Stopping first at Tortuga to unload the Huguenot peasants, Heyes discovered that the colony had been destroyed by a Spanish squadron some months earlier. This turned out to be fortunate, for the Huguenots were transported to the Delaware, making it possible to start the agricultural settlement that was all but lost with the capture of the *Salm*.

Near the mouth of the Delaware River Captain Heyes put the Huguenot peasants ashore and offloaded the granite blocks and heavy timbers. With their farm tools and livestock, the Huguenots set about putting in the first crops while several of them assisted

Gilles Honset, the partnership's construction engineer and surveyor, in building the fort. A masonry redoubt was built in accordance with plans drawn up in Amsterdam. It was duly christened Fort Oplandt. Captain Heyes then set sail for home, even though in doing so he was disobeying his orders to remain in the bay and engage in whaling. His arrival in Amsterdam with an empty ship angered the partners, who had lost a fortune on the expedition. After a heated meeting, Heyes was fired and David de Vries made the new commander with orders to sail forth immediately with a relief expedition. Before he could weigh anchor, however, news reached Amsterdam that the tiny settlement of Huguenots had been wiped out by an Indian attack.

Shaken by news of the disaster, de Vries and his partners debated the course of action. De Vries's two ships were equipped only to supply, not to rebuild the colony. The partnership nevertheless decided to send the ships to the West Indies on a privateering expedition in the hopes of regaining some of their losses.

The second expedition was plagued with problems from the outset. Off the coast of Dunkirk the lead vessel, the *Walvis*, ran aground at low tide and was freed only after a harrowing struggle. Damaged too severely to continue, she was forced to put in for repairs at Portsmouth, England. The repairs took six weeks. De Vries decided to sail directly to the Delaware to survey the damage. After an uneventful crossing, the two vessels, the *Walvis* and the two-masted *Eikhoorn*, dropped their anchors in Delaware Bay. The date was one celebrated by all Dutchmen as St. Nicolaas Dag, December 5, but there was little to celebrate on this day. De Vries put ashore in a dinghy to view the devastation. What he saw sickened him. The stone and wood fort was half-burned, and its roof sagged on one side. Human skeletons, dismembered in battle and ravaged by animal scavengers, littered the frozen fields. Around the perimeter of the compound lay the slaughtered corpses of the cattle, frozen stiff in bizarre positions. Nothing was left, save a few tobacco plants and the once thriving corn fields. De Vries turned back to sea and rowed out to the waiting ships.

This tragedy and other reverses convinced Godijn and his partners to take advantage of the West India Company's offer to buy back the patroonship for a small cash sum. Though de Vries did not lose faith in New Netherland so easily (he would later attempt to develop another patroonship in the colony), by 1636 only van Rensselaer held the rights granted him in the Freedoms and Exemptions. Rensselaerswyck was to have a colorful history under succeeding generations of van Rensselaers, and, although the colony remained a thorn in the side of Company officials, its legitimacy was never again challenged.

For all the wrangling and acrimony, however, New Netherland in the early 1630s remained underpopulated and dangerously dependent upon its trade lifeline with the United Provinces. The plan to establish seignorial estates in the colony had failed miserably. Only struggling Rensselaerswyck stood as moot testimony to the efforts of Kiliaen van Rensselaer. Perhaps O'Callaghan and Brodhead were right in arguing that a feudal order never would have worked in America. Yet the patroonship system failed before the merits of feudalism could have been tested. The English, moreover, were to have limited success with a manorial society between 1664 and 1775. The failure of the patroonship system had other less grandiose causes. It failed because the restrictions on private investors made the system unattractive to those who hoped to profit from the fur trade. It failed because only a handful of principal shareholders in the Amsterdam chamber wanted the system in the first place. It failed because even among this handful only one man could withstand the relentless attack of de Vogelaer and the contrary-minded. And it failed because ultimately the colony of New Netherland could not sustain the national interest and imagination of the United Provinces in these war years. To be sure, the patroons had wrenched important concessions from the Company during the interim between the plan of 1628 and that of 1629, but these concessions were not enough. Encumbrances to investment remained in the clauses requiring the use of Company ships, the regulation of Company supercargoes, and the payment of Company inventory fees. It should hardly be expected that a joint-stock company would be overly generous in dispensing its monopoly. Nor could the patroons be expected to be any less intransigent in their demands for free trade. Seen in a larger context, the struggle between the contrary-minded Company faction and the patroons was part of the overall dilemma facing the West India Company in its territories around the Western Hemisphere. Gradually the Company would be forced by financial problems to abandon monopoly altogether in exchange for a regulatory role in private trade within the chartered territory. Eventually the great Company evolved institutionally to assume the role of government in much the same way that the English joint-stock companies would do in Virginia and New England. The surrender of its monopoly privileges was virtually complete by the 1640s, but this was long after the patroonship system had ceased to be attractive. Private merchants with fewer ties to the colony and Company would take over the tasks of colonization, not out of any commitment to New Netherland but simply out of a commitment to profits. Before this occurred, however, New Netherland would have to deal with another threat to its existence. For though the West India Company had failed with the Walloons, and the patroons had abandoned their ephemeral hope of landed estates on the Hudson, thousands of English families were beginning to arrive in New England.

[5]

Anglo-Dutch Rivalry and the Abandonment of the Company Monopoly

I can not get over my surprise as to the changes which are said to have occurred in the fur trade at Fort Orange, when for at least 15 years in succession yearly 5,000 or 6,000 skins have come. The English on the Fresh River, by corresponding with the *Mahicans* lying about two leagues below Fort Orange and through these in turn with the *Macquaas* draw everything away from us over land.

—Kiliaen van Rensselaer, 1640

We having had formerly converse and familiarity with the Dutch, they seeing us seated in a barren quarter told us of a river called by them the Fresh River, which they often commended to us for a fine place both for plantation and trade, and wished us to make use of it.

—William Bradford, 1633

The conflicting interpretations of the English infestation of the Connecticut River valley in the above quotations reflect the widely divergent views held by the Dutch and English about the rightful ownership of land in those regions. As the English settlements grew and New Netherland languished, the threat of an English conquest of the Dutch colony loomed ever larger. The first ominous signs of trouble appeared in the 1630s.

With the need for capital pressing the West India Company, the directors of the Amsterdam chamber came under increasing pressure to make their colony of New Netherland pay its costs. The colony, as we have seen, was in a dangerous state in the 1630s. The patroonship plan, initiated with so much fanfare and so little result, had convinced some within the Amsterdam chamber that the Company must make another major effort to secure the colony. Even the Company faction on the New Netherland Commission had come to realize that the decision to colonize New Netherland a decade earlier had tied the prestige of the United Provinces and the financial fortunes of the Company to the maintenance of a Dutch presence on the Hudson. The rising strength of the English colonies to the north, however, threatened the loss of the fur trade. Already a number of angry encounters between the two colonial powers had hardened attitudes on both sides.[1] In the early 1630s, the once unthinkable prospect of war between the United Provinces and England had become a terrifying possibility. The Amsterdam chamber, with the approval of the Nineteen, decided to move aggressively to meet the threat posed by the English.

In the spring of 1633, the heavily armed *Zoutberg* arrived at Fort New Amsterdam carrying 104 soldiers, 52 combat marines, and a new commander, now called a governor-general, Wouter van Twiller.[2] Van Twiller was a former Company clerk of limited experience but powerful family connections. A nephew of Kiliaen van Rensselaer, he soon proved that his rapid rise to power was not a product of merit. His assignment was essentially military—to establish an armed garrison in New Netherland that would serve as a deterrent to English aggression. Shortly after his arrival, an example of English aggression occurred.

Early one morning, as the mist was clearing in the roadstead before Fort New Amsterdam, the sails of an English ship were

---

1. The amicable relations between New Netherland and New Plymouth were broken in 1632, when a ship carrying furs and passengers, including Pieter Minuit, out of New Amsterdam was forced by poor weather to take refuge at New Plymouth. The vessel was seized by the English on the grounds that it had illegally traded in areas belonging to "His Britannic Majesty." The ship was the *Eendracht*, under charter to the West India Company. Although the ship was released soon afterward, the Dutch made a formal protest through their ambassador in London. The protest included a long document purporting to prove Dutch rights to New Netherland. The English government stopped short of denying Dutch rights to New Netherland, although the king's possession of the entire North American continent was asserted on the basis of ancient tradition and voyages of discovery (Edmund B. O'Callaghan, *History of New Netherland; or, New York under the Dutch*, 2 vols. [New York, 1845], 1:143–45).

2. Ibid., pp. 141–42.

sighted. By midmorning the vessel had anchored beside the *Zout-berg*. She was the *William*, sailing under the authority of the New England Company out of London. Van Twiller, faced with his first diplomatic crisis, invited the captain ashore to discuss his mission. The captain turned out to be a Dutchman by the name of Jacob Eelkes, a former trader at Fort Orange in the days before the founding of the West India Company. Eelkes, who spoke English well, refused to discuss the matter in Dutch. Van Twiller, whose English was broken at best, demanded to know what was Eelkes's intention in New Netherland. When Eelkes replied that he intended to trade for furs along the banks of the Hudson River, the governor-general demanded to see his commission from the Honorable Directors of the West India Company. Eelkes countered by asking to see van Twiller's commission authorizing the Dutch to build a settlement in His Britannic Majesty's domain. Van Twiller then proceeded to get drunk, berating Eelkes and his employers as thieves and interlopers. In a state of near collapse, the governor-general ordered the *William* to remain at anchor while he called a meeting of the council to discuss the problem. Meanwhile, he ordered the guns of the fort trained on the ship.

At this juncture the intrepid David de Vries intervened. De Vries had arrived in the colony in April aboard the *Walvis* sailing with the *Eikhoorn*. The two ships were returning from an unsuccessful whaling expedition in the Delaware Bay and were loaded with contraband, including some beaver pelts obtained along the Delaware River. De Vries, who had been welcomed at New Amsterdam in an elaborate ceremony befitting his position as a patroon, now attempted to advise the inexperienced governor-general. He began by pointing out the obvious, namely, that the *William* was no match for the *Zoutberg* and could easily be sunk if need be. He counseled van Twiller to be firm. After five days, Eelkes came ashore once again and demanded that he be permitted to weigh anchor and continue his voyage. Van Twiller threatened him with arrest and denied his request. Thereafter followed a comic opera.[3]

Van Twiller ordered the flag of the Prince of Orange lofted above the fort and three cannon fired in salute. Eelkes then hoisted

3. Charles McKew Parr, *The Voyages of David de Vries* (New York, 1969), p. 191.

his colors on the mainmast of the *William* and sounded a three-cannon salute. While the cannoneers of the fort leveled their sights on the *William* and awaited the order to fire, Eelkes called van Twiller's bluff by weighing anchor and coming about. With a light breeze coming in from the sound the *William* turned into the Hudson and sailed north. The combative de Vries was enraged at van Twiller's failure of nerve. De Vries's contempt for the governor-general burst forth in an account he gave of the incident for the directors of the West India Company: "Then Director General van Twiller assembled all his forces before his board, had a cask of wine brought out, filled a bumper, and cried out for those who loved the Prince of Orange and him to do the same as he did, and protect him from the outrage of the English ship that was already out of sight and sailing up the river. The people began to laugh at him, for they understood very well how to drink the cask of wine dry."[4]

De Vries suggested that the *Zoutberg* be ordered to apprehend the intruder. The governor-general, at the urging of his council, issued the order. By the time the captain could prepare the *Zoutberg* to get under way, however, the *William* was far upstream. The *Zoutberg* caught up with her just south of Fort Orange, where the Dutch marched ashore with combat marines. To their dismay they discovered that the English were doing a brisk business trading for furs with several local Indian trappers. Trouble had already occurred, and an Indian sachem had been murdered by Hans Hunthum, van Rensselaer's old nemesis, who had defected from Company service to sign on with Eelkes.[5] The Dutch skipper lost no time in discussion but ordered his marines to tear down the tent, confiscate the furs and trade goods, and arrest the Englishmen. The English put up little resistance but protested vehemently the violation of His Majesty's subjects. With the guns of the *Zoutberg* prepared for a broadside, Eelkes surrendered the *William*. Sailing under a Dutch crew, the *William* was brought downriver to Fort New Amsterdam. Van Twiller ruled that the confiscated furs and trade goods were to be kept as an indemnity. The *William* was then released and ordered to sea, accompanied by the *Zoutberg* until she had cleared the eastern tip of Long Island.

4. Ibid., pp. 191–92.
5. Eyewitness testimony of Dirck Cornelisz Duysters in Gemeentelijke Archief van Amsterdam, Notarial no. 1040, July 14, 1634, pp. 20–21.

The incident did not end in America. When news of the events reached London via the directors of the New England Company, a formal protest was lodged with the Dutch ambassador. Accompanying the protest was a detailed account of the incident and a demand for damages from the proprietors of the New England Company. The Dutch ambassador forwarded the protest to the States General at The Hague for consideration. Their High Mightinesses passed the documents on to a special committee charged with investigating the affair. On the advice of the committee, the matter was turned over to the Nineteen, who in turn passed the buck to the Amsterdam chamber. After a number of delays, the Nineteen submitted their version of the incident to the States General with a recommendation that that body request a joint meeting of both governments to decide the boundaries of their colonies in America. Their High Mightinesses declined to participate directly in the matter and ordered the Nineteen to settle the problem through the English ambassador. Thus the matter was dropped.[6]

The *William* affair is significant for two reasons. First, the use of force by the captain of the *Zoutberg* was the beginning of several violent confrontations between the Dutch and English in North America. Second, the incident soured the relationship between the Dutch and English at a time when cooperative effort was needed to defend the European colonies against the disgruntled Algonkian tribes, who opposed the white intruders on both sides of Long Island Sound. In the Connecticut River valley a booming fur trade brought both sides to the brink of war.

The Fresh River valley, as the Dutch termed it, was a pristine wilderness in the 1630s, inhabited by a few recluse fur trappers and teeming with beaver, otter, and mink. Its strategic location had long been recognized by the Dutch, who had attempted to lay claim to the area as far back as 1624, when Cornelis Jacobsz May may have settled a few Walloon families at the mouth of the Connecticut. The valley had commercial advantages, too, rivaled only by the great valley of the Hudson. Since it offered the best opportunity for an expansion of the fur trade, the West India Company was determined to beat the English to the Connecticut River valley.

In the summer of 1633 Governor-General van Twiller sent out

6. O'Callaghan, *History of New Netherland*, 1:144–47.

Company agents to purchase the valley from the Indians or, failing that, to conclude an exclusive trade agreement that would permit the Company to shut out English traders. The agents were successful in securing title to the valley, although the Indian tribes of the area would later argue that the agreement was only to permit fur trapping. The governor-general followed up his Indian treaty with a military expedition under the command of Jacob van Curler, who sailed to the valley with a company of soldiers. Van Curler and his company sailed upstream searching for a suitable place to establish a small trading post and fort. A few miles upriver they spotted a natural clearing that offered easy access to the water and a defensible perimeter of rocks on a small hill. With tools they had brought with them they cut timber and constructed a small fort, which they christened House of Good Hope. Within days Indians were arriving at the fort with lightweight summer pelts of otter and beaver.[7]

The English had been making plans to enter the valley at about the same time. When news of Dutch activities in the summer of 1633 reached New Plymouth and Boston, Governor John Winthrop wrote a letter to van Twiller clearly stating English territorial claims to the area. Winthrop's letter warned van Twiller not to erect any fortifications in the valley lest such a move be "misinterpreted." Van Twiller received the letter some weeks later and dashed off a reply that attempted to avoid a confrontation. The governor-general's letter feigned surprise at the hostile tone of the English governor's warning and expressed dismay that two long-time allies should initiate a correspondence with such language. Van Twiller described the House of Good Hope as only a trading post. Moreover, he pointed out that Dutch claims to the valley antedated those of the English by some years. Van Twiller closed the letter with a respectful but firm refusal to abandon the area. In the meantime, events were moving fast in the valley.[8]

Governor Edward Winslow and William Bradford of New Plymouth had already started negotiations with local Indian sachems in the valley, seeking permission to establish a fur trading post somewhere along the upper Connecticut River. Winslow and Bradford informed Governor Winthrop of their plans and sug-

7. Ibid., pp. 149–50.
8. Ibid., p. 152.

gested that the Bay Colony support the scheme as a way of preventing further Dutch encroachments in the region. Winthrop was less enthusiastic than they might have hoped and declined to support the plan. In New Plymouth news of the building of the House of Good Hope excited near panic. Merchants pressed for action. Without the support of the Bay Colony, Winslow and Bradford outfitted a coastal sloop with materials to construct a frame house on the Connecticut River.[9]

When the English arrived opposite the House of Good Hope, they were hailed by Dutch soldiers who ordered the sloop brought about at anchor. The Dutch commander then questioned the English about their intentions in the region, warning them that the entire area was under the jurisdiction of the West India Company. The English skipper replied that he intended to sail up the river to trade for furs, as was his right in the domain of His Majesty King Charles. The Dutch commander decided to detain the ship until he could receive instructions from Fort New Amsterdam. He then ordered the English skipper to strike his flag and heave to or risk being fired upon by the three-pounder that was trained on the sloop. The skipper refused and, unfurling his sail, moved past the Dutch fort. Once again a Dutch commander had failed to fire on an English ship, no doubt a wise decision in this case given the dangerous situation facing the Dutch in their rivalry with the more populous English colonies. The English had showed courage in challenging the Dutch to fire upon them, but the incident may have given the false impression that the Dutch were not willing to use force to protect their rights. In any case, the sloop continued upstream to a point some miles above the House of Good Hope. There the English skipper ordered the frame house set up. Within a few days local Indians gathered to conduct an active trade in furs and skins.[10]

When Governor-General van Twiller received the report of the events in the valley, he immediately dispatched Jacob van Curler to the House of Good Hope. From there van Curler was to proceed with a company of soldiers to the English post upstream. His written instructions directed him to deliver an official demand that the

9. *New-York Historical Society Collections*, 2d ser., 1 (1841): 366–67.
10. O'Callaghan, *History of New Netherland*, 1:153–54.

English evacuate the post. His verbal orders, however, forbade him to use force. He was to bully the English into leaving by a show of strength, for van Twiller believed that the English could be dislodged without bloodshed. The English proved to be supremely confident of their rights, however, and their commander, William Holmes, refused to be intimidated by van Curler and his soldiers. Unable to use the soldiers, van Curler retired humiliated to the House of Good Hope and from there to Fort New Amsterdam, where he conferred with the governor-general and council about what other action to take.[11]

The young governor-general was in a difficult situation, and his position was not helped by his recent conduct in the *William* affair, which had made him the butt of many unkind jokes on the streets of New Amsterdam. He decided to dislodge the English by force and dispatched two companies of soldiers to their encampment. Once again the English refused to leave, and the Dutch commander disobeyed his orders by refusing to fire on them. Meanwhile, the fur trade at the House of Good Hope had slowed as Indians began to deal with the English upstream. Van Twiller was soon involved in other serious concerns, and the situation in the Connecticut Valley remained unresolved.[12]

The foothold obtained by the English on the Connecticut River would prove to be the beginning of the end of Dutch hopes to make the valley part of New Netherland. William Bradford would later justify English actions by denying that any injuries had been done to Dutch trade. "We did the Dutch no wrong," he wrote, "for we took not a foot of any land which they bought, but went to the place above them, and bought that tract of land which belonged to the Indians."[13] What Bradford neglected to say was that the title to the land was largely incidental to the fur trade. The creation of a trading post upriver from the House of Good Hope enabled the English to tap the interior of the Connecticut Valley, thus leaving the Dutch only that area south of the English position.

A more candid analysis of English motives was given by John Winthrop, who though not approving the action taken by the peo-

11. John Winthrop, *Winthrop's Journal: "The History of New England, 1630–1649,"* ed. James K. Hosmer, 2 vols. (New York, 1908), 1:144–45.

12. O'Callaghan, *History of New Netherland*, 1:157.

13. *New-York Historical Society Collections*, 2d ser., 1 (1841): 368.

ple of New Plymouth, nonetheless understood the goals they had in mind:

> This river [Connecticut] runs so far northward, that it comes within a day's journey of a part of [the] Merrimack called _____ and so runs thence N.W. so near the Great Lake, as [allows] the Indians to pass their canoes into it over land. From this lake, the hideous swamps about it, come most of the beaver which is traded between Virginia and Canada, which runs forth of this lake; and Patomack River in Virginia comes likewise out of it, or very near, so as from this lake there comes yearly to the Dutch about ten thousand skins, which might easily be diverted by [the] Merrimack, if a course of trade were settled in that river.[14]

Winthrop's geography was obviously in error, but his business sense was sound. The rich fur trade of the Connecticut Valley was part of the same trade that thrived on the Hudson. If the Indians could be attracted to the Connecticut, a portion of the furs usually traded at Fort Orange would make their way overland and by small tributaries to the English. Indeed, this is exactly what happened in the years to follow, as Kiliaen van Rensselaer's lament suggested. Furthermore, the Dutch could not be expected to stay long on the Hudson if the revenue from furs declined dramatically. And the removal of the Dutch from the Hudson would open up enormous new territories for English settlement.

The first confrontation in the Connecticut Valley had been won by the English. They would win many more. By the end of the decade, English traders dominated the fur trade in the valley, and the vanguard of the force that would spell the end of the trade had already arrived. Farmers by the dozen, then by the score, and finally by the hundreds would make the valley indisputably English. The farmers would oust the unmarried, rough fur traders who plied the tributaries of the Connecticut and lived Indianlike in the wilderness. The valley would begin to yield up its riches to the plow rather than the trap, and with their families the farmers would transform the valley forever. Coming from the older villages of Watertown, Dorchester, Cambridge, and Newtown, the tillers of the soil would replace the trapper, the trader, and the Indian.

14. Winthrop, *Winthrop's Journal*, 1:110.

The Dutch would go with the others, too few to offer resistance to the onslaught of English settlers and too inclined to seek their fortunes elsewhere to attempt a stemming of the tide.

As the Dutch became strangers in the valley, their contacts with the English became more heated. A minority within a majority culture by 1640, they complained of harsh treatment by the English. At New Amsterdam a litany of complaints flowed from Dutch trappers and traders who told of being driven from their posts by Englishmen, while they were ridiculed for their language and accused of crimes they did not commit. The English complained of the Dutch, too. Chief among the accusations was that the Dutch sold liquor and firearms to the Indians. Not only were the Dutch arming the savages, but they debauched them as well. Such charges were probably based on some fact, for the Dutch had earned an unsavory reputation for their willingness to sell guns and brandy to the Indians. Most of the complaints, however, were simply echoes of the cultural rivalry that would assume political and military form in later years.[15] Eventually, the charges and countercharges found their way to the respective home countries, where statesmen unfamiliar with the circumstances came to regard

---

15. Lord Say and Sele received numerous letters from Connecticut complaining of the Dutch. In 1642 he became convinced that some government-level action needed to be taken. In an angry letter to the Dutch ambassador residing in London, the proprietor of Connecticut reviewed the charges against the Dutch in "his" valley and ended the epistle with an interesting interpretation of English and Dutch claims to the area. "'Tis true," he wrote, "the Netherlanders sometimes aver that they purchased a portion of land, situate on the aforesaid river [Connecticut], from the Pequod Indians, and pretend a right thereto by virtue of said purchase. But it is very well known, (if any such purchase has been made, which as yet has never appeared) that the Pequods had no other than an usurped title. And herein the weakness of their pretensions becomes apparent." In short, the Dutch had been swindled and therefore must suffer the consequences of their gullibility (quoted in O'Callaghan, *History of New Netherland*, 1:256). Dorothy Dening, in *The Settlement of the Connecticut Towns* (New Haven, 1933), pp. 2–3, denies the Dutch claim to the valley on similar grounds. Dutch complaints about the English are found in several notarial documents, many of which were testimonies given at the request of the Amsterdam chamber to support the chamber's request for more troops. Jacob van Curler, van Twiller's unfortunate commander in the 1633 fiasco, testified that the English were always haughty and disrespectful of the Dutch (Gemeentelijke Archief van Amsterdam, Notarial no. 1065, October 24, 1643, pp. 186v–187v).

them as examples of a systematic policy of harassment and humiliation. Although the legal question of territorial jurisdiction could be sidestepped for years, the growing distrust between the peoples of New England and New Netherland would eventually make any solution short of war and conquest unacceptable.

Elsewhere in New Netherland the Dutch were experiencing difficulties in the 1630s. The settlements begun by Blommaert and de Vries on the Delaware had been destroyed by Indians, and within a decade the area would be occupied by Swedes, who, having taken on the services of Pieter Minuit, would found the colony of New Sweden not far from the site of Swanendael.[16] At Fort Orange, the center of the Company's fur trade, the conflict of interest between the Company and Kiliaen van Rensselaer had resulted in bidding wars for furs. Moreover, the Iroquois and the French were negotiating a trade agreement that threatened to cut off the northern supply of pelts by diverting the highly valued winter pelts north to Canada.[17] On Manhattan Island the repatriation of farmers had created a labor shortage on Company farms, and food had to be imported from the fatherland in some years.[18] Faced with such difficulties, the Amsterdam chamber began to look for ways to save money. One method was to scale down the building plans for New Amsterdam.

In the decade of the 1630s New Amsterdam was hardly worthy of the name. The island of Manhattan boasted few structures with the appearance of permanence other than the fort, a stone warehouse for the Company's pelts, and two or three wooden frame houses for the governor-general and his staff. Beyond the compound, the thirty log houses reported by Isaac de Rasiere in 1626

16. Amandus Johnson, *Swedish Settlements on the Delaware*, 2 vols. (Philadelphia, 1911). For a more concise and better-balanced account of the Swedish colonization of the Delaware, see C. A. Weslager, *The English on the Delaware, 1610–1682* (New Brunswick, N.J., 1967), pp. 55–71.

17. J. Franklin Jameson, ed., *Narratives of New Netherland, 1609–1664* (New York, 1909), p. 139.

18. Conditions were hardly better at Rensselaerswyck. In 1636 Kiliaen van Rensselaer and Gerrit de Forest jointly purchased a small vessel, which they named the *Rensselaerswyck*, for a voyage to the patroonship. A partial cargo list contained in a notarial document reveals that among other food items a load of wheat (*tarwe*) was being sent to the colonists (Gemeentelijke Archief van Amsterdam, Notarial no. 1045, August 8, 1636, pp. 120–120v).

were still standing, although many had been converted into stables and shelters for sheep and pigs. There was no church and would be none for years to come. Jonas Michaëlius, the colony's first preacher, conducted his services in the loft of a stone mill (used for crushing tree bark for the tanneries), which because of its size was the most imposing structure in the compound. The main thoroughfare of the town was Breed Straat (Broad Street), which ran through the middle of the compound. Down the center of the street stretched a canal, which was a befouled and stinking sewer in the warm months of summer and a treacherous ice floe in the winter. A wooden fence, constructed of timbers sunk in mud and secured by pegs and rope, crossed the island on the leeward side of town. Beyond the fence were the farms, or *bouwerijen*, where the town's food was grown and where most of the free colonists (about 150 in 1635) lived with their families. With so many wooden structures, fire was always a threat, and Pieter Minuit had established the first night watchman in the 1620s. Every hour from dusk until dawn the watchman would circle the compound calling out the time and announcing all was well, or if a fire was spotted, alerting the town. The island was shrouded in darkness at night, although a town ordinance required every seventh structure to keep a lantern burning during the dark of the moon.[19]

The Company planned a major rebuilding and expansion of New Amsterdam as part of the new aggressive posture that had brought the *Zoutberg* to Manhattan in 1633. The fort was to be rebuilt as a quadrangle with bastions at each corner. The northwest bastion, which would have to withstand gunfire in case of a naval attack, was to be constructed of stone, the remaining bastions to be of earth and timber. The quadrangle was to be approximately 300 feet along the north-south wall and 250 feet along the east-west wall. At a cost of nearly 4,500 fl. it was the most expensive construction project yet undertaken by the Company. In addition, the Company

19. This description of New Amsterdam in the 1630s comes from a variety of sources. See Dingman Versteeg, *Manhattan in 1628 as Described in the Recently Discovered Autograph Letter of Jonas Michaëlius Written from the Settlement on the 18th of August of that Year, and Now First Published; with a Review of the Letter and an Historical Sketch of New Netherland to 1628* (New York, 1904), pp. 84ff.; Parr, *Voyages of David de Vries*, p. 189; and Maud Wilder Goodwin, "Fort Amsterdam in the Days of the Dutch," in *Historic New York: The Half Moon Papers*, 4 vols. (Port Washington, N.Y., 1897; rpt. 1969), 1:1-7.

planned a wharf, a new warehouse, and two new mills. Carpenters, bricklayers, stone masons, and millers had arrived on the *Zoutberg* to begin the construction.

The workers had no sooner begun tearing down the old earthen ramparts then the troubles in the Connecticut Valley had forced van Twiller to draft many of them into military service. The fort was eventually completed by Company slaves brought from the West Indies, but its construction took two years.[20] In the meantime, the plans for the wharf and warehouse were scrapped, and the mills were completed with private funds. The men who had come out on the *Zoutberg* to work in the construction projects were angry at being made soldiers. When they returned to the United Provinces at the end of their contract terms, they found the Company unwilling to pay them the wages originally promised. One man's plight may serve as an illustration of the general discontent prevailing among Company employees in these years.

Luycas Jansz Sprangh, a master bricklayer, had been recruited by the Company in July 1632 to go to New Netherland to supervise the rebuilding of Fort New Amsterdam. He had been reluctant to leave his family, but he was heavily in debt to his brother-in-law, who prevailed on him to accept the offer of a two-year contract at an annual salary of 1,000 fl. Sprangh increased his indebtedness by purchasing tools, for which the Company was supposed to reimburse him. He sailed with Governor-General van Twiller aboard the *Zoutberg*, leaving behind a wife, four children, and an army of anxious creditors. In New Netherland he organized the labor force and began selecting timber for use in the palisades. In addition, he supervised the masonry work for the fortified bastion and had completed much of the preliminary foundation work on the fort when van Twiller drafted most of his crew for military service. When work on the fort seemed all but abandoned, Sprangh took a ship for home. Arriving in Amsterdam, he filed suit against the Company for back wages, complaining that he had not received any of his contracted salary. He noted that two carpenters, four laborers, and a journeyman bricklayer were also unpaid after a year's work in New Netherland.[21]

20. Goodwin, "Fort Amsterdam," p. 6.

21. Gemeentelijke Archief van Amsterdam, Notarial nos. 914, July 8, 1632, p. 99; 915, September 29, 1633, p. 213v.

Sprangh and his coworkers were just a few of the angry Company employees walking the streets of Amsterdam, pestering Company officials and filing suit after suit for back wages and damages. During these same years the directors of the Amsterdam chamber were deadlocked over the uncertain future of the patroonship system, and stockholders once more were clamoring for dividends. In this charged atmosphere the question of how to deal with New Netherland's myriad problems came up for discussion again.

By 1636 supporters of the patroonship system had lost faith in the scheme. Only Kiliaean van Rensselaer, whose dogged determination had enabled him to make a modest success of Rensselaerswyck, continued to defend the system as the colony's best hope for the future. Others believed that the only way to make the colony thrive was to abandon the Company monopoly. The reports coming back from America only confirmed the directors' worst fears: the fur trade was being lost to the English, the Connecticut River valley would have to be abandoned, colonists were returning home, the Indians were restless, and the red ink was beginning to gush forth as the costs of rebuilding New Amsterdam and paying the troops now stationed in the colony increased the Company's expenses without any appreciable increase in trade revenues. It was becoming difficult to hire soldiers and laborers for New Netherland, and the labor shortage alone was enough to make a few directors see the need for sending slaves to the colony.[22] Something had to be done if the efforts of the last ten years were not to be in vain. As the list of New Netherland's problems seemed to lengthen daily, long-term solutions were set aside and expedients were grasped.

Some of the directors put the blame on Wouter van Twiller, whom David de Vries and others charged with mismanagement and cowardice. The governor-general's disfavor may also have been attributable to his close relationship with his uncle, Kiliaen van Rensselaer. It was rumored that van Twiller had used his position to assist his uncle in acquiring livestock and shipping space aboard

---

22. The slaves were probably first transported to New Netherland aboard the *Eendracht* in 1635. The testimony of a former Company employee, Gijs Jansz, noted the unloading of "some soldiers, blacks, and other persons" at New Amsterdam on or about April 15, 1635 (Gemeentelijke Archief van Amsterdam, Notarial no. 917, December 1, 1635, p. 309v).

Company ships. One source of the gossip was the Company's *schout-fiscaal* (a combination customs officer and chief accountant), Lubbertus van Dinclage, who had clashed with the governor-general on many occasions, most frequently over the issue of the Company's interest and the patroon's rights. When van Dinclage tried to prevent the governor-general from selling Company yearlings to Kiliaen van Rensselaer, van Twiller threw him in jail. After bribing his jailer, van Dinclage was able to escape to Virginia, where he caught a ship for Europe. When he finally arrived in Amsterdam, the tale he told confirmed what de Vries and others had been saying. With the backing of Kiliaen van Rensselaer's enemies in the Amsterdam chamber he filed a long deposition before a notary, which was to be used as evidence for the removal of van Twiller as governor-general.[23]

Van Twiller's problems were mostly self-inflicted. By 1635, the governor-general's alcoholism had caused several disasters. On one occasion, upon receiving a fine bottle of claret from a friend, the governor-general invited his staff to a drinking contest. Near the end of the evening, when the claret had long since been exhausted and the inebriated company had started on a keg of cheap brandy, a fight broke out. To break it up, the governor-general fired off a cannon in the middle of the compound. A spark from the powder landed on the thatched roof of a nearby building, and the immobilized crowd let the structure burn to the ground. The fort might have been consumed by the flames had not others responded to the alarm with a bucket brigade.[24] The directors of the Amsterdam chamber heard about this and other incidents from van Twiller's enemies long before they were informed by him. Indeed, van Twiller seldom corresponded with his employers, and months passed without a single word from him. The directors finally acted in 1637 by recalling van Twiller and appointing Willem Kieft in his stead.

Willem Kieft was a former merchant with a reputation as a disci-

23. Van Dinclage's testimony is contained in Gemeentelijke Archief van Amsterdam, Notarial no. 856, December 18, 1635, pp. 174ff. Further references to the business dealings between Wouter van Twiller and his uncle, Kiliaen van Rensselaer, are found in Arnold J. F. van Laer, ed. and trans., *The Van Rensselaer–Bowier Manuscripts* (Albany, 1908), pp. 254, 255, 257, and 258.

24. Gemeentelijke Archief van Amsterdam, Notarial no. 856, December 18, 1635, p. 174.

plinarian. The directors of the Amsterdam chamber no doubt looked upon him as a savior for the faltering colony. Moreover, as a merchant he was experienced in commercial matters and much less likely to be bullied by Kiliaen van Rensselaer and others who would pursue their own interests at the expense of the Company's. His appointment must have signaled a defeat for the patroon's cause within the chamber because his actions in New Netherland suggest that he arrived in the colony with a mandate to curb van Rensselaer's influence. The new governor-general sailed from Amsterdam aboard the *Haring* in the last months of 1637. After an uneventful winter crossing by the South Atlantic route, the *Haring* dropped anchor before Fort New Amsterdam in the first months of the new year.[25] Kieft lost no time in taking the reins of authority. His first task was to reduce the power of the governor's council.

Under van Twiller the governor's council had become a hotbed of opposition to Company policy. Kieft was determined to re-establish the council as an advisory body. As was his custom, Kieft plunged headlong into a confrontation. He began by reducing the council to two persons, himself and an "adviser," giving himself two votes to the adviser's one. Others were to be permitted to sit in on council meetings at the governor-general's invitation, but they were to have no voting rights. This abbreviated council, furthermore, was to be called only when the governor-general deemed it necessary. Within days of Kieft's arrival in New Netherland the "council" held its first meeting to consider a petition from Jacob Planck, the chief administrator of Rensselaerswyck. Planck requested permission to use a company sloop to transport some cattle from Manhattan Island to the patroonship. Kieft exploded in an angry tirade upon hearing the petition, fuming that he would not be a party to the patroon's efforts to impoverish Manhattan Island. The island was already "vacant and stripped of animals and not fit for cultivation," and Planck's petition was nothing less than an attempt to enrich the patroon with seed stock from the company's

25. The voyage of the *Haring* produced several notarial documents which permit a fairly accurate reconstruction of its cargo and mission. Among the more interesting documents is one confirming that the company had sent four experienced tobacco merchants to New Netherland to explore the possibilities of establishing tobacco plantations in the colony (Gemeentelijke Archief van Amsterdam, Notarial no. 1420, September 3, 1637, p. 121).

farms. Although the cattle in question had been purchased from free colonists on the island, Kieft denied the petition and ordered the cattle confiscated in the name of the Honorable West India Company.[26]

On the same day that Planck's petition was denied, the council passed a new ordinance prohibiting Company employees from engaging in the fur trade. The ordinance was nothing more than a clarification of the Company's long-standing position, but the penalties imposed upon violators signaled a new get-tough attitude. Wages were to be forfeited, all trade goods were to be confiscated, and even the personal belongings of a convicted employee were to become Company property. The ordinance warned "all free persons not in the Company's service to govern themselves according to the granted charter," a clear signal to the free colonists that smuggling was about to be curbed. Sailors aboard ships docked at New Amsterdam were forbidden night shore duty unless specifically approved by the governor-general. Moreover, all ship personnel were to "return on board by sundown," and the ships' captains were to be held responsible for any violations by their crews. These regulations were clearly aimed at curtailing the thriving smuggling business that had grown up over the years between Company sailors and free colonists. Kieft also attempted to improve the moral demeanor of New Amsterdam by providing severe penalties for "adulterous intercourse with heathens, blacks, or other persons; [as well as] mutiny, theft, false testimony, slanderous language and other irregularities."[27]

How successful such measures were is debatable. Smuggling remained a chronic problem for the Company, and the other laws were only as valid as the government's ability to enforce them. Still, the flurry of laws and "amplifications" marked a change in the West India Company's relationship with the colony of New Netherland. The Company had never intended to become a government with responsibilities over free citizens or to involve itself in the complexities of ruling a society. Like the ill-fated Virginia Company, the West India Company found itself shackled to a society of its own creation. What Sigmund Diamond has written of the

26. Arnold J. F. van Laer, trans., *New York Historical Manuscripts: Dutch*, 4 vols. (Baltimore, 1974), 4:2.

27. Ibid., pp. 3–4.

Virignia Company applies with uncanny precision to the situation in New Netherland in the 1630s: "The Company had been faced with the problems of motivating its members to work for the ends which it was created to achieve and, at the same time, of maintaining the discipline that was essential for its organizational integrity. The solution it adopted for the first problem made it impossible to solve the second; and the burden of achieving order and discipline now became the responsibility not of an organization but of a society."[28] The Company's new responsibilities were to become crushing in the years ahead. In the meantime, the directors of the Amsterdam chamber were frantically searching for a way to increase the colony's population.

In 1638, while Kieft was in the process of reorganizing the council and establishing order in New Netherland, the situation in the distant colony became a point of discussion in the States General. New Netherland had become a diplomatic problem for the United Provinces. The recent confrontations in the Connecticut Valley and the complaints of the proprietors of the New England Company had forced the government at The Hague to intervene. In the spring session of the States General a resolution passed which directed the Nineteen to improve the colony or risk its confiscation. The chief problem was a lack of population, which invited conquest by the rapidly growing English colonies. An underpopulated New Netherland could not be defended, and if the West India Company was unwilling to populate the colony, the States General was prepared to undertake the task itself. Thus the resolution was a virtual ultimatum to increase the number of colonists in New Netherland or lose it.[29]

Throughout the summer the directors of the Amsterdam chamber pondered the problem of how to increase New Netherland's population with a program of incentives concrete enough to entice people to settle in a colony that had never been very attractive to the average Hollander. At the end of August the chamber submitted a set of "Articles and Conditions" to the Nineteen. The docu-

28. Sigmund Diamond, "From Organization to Society: Virginia in the Seventeenth Century," *American Journal of Sociology* 63 (1958): 474.

29. John Romeyn Brodhead, comp., Edmund B. O'Callaghan and Berthold Fernow, eds. and trans., *Documents Relative to the Colonial History of the State of New York*, 15 vols. (New York, 1856), 1:106; hereafter cited as *DCHNY*.

ment was forwarded without comment to the States General for approval.

The Articles and Conditions represented the final act in the long drama to maintain the Company monopoly on trade. Under the new regulations, all colonists, and not just the patroons, would be allowed to engage in the fur trade, provided they were willing to settle permanently in the colony as farmers. The Company would still control the transoceanic trade, and furs obtained by the colonists would have to be registered with the Company before being shipped to the fatherland in Company ships. Low freightage rates were promised the colonists for their goods, and the Company pledged itself to provide passage to New Netherland for all settlers at rates below those of privately chartered ships. The Company reserved the right to tax all imports and exports at rates to be determined by the directors. And finally, the colonists were prohibited from using their own ships unless licensed by the Company. This last restriction was clearly intended to provide the Company with profits from the carrying trade, although the opponents of the Articles and Conditions pointed out that the plan simply replaced the fur trade monopoly with a monopoly in shipping.

The one asset the Company had at its disposal was land, and the Articles and Conditions offered it free to any colonist who would promise to farm it. Once again the parallels with the Virginia Company are striking. In Virginia the problems of maintaining a sufficient number of colonists had been exacerbated by disease and the severe regimen of martial law in the early years. Yet years after the infamous starving time, Virginia could not attract large numbers of permanent settlers. The solution reached by 1619 and followed consistently thereafter was the offer of free land as an incentive for migration. This policy strengthened the colony and weakened the Virginia Company. Diamond's succinct analysis is worth repeating:

> Once all land had been owned by the Company. Now much of it was owned by private persons, and even more had been promised to them, and the opportunities for the creation of private fortunes involved the planters in a new relationship with the Company. No longer was the planter willing to have his tobacco exported through the Company at a fixed price, when, as a free landowner, he might

strike his own bargain with the purchaser. No longer was the planter willing, at a time when labor meant profit, for the Company to commandeer his servants. . . . Indeed, it became increasingly difficult to get planters to accept Company positions. . . . The increase in private wealth tended to subordinate status in the Company to status in a different relationship among the planters.[30]

A similar pattern would evolve in New Netherland in the 1650s and 1660s, for once the West India Company released its hold on trade and land, it lost its ability to enforce its authority on the colonists. In fact, once the Company ceased to be the main employer of labor in the colony, it found itself burdened with all the responsibilities of government but little of the privileges and virtually no respect. Even the 10 percent "farm tax" imposed by the Articles and Conditions on the produce of all farms starting in their fifth year of production was not an effective device to maintain the Company's authority because the revenue was not to go into the Company's dividends but to pay the salaries of preachers and schoolmasters. Clearly, with the Articles and Conditions the West India Company had ceased to function as a joint-stock company. It had become a government.

The Articles and Conditions had nullified the Company charter by eliminating nearly all of the monopolistic privileges once held by the directors in the territories of the chartered domain. Thus it must have come as a shock to the Nineteen when the States General rejected the plan. The delegates at The Hague found the plan limited and too cautious. They noted, for example, that incentives for colonists applied only to farmers. Traders, artisans, and others were not likely to be attracted to the colony if the only way they could engage in their business was to farm the land. Furthermore, the Company was nearly bankrupt, and the promise of sufficient shipping to meet the increased demand envisioned in the plan seemed unlikely to be kept. The States General directed the Nineteen to devise a better plan.

The Nineteen referred the matter to the Amsterdam chamber, which discussed the problem through the fall of 1638 and produced a heavily revised Articles and Conditions in January 1639. The new plan kept all of the provisions of the older one but expanded the

30. Diamond, "From Organization to Society," p. 472.

colonists' trade privileges to encompass a virtual free trade in all commodities. The fur trade was opened to all citizens of the United Provinces and not just to residents of New Netherland. Private shipping was permitted to and from the colony, provided a Company supercargo was on board. The only vestige of the Company monopoly that remained was its right to tax certain imports and exports, but even this right was aimed more at regulation than revenue. Not surprisingly, the new Articles and Conditions were readily approved by the States General. The following year the Company issued a revised set of Freedoms and Exemptions based on the provisions in the Articles and Conditions. The Freedoms and Exemptions of 1640 provided two hundred acres of free land to each colonist who brought with him five family members or servants. The trade privileges of the 1639 Articles and Conditions were kept, and even the patroonship scheme was revived in a modified form. The new patroons were to receive much less land and slightly less authority over their tenants, but the manorial foundation of authority was retained. Various other sets of Freedoms and Exemptions would be issued in the years to come, but none would go further in opening up New Netherland to settlement than those of 1640.[31]

The private merchants of Amsterdam had awaited such an opportunity for nearly twenty years. They had already developed plans for financing the trade with New Netherland, in which many had been engaged illegally for some time as smugglers and licensed Company traders. With their enormous pools of capital and influential connections, they would succeed where the Company had failed. Within a decade of the abandonment of the monopoly, the private merchants of the fatherland would achieve a lively and profitable trade with the colony on the Hudson. The next three decades of New Netherland's history would witness some astonishing contrasts. Large numbers of colonists would come to stake out farms and begin new lives. Disastrous Indian wars would threaten the very existence of the colony. New institutions would be established, as the Company struggled to handle the complexities of human relationships that evolved naturally with population growth. And finally, when the colony seemed to have at last

31. *DCHNY*, 1:110–15.

achieved a stable population of permanent colonists, English war-ships would appear in Long Island Sound to snatch by conquest the only victory the Dutch colony had won in its struggle to survive. Before this ignominious conquest, however, would come years of success in expanding the fur trade, in establishing colonial bound-aries, and in increased population as the tide of immigration finally surged. That tide brought a fascinating variety of folk to New Netherland. It is time to examine these people in some detail.

[6]

The People of New Netherland

It was thus that many men of many creeds and tongues were drawn to New Amsterdam. During Stuyvesant's rule there was a great influx of Waldenses from Piedmond and of Huguenots from France, and besides these there were Scotch Presbyterians, English Independents, Moravians, Anabaptists, and Jews. In 1655 you might have gone from the Penobscot all the way to Harlem River without meeting any other civilized language than English, but in crossing the island of Manhattan, you might have heard a dozen or fifteen European languages spoken. At that early stage the place had already begun to exhibit the cosmopolitan character which has ever since distinguished it.

—John Fiske, *The Dutch and Quaker Colonies in America*, 1899

The migration of Europeans to New Netherland has not received the scholarly attention given to the much larger movements of people to New England and the Chesapeake Bay. Although the lively interest in genealogy and the increasingly sophisticated studies on colonial demography have uncovered much that is of importance in any analysis of New Netherland's population, the colony's specific immigration history has never been carefully examined in the light of questions commonly posed by demographers and social historians.[1] Generalizations about New Netherland's population

1. The interest in colonial demography is more acute than ever judging from the recent flurry of articles on the subject. See Mildred Campbell, "Social Origins of Some Early Americans," in James Morton Smith, ed., *Seventeenth-Century America: Essays in Colonial History* (Chapel Hill, 1959), pp. 63–89. For a recent assessment of Campbell's findings, see David W. Galenson, " 'Middling People' or 'Common Sort'?: The Social Origins of Some Early Americans Reexamined," *William and Mary Quarterly*, 3d ser., 35 (1978): 499–524, and Campbell's response following on pages 525–40, as well as the rejoinder and reply in *William and Mary*

have abounded, although for the most part they have been based on little more than the handful of written descriptions that have survived from the Dutch period. The historian John Fiske, for example, based his description of New Netherland's multiethnic and multilingual population solely on the brief account given by Adriaen Van der Donck in his *Description of New Netherland*. Several modern historians have relied on English records produced after 1664 or on ethnic analysis of family names on tax lists.[2] The result has been a set of generalizations about the people of New Netherland that has achieved a status which is, considering its narrow data base, all out of proportion to the documentation upon which it is founded.

The purpose of this study is to analyze the history of New Netherland from the perspective of the Dutch documents that have survived in various archives in the United States and Holland. Therefore, this chapter attempts a broad-based documentation for the demographic history of the colony, which tradition has rendered almost lifeless by simply repeating the time-worn generalizations that describe the heterogeneous population of New Netherland as part Dutch, part English, totally philistine, and politically factious. We need to ask some familiar questions about the people who chose to live out their lives in the obscure villages and settlements along the Hudson River. Who came and why? What were the family type and size, sexual balance, ethnic composition, and socioeconomic standing of those who lived in New Netherland? How many were there, and when did the ebb and floodtides of migration take place? Such questions are best answered quantitatively. When posing questions about categories of family type and ethnicity that can be isolated and

---

Quarterly, 3d ser., 36 (1979): 264–86. For regional and provincial studies, see Timothy H. Breen and Stephen Foster, "Moving to the New World: The Character of Early Massachusetts Immigration," *William and Mary Quarterly*, 3d ser., 30 (1973): 189–222; Russell R. Menard, "From Servant to Freeholder: Status Mobility and Property Accumulation in Seventeenth-Century Maryland," *William and Mary Quarterly*, 3d ser., 30 (1973): 37–64; James T. Lemon, *The Best Poor Man's Country: A Geographical Study of Early Southeastern Pennsylvania* (Baltimore, 1972), pp. 42–70; and Richard S. Dunn, "Barbados Census of 1680," *William and Mary Quarterly*, 3d ser., 26 (1969): 3–30.

2. Certainly the most interesting of the latter is the work of Thomas Archdeacon, *New York City, 1664–1710: Conquest and Change* (Ithaca, 1975).

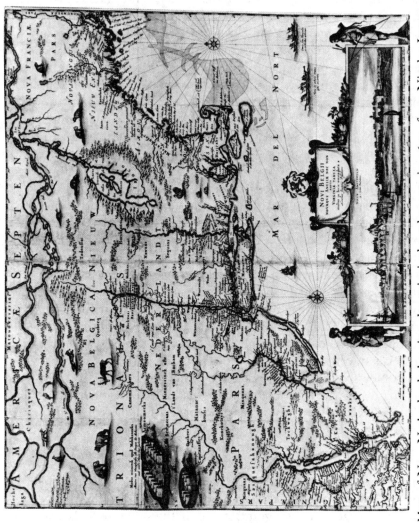

Map of New Netherland showing the principal settlements in 1655, from Nicolas Jansz Visscher, *Novi Belgii Novaeque Angliae nec non partis Virginiae tabula* (Amsterdam, 1655). Courtesy of the New York State Library, Albany.

made exclusive, numbers must carry the interpretive burden, if only because they suggest an objectivity seldom found in qualitative descriptions. Yet it is all too easy to assume that that which is quantifiable is somehow truer than that which is not. Hence, when the larger questions of causation come into play, numbers can easily lead us astray, suggesting a cause from a result or confusing the result as the product of some conscious motivation. We may, for instance, use numbers to pin down certain locations in Europe that contributed significant numbers of colonists to New Netherland, but it is another matter to determine why people left those areas for New Netherland. Such analysis requires interpretation beyond numbers. For New Netherland, moreover, quantifiable data are hard to find. What information exists must be assembled from scattered sources and subjected to careful scrutiny before being used to support generalizations. Some periods of New Netherland's history produced virtually no quantifiable data; other periods are surprisingly rich. In fact, the unpredictable survival of historical documents provides an artificial periodization for the colony's demographic history.

For the first colonization expeditions in the 1620s, specific information about individuals and their families is not available in large enough numbers to make possible any quantitative analysis. The period between 1630 and approximately 1644 produced some valuable quantitative data on immigrants settling the patroonship of Rensselaerswyck, and tentative projections about the overall migration to New Netherland are possible. The twelve-year span from 1645 to 1657 is the least amenable to quantitative method because little evidence survived the tragic Indian wars of the era, and the papers of the governor-general perished in a shipwreck. For this decade little more than sketches and impressions drawn from the traditional qualitative sources are possible. The last years of New Netherland's existence, however, offer a treasure of information. The seven-year period between 1657 and 1664 produced more quantifiable data on immigrants than all the other periods combined, and much that is new in our understanding of the history of this unique colony comes from information recorded by Amsterdam notaries and West India Company clerks in the last years of Dutch rule. Thus we have a four-part periodization for the analysis of the demographic history of New Netherland. Artificial it may be, yet the periods correspond well enough to the colony's political and administrative history, and for this reason little of substance is lost in using the periods offered by the documentation. Indeed, it is arguable that the periodization reflects the vicissitudes of New Netherland's fortunes more accurately than does the traditional division of the colony's history by the terms of office of its governor-generals.

Except for fur traders, itinerant sea adventurers, whalers, an occasional off-course fisherman, or a marauding pirate, the shoreline of New Netherland remained nearly devoid of Europeans until the coming of the Walloons in the mid-1620s. These French-speaking refugees from the southern Netherlands were the first to undertake the tasks of colony-building along the Hudson. As we have seen, the West India Company provided generous incentives to ensure that the Walloons would remain in the colony. And although many left New Netherland, many stayed. They came to form the core of free settlers in an otherwise Company colony, and as farmers they provided New Netherland with its first agricultural base.

Historians know much less about the Walloons than they would like. That they came largely as a family migration is established. Among them were to be found a number of future families of singular importance in the colony's history, including the de Forest clan. Later waves of French-speaking immigrants would add to the Huguenot culture founded by the Walloons, but their numbers were small. The Walloons were eventually relegated to a minority as Company operations expanded in the late 1620s and early 1630s. Company employees, clerks, sailors, and fur traders inundated the small settlements founded by the Walloons, making them outcasts in the colony they had helped establish. Moreover, the patroonship plan envisioned a string of private colonies each financed by private capital and each exercising extensive privileges in matters of trade through the auspices of the patroon's Freedoms and Exemptions. In the changed circumstances of the 1630s, the once dominant Walloons could not help but see their status as free colonists eroded. Many of them repatriated or drifted off to other parts of the Dutch seaborne empire. A few may have found their way to New Holland, where the West India Company's attempt to establish a colony in the heart of Portuguese Brazil turned to disaster in the 1650s.

Others remained in New Netherland, forming a family-based settlement in stark contrast to the rough-hewn free male society formed by the migration of Company employees.

By 1630 New Netherland contained perhaps no more than 300 Europeans, most of whom were still Walloon. On Manhattan Island, where roughly 270 colonists lived, the Walloons had set up small farms beyond the compound of Fort New Amsterdam. There they lived quietly, protected by the proximity of the fort, engaged in livestock raising and the cultivation of Indian maize and European wheat. They bought tools and small luxury items from the Company store at the fort and conducted a thriving smuggling trade in furs with the sailors who arrived infrequently in the colony aboard company ships. They remained a clannish lot, refusing to learn Dutch or to attend the services held by Jonas Michaëlius in the loft of the mill.

Much information about the immigrants who settled in Rensselaerswyck has survived in the notarial archives of Amsterdam, in the papers and correspondence of the van Rensselaer family, and in numerous genealogical studies. The various pieces of data can be combined in such a way as to provide a quantifiable base for generalizations.

Rensselaerswyck immigrants usually had their contracts recorded by public notaries in Amsterdam before boarding ships for New Netherland. In the colony, the patroon's agent frequently reported their arrival, noted the number of dependents, their occupations and skills, and their home villages in Holland. Notarized charter contracts for ships and testimonies of individuals made before Dutch notaries for court cases involving breach of contract and other litigations provided further evidence on the colonists emigrating to Rensselaerswyck. With the genealogical indexes in the Van Rensselaer–Bowier Manuscripts, one may reconstruct partial passenger lists for some fifteen voyages to the colony between 1630 and 1644.[3] Cross-referencing by surname, ship departure dates, and the protocols of public notaries in Amsterdam permits an analysis of family type, occupation, sexual distribution, and geograph-

3. Arnold J. F. van Laer, ed. and trans., *Van Rensselaer–Bowier Manuscripts* (Albany, 1908), pp. 805–34. The genealogical indexes after 1645 are incomplete and are based on the first appearance of the individual in the Rensselaerswyck Manuscripts.

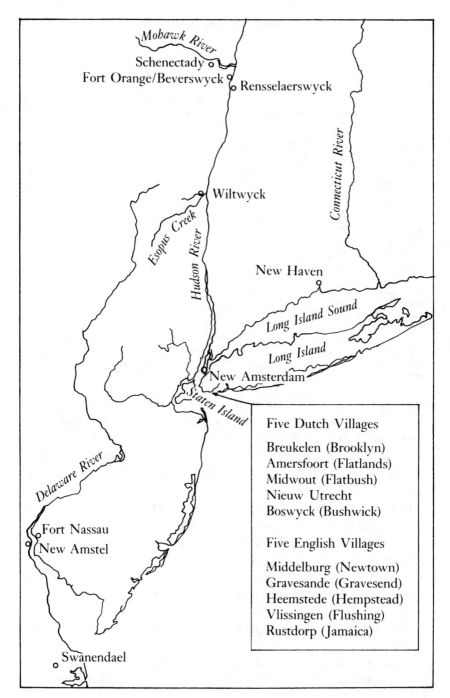

Population centers of New Netherland, ca. 1660.

Table 6.1. Rensselaerswyck immigrants, 1630–1644

Ship	Year	Total	Named passengers	Unnamed dependents	Single men	Single women	Families	Wife & no child
Eendracht	1630	15	9	6	7	0	1	0
Eendracht	1631	11	6	5	4	0	2	0
Zoutberg	1633	5	5	0	5	0	0	0
Eendracht	1634	12	6	6	4	0	2	0
Rensselaerswyck	1637	35	27	8	25	0	1	0
Harinck Chalmer	1638	4	3	1	3	0	1	1
Sleutel	1638	6	6	0	6	0	0	0
Wapen van Noorwegen	1638	19	11	8	7	0	2	1
Harinck	1639	6	5	1	5	0	1	1
Waterhondt	1640	13	13	0	13	0	0	0
Eijckenboom	1641	3	3	0	3	0	0	0
Coninck David	1641	7	4	3	3	0	1	0
Houttuijn	1642	22	13	9	8	0	4	3
Wapen van Rensselaerswyck	1644	16	12	4	9	2	1	0

Sources: Arnold J. F. van Laer, ed. and trans., *The Van Rensselaer-Bowier Manuscripts* (Albany, 1908), pp. 805–34; notarial archives of the Gemeentelijke Archief van Amsterdam; Edmund B. O'Callaghan, ed., *Documentary History of the State of New York*, 4 vols. (Albany, 1849–51), 3:33–42.

ical origin for about 174 immigrants (see Table 6.1). Although 174 is admittedly a small number for making projections about the character of the overall migration to New Netherland (a migration that may have been ten times this large), it is a respectable sized sample of the immigrants who settled in Rensselaerswyck in this period.[4]

Extrapolations from this sample apply to the rest of the colony because parallels in the demographic development of the two areas are evident. The unsettled wilderness of Rensselaerswyck and the still sparsely inhabited regions under Company control were more alike than not in this period, and it may be assumed that, on the whole, the two areas attracted the same type of immigrants in relatively similar proportions.

The immigration to Rensselaerswyck appears to have been domi-

4. As late as 1660 Rensselaerswyck consisted of about forty houses and some two hundred inhabitants. It never contained more than three hundred people. See J. Franklin Jameson, ed., *Narratives of New Netherland, 1609–1664* (New York, 1909), p. 207.

Wife & 1 child	Wife & 2	Wife & 3	Wife & 4 or more	Minor-age servants & apprentices	Foreigners	United Provinces	Farmers	Other occupations
0	0	1	0	2	4	5	9	0
2	0	0	0	1	2	4	4	2
0	0	0	0	0	0	4	5	0
1	0	1	0	0	0	2	3	3
0	0	0	1	0	5	15	11	8
0	0	0	0	0	0	2	0	3
0	0	0	0	0	0	6	1	5
1	0	0	0	5	1	6	7	2
0	0	0	0	0	1	1	1	4
0	0	0	0	0	0	10	7	2
0	0	0	0	0	0	1	2	1
1	0	0	0	1	1	2	0	4
0	0	0	1	1	5	7	5	5
0	0	0	1	0	1	9	3	5

nated by single young men. Of the 174 people in the sample, 123 were identified by name, and 104 of these listed their marital status as single. Only 2 of the 104 were women (two minor-age daughters of a man who had made the crossing a year earlier). Most of these single men were in their late teens and early twenties when they arrived in America.[5]

Fifty-one unnamed dependents shared shipboard with these young men. This sizable group included wives, children, unnamed minor-age apprentices and servants, and an occasional cousin, niece, or nephew. Grandparents were totally absent from the sample. It is possible to argue from this evidence that, although roughly a third of the immigrants arrived as members of households, Rensselaerswyck did not experience a nuclear family migration such as

5. Apprentices and servants under fourteen years of age were contracted for a minimum of four years and a maximum of seven years. Contracts invariably expired when the apprentice or servant reached majority, usually twenty-one years for males. Applying this rough age determinant to the approximately one hundred *dienstcontracten* (literally "service contracts") suggests that the average age for this group was about nineteen years.

occurred in New England. What sketchy evidence has survived on these unnamed dependents, moreover, suggests that many were teenaged offspring in a few large families. Eighteen percent of these immigrants arrived as members of families with three or more children, while less than 5 percent were members of conjugal units without children. The largest family contained nine children, one of whom was referred to as a "suckling," suggesting that the mother was still in her childbearing years. The other siblings of this family ranged in age upward to eighteen years. One family had six children, five of whom were sons between sixteen and twenty-two years of age. These exceptions to the general pattern of unmarried male immigrants did not affect the serious sexual imbalance in the colony. The few large families may even have contributed to it because families with large numbers of sons outnumbered those with daughters by a ratio of three to one. The overriding need for agricultural labor may have discouraged the immigration of families with daughters.

That the migration was dominated by single young men should not make us forget that for nearly a third of these people the decision to migrate to New Netherland constituted the beginning of a new life as members of transplanted households. For the single men in the sample, New Netherland may well have represented a rite of passage to adulthood, an adventurous sacrifice of the amenities of civilization for the brief experience of life in the wilderness. For the families it certainly meant much more.

Abraham Staas was twenty-four when he arrived in Rensselaerswyck in 1642. He had wed Trijntje Jochims just before his departure, going on ahead to prepare a place for his bride. A year later Trijntje arrived, and the young surgeon from Amsterdam began life as a colonial. In Amsterdam Staas's prospects must have been encouraging. The city by the Zuider Zee was the hub of a commercial empire experiencing a population boom seldom rivaled in the seventeenth century. Opportunities surely existed for a young surgeon. Still he chose to leave, signing a six-year contract with Kiliaen van Renssealer as the only trained medical professional in the colony. For Abraham Staas and Trijntje the promise of life in America was more attractive than the guaranteed rewards in the fatherland. Their decision turned out to be a wise one. In New Netherland Staas prospered. He became an important trader, counselor to the patroon's agents, a presiding officer and magistrate of Rensselaerswyck's manorial court, and the owner of a coastal sloop engaged in the trade to Virginia.[6]

Not all immigrants were so successful or happy in their new homes. For a few the decision to leave Holland arose from a desire to start afresh. For others the attraction lay in the opportunity to strike it rich in the fur trade or perhaps to discover gold mines and other precious commodities that could be turned for a quick guilder back home. Such dreams played upon the imaginations of all who made the crossing, pandering to their greed and sense of expectancy. The Walloons had fallen prey to these ambitions when they transformed the orderly fur trade into a panic market for profiteers in the late 1620s. Jamestown had nearly starved in pursuit of similar goals. The same pattern would occur again and again in many colonies. In New Netherland such attitudes became a fact of life for the West India Company officials, who constantly had to struggle against the impermanence of a sizable portion of the colony's inhabitants.

The men who emigrated with large families generally stayed in the colony. Albert Andriesz, whose entourage in 1637 included his pregnant wife and seven children, was one of these. The twenty-nine-year-old Andriesz, from Frederikstad in Norway, came to mill van Rensselaer's grain. An experienced miller, he contracted with the patroon to oversee the operation of the estate's mills for five years. Later he became a farmer of tobacco and wheat. In 1662, upon the death of his first wife, he married again, having discarded the patronymic Andriesz for Albert Andriesz Bradt. He died June 7, 1686, having spent forty-three of his seventy-two years in the colony.[7]

These men and their families, though a distinct minority of the immigrants in this period, made up (along with the Walloons) the stable core of the colony's population. Their numbers were constantly added to as the much larger migration to Company lands became a family migration in later years.

Whether family head or single young man, most came to work the land. Of the 123 named immigrants, 68 percent reported their

6. Van Laer, *Van Rensselaer–Bowier Manuscripts*, pp. 828–29.
7. Ibid., pp. 809–10.

occupations to public notaries in Amsterdam. These eighty-four individuals and eighteen others identified by occupation in the colony's records were spread across thirty-two occupational categories (see Table 6.2). The six agricultural categories constituted 38 percent of all those listing occupations, but there is reason to suspect that this figure is too small.

Those listed simply as servant (*dienaar*) or laborer (*arbeidter*) were probably under contract to their masters for agricultural work. If this assumption is valid, another twenty-six people may be added to the group of farm occupations. Furthermore, the occupations of those failing to list a previous trade or craft may well have been agricultural in the main because, unlike the relatively free immigration to Company lands, the movement of people to the patroonship of Rensselaerswyck was a planned migration, consciously recruited and paid for by the patroon.

The patroon was intent upon making his domain a self-sufficient agricultural enterprise. In a letter to his overseer in 1638, Kiliaen van Rensselaer made his views clear on the importance of farming to his colony: "I do not care to suffer in my colony those who have their eye mainly on the fur trade. That some trifles should be overlooked is a different matter, but those who make purely a business of it, I do not care to have . . . as my principal object is directed toward farming and things connected therewith."[8] Two years later he revealed his dream for the colony when he outlined his plans to Governor-General Willem Kieft: "I think that my farming people will, in proportion man for man, grow more grain than any others and thus help to make the country rich in grain so as in time to nourish Brazil and bring home sugar in return for meal sent there; then New Netherland would flourish."[9] Van Rensselaer was as good as his word in these matters, for 60 percent or more of the colonists in the sample came to farm the land.

Artisans and professionals came to Rensselaerswyck expecting to pursue their trades in the colony. Those in the building and construction crafts made up the largest portion of this group. Of those who listed occupations, 14 percent were carpenters, masons, wheelwrights, millwrights, or carpenter's apprentices. The next largest group were those skilled in the production of commodities.

8. Ibid., pp. 411–12.
9. Ibid., p. 482.

Table 6.2. Occupational distributions for
102 immigrants to Rensselaerswyck, 1630–
1644

Farmers (*boeren*ᵃ)	11
Farm servants (*bouwerijdienaar*)	5
Farmhands (*bouwerijwerker*)	10
Farm laborers (*bouwerijarbeiter*)	10
Farmboy (*bouwerijjongen*)	1
Farmer's apprentice (*bouwerijleerling*)	1
Servant	19
Laborer	7
Magistrate (*schepen*)	1
Sheriff (*schout*)	1
Carpenter/mason	1
Wheelwright	2
Journeyman carpenter	1
Carpenter	7
Master carpenter	1
House carpenter	1
Millwright	1
Miller	2
Shoemaker	4
Blacksmith	1
Hog Dealer	1
Baker	1
Cooper	1
Clerk	1
Weaver	1
Tailor	4
Wagoner	1
Foreman	1
Brewer	1
Surgeon	1
Minister	1
Skipper	1

Sources: Arnold J. F. van Laer, ed. and trans.,
The Van Rensselaer-Bowier Manuscripts (Albany,
1908), pp. 805–34, and work contracts in the
notarial archives of the Gemeentelijke Archief
van Amsterdam.

ᵃ Dutch word appearing in notarized work
contracts.

Four cobblers and four tailors emigrated to Rensselaerswyck along with a brewer of beer, a cooper, a baker, a weaver, and a blacksmith. To these the patroon added a surgeon and a preacher.

Persuading these skilled workers and professionals to emigrate was expensive. Van Rensselaer agreed to pay wages and salaries that, on the average, exceeded those in the fatherland by some 25 percent (see Table 6.3). In addition, lucrative financial arrangements were made with colonists to attract them to the estate. To Reyniert Stoffelsz, a blacksmith and iron worker from Essen in Germany, the patroon granted free passage for his wife and sister-in-law as well as all the iron ore and other materials necessary to start a foundry. At the end of four years in the colony, Stoffelsz agreed to pay van Rensselaer 70 percent of the value of his materials. This arrangement amounted to a 30 percent subsidy.[10]

Wages were paid in pelts, tobacco, and occasionally grain. The colonists seldom came out ahead in these transactions because the prices of commodities and especially of livestock, the auxiliary industry of almost every tenant, outpaced the prices the Company and patroon allowed for furs. A revealing document from 1639 listed livestock prices at the Company auction on Manhattan Island for the years 1634 to 1638. In a deposition given before Hendrick Schaeff, public notary in Amsterdam, Jacques Bentin and Jan Jansz Damen, two former West India Company farmers in New Netherland, testified that livestock prices in the colony were in some cases nearly 100 percent higher than those in Holland.[11]

Such conditions created animosity toward the Company and the patroon and encouraged speculation in furs as a hedge against the rising prices of consumer goods and farm tools.[12] In the long run the chronic lack of a stable currency caught the tenants in a vise between the hated Company store and an increasingly avaricious

10. Gemeentelijke Archief van Amsterdam, Notarial no. 1054, April 18, 1639, pp. 65–65v.

11. Gemeentelijke Archief van Amsterdam, Notarial no. 1280, May 5, 1639, pp. 60v–61. In 1664 prices in New Netherland were still very high. A notarial document from that year revealed that thirty-five pair of shoes purchased for 120 fl. in Amsterdam sold for 280 fl. at the Company store on Manhattan Island (Notarial no. 2855, January 12, 1664, Folio 361–62, unpaginated).

12. This practice accelerated the eradication of fur-bearing animals, and by the 1650s pelts were in short supply, forcing the Company to accept tobacco as legal tender. The thriving Virginia trade soon flooded New Netherland with tobacco in

Table 6.3. Annual salaries by occupation for Rensselaerswyck immigrants, 1630–1644 (in florins)

Occupation	Lowest	Highest	United Provinces
Farm servant	80[a]	110	84
Farm laborer	30	32	no data
Foreman	–	140	100
Shoemaker	40	100	65
Carpenter's boy	–	40	25
Journeyman carpenter	–	120	115
Master carpenter	–	550	410
Cooper	90	168	200
Servant	25	140	no data
Minister	1,000	1,200	1,000

Sources: Notarized work contracts in the Gemeentelijke Archief van Amsterdam and van Laer, ed. and trans., *Van Rensselaer-Bowier Manuscripts*, pp. 805–34.

The high and low salaries are deduced from a comparison of work contracts drawn up before Amsterdam notaries in the 1630s. Since most Rensselaerswyck contracts included provisions for passage and victuals upon arrival, their real value was higher than those shown here. The figures for the United Provinces are averages calculated on the basis of day labor rates that appear in work contracts in the Gemeentelijke Archief van Amsterdam.

[a]The Dutch florin contained 20 stuivers and was frequently referred to as a guilder. For the first half of the seventeenth century, 48 stuivers, or roughly 2 1/2 fl. equaled a Spanish-American rial-of-eight. In New Netherland, a good-quality beaver pelt was worth about 8 fl. and a 240-pound hogshead of Virginia tobacco was worth about 114 fl. (Charles R. Boxer, *The Dutch Seaborne Empire, 1600–1800* [New York, 1965], pp. 304–5; Gemeentelijke Archief van Amsterdam, Notarial no. 1119, October 2, 1656, p. 3).

Indian population and may have contributed to the disastrous Indian wars of the 1640s that nearly wiped out the Dutch presence in the lower reaches of the Hudson River valley and threatened the security of Long Island and Manhattan.[13]

1656, causing a 150 percent inflation in prices (calculated in tobacco) over those that had prevailed just three years before (Gemeentelijke Archief van Amsterdam, Notarial no. 1119, October 2, 1656, p. 3).

13. Thomas Elliot Norton, *The Fur Trade in Colonial New York, 1686–1776* (Madison, 1974), pp. 9–12; J. W. Schulte-Nordholt, "Nederlanders in Nieuw Nederland, de oorlog van Kieft," *Bijdragen en Mededelingen van het Historisch Genootschap* 80 (1966): 38–94.

For Rensselaerswyck the situation meant a continuing attrition of settlers as colonists failed to complete their contracts and moved to unoccupied land farther south or in some cases abandoned farming altogether to pursue the elusive riches of the fur trade. Faced with these difficulties, the patroon could do little more than expand his recruitment of colonists in Europe and complain to his friends. In a fit of pique van Rensselaer wrote to Reyniert Stoffelsz in 1640 revealing his frustration: "I trust that you will serve me faithfully and live up to your contract, unlike others, who I understand do nothing but misconstrue my contracts and seek to stir up others."[14]

The patroon would continue to have difficulties with his tenants, and Rensselaerswyck ceased to be attractive to colonists after the Company monopoly was abandoned in 1639. Those whom van Rensselaer could persuade to settle on his estate all too frequently had little reason to stay in the fatherland. Of the ninety-six immigrants who gave their origins to Amsterdam notaries, seventy-six were from the villages and towns of the United Provinces. Almost 30 percent of these came from the province of Utrecht, the inland center of resistance to the burgher oligarchs of Amsterdam and one of the most economically depressed areas in an otherwise booming Dutch economy. After 1620, the rising popularity of the so-called "new draperies" (a lightly woven linen cloth) disrupted the Utrecht-based heavy linen industry, causing an exodus of skilled linen workers to other areas. Utrecht's once formidable position in the Dutch textile economy had been eclipsed by Gouda, Delft, and Haarlem in mid-century. Leiden led the nation in textile production, and Amsterdam, with its immense capital reserves and rising population, threatened to drain Utrecht Province of every able worker.[15] Thus when the call went out for colonists for Rensselaerswyck, the patroon received more responses from Utrecht than any other province. Farmers and laborers, denied the market for their products and skills in Utrecht and unable to compete effectively in the dislocated provincial economy, drifted to Amsterdam, where the patroon's agents enticed them with tales of riches and prosperity awaiting them in New Netherland. So effective was this combination of forces in encouraging inhabitants of Utrecht Province to emigrate

14. Van Laer, *Van Rensselaer–Bowier Manuscripts*, p. 502.
15. J. G. van Dillen, *Van Rijkdom en Regenten: Handboek tot de Economische en Sociale Geschiedenis van Nederland tijdens de Republiek* (The Hague, 1970), p. 186.

that the inland province contributed more colonists to Rensselaerswyck than South Holland and North Holland combined— an astounding fact when one considers that the three largest concentrations of Dutch population were located in the latter two provinces.

Fifteen immigrants in the sample listed their origins as North Brabant (a frontier area between the Protestant North and the Catholic South) and Overijsel, a province noted for its dairy farming. Only two immigrants came from Amsterdam. Perhaps just as surprising was the presence of so many foreigners among the colonists.

Twenty immigrants were identified as non-Dutch. Half of these came from places in the Germanies; six were Norwegian; and Sweden, France, Denmark, and England contributed one each. These foreigners outnumbered those from the populous province of North Holland and constituted more than a fifth of all immigrants listing an origin. Although these numbers are certainly significant for the migration to Rensselaerswyck, other studies based on a thorough reading of genealogical materials suggest that the proportion of foreigners in New Netherland was much larger, constituting perhaps as much as 50 percent of the colony's population.[16] If such estimates are accurate, the Rensselaerswyck sample is indicative of the overall demographic trends in the colony. The presence of so many foreigners in the Dutch colony, moreover, requires an explanation.

Unlike England, where the centripetal forces of Puritan radicalism and attempts by the Stuart monarchs to enforce political and religious conformity encouraged a swarming of the population out of the realm, the United Provinces beckoned thousands to their shores. A study of immigrants in the Great Migration to New England notes that for many Englishmen the choice was between America and Holland, with the latter frequently winning out.[17] Indeed, so popular had the United Provinces become as a center for refugees that a 1631 tax assessment in the city of Amsterdam revealed that of the 685 wealthiest individuals no less than 160 were

16. David Cohen, "How Dutch were the Dutch of New Netherland?" *New York History* 62 (1981): 51.

17. Breen and Foster, "Moving to the New World," p. 206.

Flemish or Walloon, 30 were German, and numerous Italian, English, and Scandinavian names dotted the list.[18]

The largest number of refugees came from the southern provinces, where Spanish oppression forced perhaps a tenth of the population to flee north, but no national group seemed to lack representatives. English Brownists had found temporary refuge in the university town of Leiden; Spanish Jews concentrated in The Hague; Rotterdam, with its busy wharves, housed sailors and soldiers from every land; and Amsterdam teemed with all nationalities of folk seeking their fortunes.[19] In this intoxicating period of Holland's aptly named *goude eeuw* (golden century), the overseas possessions of the fatherland competed for colonists.

Asia had the greatest attraction, seducing young men with promises of Oriental treasures and adventure in the service of the VOC. Brazil, for thirty years the center of West India Company operations in the New World, drew its share of young men and women to the sugar plantations of New Holland. The West Indian islands had a similar attraction, and there the opportunity to smite the Spanish enemy proved heady brew to three generations of Dutchmen seeking to earn their spurs. New Netherland, without gold or glory, ran a poor fourth in this competition for colonists.

New Netherland in general and Rensselaerswyck in particular were the have-nots of the Dutch seaborne empire. Always underpopulated and chronically mismanaged, New Netherland could not attract enough colonists to survive in an English-dominated North America. Those who could be persuaded to emigrate to the colony, moreover, were often those with few ties to the fatherland—foreigners drifting in and out of Holland's economy as unemployed or underemployed sailors, soldiers, and adventurers; dispossessed farmers and their families fleeing deteriorating economic conditions or the ravages of a war that seemed never to end; clannish ethnic or religious minorities who could not find comfort in the tolerant secularism that pervaded Dutch culture; and the young from all groups whose restlessness and poverty made them suscep-

18. J. G. van Dillen, *Bronnen tot de Geschiedenis van het Bedrijfsleven en het Gildewezen van Amsterdam, 1512–1632*, 2 vols. (The Hague, 1929–33), 2:xli–xlii.

19. J. A. van Houtte, "Het economisch verval van het Zuiden," in *Algemene Geschiedenis der Nederlanden* 5 (1952): 193–200.

tible to promises of independence overseas. The notarial records of Amsterdam chronicled some of these people and their aspirations.

Jacob Swenthorst of Hamburg had traveled the world by his twenty-fifth birthday. Illiterate and poor, he would sign on with any skipper who could pay him. He faced an important decision in 1632 when the West India Company advertised for colonists to go to New Netherland. Down on his luck, Swenthorst needed 300 fl. to support his illegitimate daughter in the local orphanage. His unusual sense of responsibility in this matter and his chronic restlessness persuaded him to sign on with the Company for three years as a farmhand (*bouwerij werker*) for the Company farms on Manhattan Island. Shortly before his departure, he signed over all his wages to his friend Bartel Goelits, a laborer in the canal works around Amsterdam. Goelits swore to pay Swenthorst's wages to the orphanage and care for the child while her father was in America. Taking sail, Swenthorst emigrated to New Netherland in the summer of 1632 and disappeared from history.[20]

For some colonists New Netherland was not so much a destination as a stopping point in their wanderings around Holland's worldwide empire. Pieter Pietersz Bijlevelt lived in the colony with his wife and three children from 1630 to 1638. Failing to find his pot of gold, he packed up his family and returned to Amsterdam. There he roamed the streets aimlessly looking for work while his family survived on public charity. In 1639 Pieter deserted his wife and children to sign on with the VOC for a two-year voyage to Java. Geertruijt Bijlevelt, pregnant with her fourth child, sued the West India Company for failing to buy back the livestock and grain the family had left behind on Manhattan Island. An inventory submitted with the notarized claim revealed that the Bijlevelts had abandoned a prosperous farm with two mares, six milch cows, and twenty acres of maize. At prices then prevailing in the colony, the livestock and grain were worth more than three times the wages Pieter Bijlevelt could hope to earn in the service of the VOC in Asia.[21]

20. Gemeentelijke Archief van Amsterdam, Notarial no. 788, June 14, 1632, p. 366.

21. Gemeentelijke Archief van Amsterdam, Notarial no. 1187, March 3, 1639, p. 2.

For such people no place could be home for very long, and the imprint they left on the colony was faint. Others, how many we will never know, would follow in this senseless pattern of migration, rendering in the process a New Netherland dangerously underpopulated and vulnerable to Indian attack and foreign conquest.

The indexes of immigrants to Rensselaerswyck do not extend beyond 1644, and the next quantifiable data begin in 1657. Amsterdam notarial records, however, indicate that this thirteen-year interval was the busiest yet for the West India Company and the private merchants and settlers of New Netherland. Scattered references to immigrants aboard approximately two-thirds of ships chartered for the colony suggest that a large influx of colonists arrived in these years.[22] Estimates of New Netherland's population vary widely depending on the source and the data used, but the best guess is that the colony contained no more than five hundred inhabitants in 1628, when the patroonship plan was first proposed, two thousand five hundred in 1645 following the Indian wars of 1639–43, and certainly no more than nine thousand in 1664, when the colony fell to the English.[23] If these estimates are correct, New Netherland must have experienced its own version of a great migration in the last years of its existence.

The character of the migration between 1644 and 1657 is difficult to judge, and historians know virtually nothing about the immigrants in this period. References in the notarial records to groups of

22. Sixty separate references to immigrants aboard thirty-six of fifty-three ships sailing to New Netherland were found in the notarial archives. Most of these references, unfortunately, were made in connection with other matters, and it is impossible to infer much about the character of the migration in these years. That it was a substantial migration seems assured.

23. These estimates are mine and are based on a number of sources, the most important of which are Henry R. Friis, "A Series of Population Maps of the Colonies and the United States, 1625–1790," *Geographical Review* 30 (1940): 463–70; Julius M. Bloch, Leo Herschkowitz, Kenneth Scott, and Constance D. Sherman, eds., *An Account of Her Majesty's Revenue in the Province of New York, 1701–09: The Customs Records of Early Colonial New York* (Ridgewood, N.J., 1966); W. R. Menkman, "De Nederlanders in West-Africa en de Nieuwe Wereld," *Algemene Geschiedenis der Nederlanden* 6 (1953): 110–13; and thirty-three notarial documents contained in the protocols of Hendrick Schaef, Hendrick Rosa, Cornelis Trouw, Arnout van Zurck, and Jan Leuven in the Gemeentelijke Archief van Amsterdam. These last-named documents are especially useful for estimating the number of West India Company soldiers in New Netherland.

families aboard the ships sailing to New Netherland suggest that the once dominant trend of single males was being challenged by a family migration. Whether family migration in these years was large enough to change the sexual imbalance in the colony cannot be ascertained with any degree of certainty. In the fleet of four vessels carrying the new director-general, Pieter Stuyvesant, to New Amsterdam in 1646–47, West India Company soldiers made up the largest proportion of passengers. The *Groote Gerrit*, a three hundred-ton ship accompanying the Stuyvesant fleet, carried at least a few families to New Netherland, though their names and everything else about them is unknown.[24] In 1646, the owners of the *Wapen van Nieuw Nederland* and the *Witte Doffer*, two privately chartered ships, publicly solicited passengers and cargo for New Netherland. Presumably these ships carried immigrants to the colony.[25] More reliable data come from the notarial records of the *Gelderse Blom* and the Swedish-owned *Keyser Karl*.

The *Gelderse Blom* carried twelve colonists to Rensselaerswyck. All were single men ranging in age from fourteen to forty years. Their contracts with the patroon indicated that none of those below twenty-one years was literate enough to sign his name, and only forty-year-old Adriaen Dircksz listed his occupation as a farmer. The other eleven were apparently without a trade or vocation. All twelve were indebted to the van Rensselaer family for their lodgings and board in Amsterdam, and all were from the countryside. This group of ne'er-do-wells, snatched off the streets of the city where they had drifted from the hinterland, conformed to the pattern of migration established in the 1630s.[26]

The immigrants aboard the *Keyser Karl* were of a different character: they included "many colonists and their children who wished to settle in New Netherland."[27] These families were mostly Swedish and represented the first sizable migration under the auspices of the Swedish West India Company. Their destination was the Dela-

24. Gemeentelijke Archief van Amsterdam, Notarial no. 1340, August 1, 1647, p. 72.

25. Ibid., Notarial nos. 817, March 29, 1646, unpaginated; 1573, June 24, 1646, p. 323.

26. Ibid., Notarial no. 1096, March 20, 1651, pp. 286–287v.

27. Ibid. Notarial no. 2279, April 5, 1652, pp. 44–45v.

ware River, where they would be engaged in establishing the colony of New Sweden. C. A. Weslager, the leading scholar on the subject, has suggested that more than half the settlers in this small colony were ethnic Finns taking up residence beside the "lawbreakers, poachers, persons guilty of breaking forest ordinances, deserted soldiers, and debtors" who made up the roughly four hundred people living in New Sweden at the time of the Dutch conquest and annexation in 1655.[28] Whether any of the families on the *Keyser Karl* were Finnish cannot be known, but one of the crewmen who later testified on behalf of the West India Company listed his home as "Helzinkvoors," the Dutch phonetic spelling of Helsingfors, or Helsinki.[29]

Another group of immigrants who began to arrive in larger numbers in these years were African slaves. It is not known when the first slaves arrived in New Netherland, but by 1639 West India Company maps showed a slave camp some five miles north of Fort New Amsterdam on Manhattan Island. Brief references to slaves appear in the written records as early as 1630, and in the late 1650s fully loaded slavers were docking in New Amsterdam with human cargo for sale.[30] Little more is known of these people. The first slaves to be forcibly transported to New Netherland were probably booty taken by Company warships in their incessant preying on Iberian shipping. A few references to slaves and freedmen in the Council Minutes of Willem Kieft suggest that some of these slaves had become freedmen and property owners by 1640. In 1638, for example, Anthony the Portuguese (presumably a former slave) sued Anthony Jansen for injury done to a hog. In June of the next year the governor-general's council heard the suit of Pedro Negret-

---

28. C. A. Weslager, *The English on the Delaware, 1610–1682* (New Brunswick, N.J., 1967), p. 71.

29. Gemeentelijke Archief van Amsterdam, Notarial no. 1576, March 15, 1652, p. 285.

30. For facsimiles of early maps showing the slave camp, see Isaac Newton Phelps Stokes, *The Iconography of Manhattan Island*, 6 vols. (New York, 1915–28), 2:186–87 and map plates 41, 42, and 42a. For an excellent analysis of the written evidence for slavery in New Netherland, see P. C. Emmer, "De slavenhandel van en naar Nieuw Nederland," *Economische- en Sociaal-Historisch Jaarboek* 34 (1974): 94–147.

to, a day laborer and farmhand, who claimed back wages against Jan Celes for work done in tending the defendant's hogs.[31] Slaves were undoubtedly subjected to all the cruelties that have attended the institution of slavery since its inception. Still, there is reason to suggest that slavery in New Netherland lacked the life-taxing brutality it did elsewhere in the Dutch seaborne empire.

With no plantation economy or even a cash crop upon which to base one, New Netherland's potential use for slaves was dubious. Until the 1650s, however, slaves were needed to man Company farms, tend Company livestock, load and unload the occasional Company ship, and even take up arms to help protect the lives and property of their masters. In 1641, at the height of the Indian hysteria, a frightened Willem Kieft asked the heads of families and householders in New Netherland to approve the use of slaves as fleet-footed hit-and-run teams armed to disrupt Indian hunting parties along the lower banks of the Hudson. The teams would employ "many Negroes from among the strongest and fleetest," and each would be armed with "a hatchet and a half-pike."[32] Such trust in one's slaves reflects a special relationship between master and slave in New Netherland. The Company had adopted a practice of giving its slaves "half-freedom" after years of faithful service, which entitled the slave to freedom of travel in the colony, the right to own or acquire some property, and the freedom to marry. The half-slave was obligated to pay the Company a fixed sum per annum, usually in the form of grain, furs, or wampum. Many slaves were manumitted by their owners and given land by the Company.[33] Certainly, slavery was not a growing institution in New

31. Arnold J. van Laer, trans., *New York Historical Manuscripts: Dutch*, 4 vols. (Baltimore, 1974), 4:23, 53.

32. Ibid., pp. 124–25.

33. Charles T. Gehring, ed. and trans., *Land Papers* (Baltimore, 1980), pp. 34–36. In other matters, too, New Netherland's blacks appear to have enjoyed several civil privileges, not the least of which was the right to marry legally and have the matrimonial bonds proclaimed in the Reformed church. The marriage records for the New Amsterdam Church indicate that between 1639 and 1652 (the only years for which there exists documentation) fourteen marriages involving blacks were recorded. These fourteen marriages represent about 28 percent of all marriages recorded in that period. Thirteen marriages involved black men marrying black

View of New Amsterdam, ca. 1655. Inset view from map in Nicolas Jansz Visscher, *Novi Belgii Novaeque Angliae nec non partis Virginiae tabula* (Amsterdam, 1655). Courtesy of the New York State Library, Albany.

Netherland, although in the last years of the colony's existence Company management considered making New Amsterdam a slave market for North America.

The *Witte Paert* took her anchorage in the roadstead before Fort New Amsterdam on September 15, 1655. The reeking hull alerted everyone on the island that a slaver had docked. Below decks the *Witte Paert* carried nearly three hundred Africans, writhing in the agony of the sweltering late summer day. The arrival of the slaver was an important event in the colony's history, for it marked the first direct slave trade between New Netherland and the Guinea coast. A few weeks later, when the slaves sold for nearly 1,200 fl. each at auction, some enterprising colonists and company officials saw the possibility of more profits.[34]

In 1656 the *Bontekoe* arrived in the colony as the first of three slavers to sail from West Africa via Curaçao with a cargo of humans. Under an agreement reached between the West India Company and a syndicate of Spanish merchants living in Amsterdam, one-third of the slaves would be unloaded at Curaçao, where agents of the Spanish syndicate agreed to pay the sum of ninety-five pieces of eight for each healthy male slave. The other two-thirds were bound for New Netherland.[35] For some time the Amsterdam chamber of the company had contemplated and debated the financial returns that might accrue from the establishment of a slave auction at New Amsterdam. In the late 1650s the debate may have turned to policy. Although no reliable estimates can confirm the existence of an ongoing slave market, some admittedly sketchy evidence in the Stuyvesant Papers suggests that New Amsterdam may have become a budding entrepôt for slaves in the last years before the English conquest. Company contracts and charter agreements for slave ships sailing directly to New Netherland had become so commonplace that Pieter Stuyvesant had several forms printed. The form left blanks for inserting the name of the ship and

---

women, and one marriage was interracial—a European man married a black woman from Angola. Five of the marriages involved widows or widowers marrying for the second time. Samuel Purple, ed., *Index to the Marriage Records of the Dutch Reformed Church in New Amsterdam and New York* (New York, 1890).

34. Emmer, "De slavenhandel," pp. 114–15.

35. Gemeentelijke Archief van Amsterdam, Notarial no. 2117, November 23, 1656, p. 161.

her captain as well as the specific destinations on the West African coast where gangs of slaves could be picked up.[36]

Whether slaves ever made up a significant percentage of New Netherland's population, it is unlikely that their presence in the colony was very permanent. Enough evidence has survived to suggest that many of the slaves arriving in New Netherland were quickly sold down the coast in English Maryland and Virginia. That the practice had become common was revealed by the levying of a 10 percent export tax on all slaves sold to the English colonies. Possibly this tax was aimed at prohibiting the traffic in humans; more likely it represented a Company effort to profit from an ongoing trade.[37] In any case, black Africans had joined other ethnic and national groups in the 1650s to make New Netherland the most culturally heterogeneous European colony in North America.

New Netherland's last years are the most fully documented. Edmund B. O'Callaghan compiled passenger lists for thirty-five ships that sailed to the colony in the years 1657–64.[38] These lists, although ostensibly made for genealogical research, provide a good deal of information on the marital status, family size, and general character of the migration to New Netherland in this period. O'Callaghan's lists do not include all of the vessels that arrived in the colony, and the notarial records of Amsterdam show that a few of those he cites failed to make the crossing. Nevertheless, these same records indicate that O'Callaghan's work was accurate generally, and most, if not all, passenger-carrying ships were accounted for. When checked against the various charter contracts and bottomry bonds in the notarial archives, the list can be augmented, reduced in some cases, and made more complete and accurate. The result (see Table 6.4) is the closest approximation to an index of immigrants that we are ever likely to have for New Netherland.

The revised O'Callaghan lists provide data on 1,079 individuals. What proportion of the period's total immigration this sample represents is difficult to determine. A conservative estimate of the colony's population in 1655 placed it at 2,000 inhabitants. The

36. Emmer, "De slavenhandel," pp. 140–41.
37. Ibid., p. 115.
38. Edmund B. O'Callaghan, ed., *Documentary History of the State of New York*, 4 vols. (Albany, 1849–51), 3:33–42.

highest estimate for that same year was 3,500. For 1664 the estimates ranged upward to 9,000. Assuming the shortest range for
population increase to be the difference between the highest estimated population in 1655 and the lowest in 1664, it would seem
that an increase of at least 5,900 people occurred in these years.
From these figures, we must subtract about 2,000 for the New
Englanders on Long Island and elsewhere whose intercolonial migration affected the overall population estimates at the time of the
English conquest in 1664. We are left with an estimated population
increase in this period of approximately 3,900. How much of this
growth was attributable to natural increase cannot be estimated,
but the chronic shortage of women in New Netherland probably
kept natural increases at a low level throughout most of the colony's
history. Thus the sample of 1,079 immigrants represents about 27
percent of the total Atlantic migration from the United Provinces in
this period.[39]

That the sample is representative, moreover, seems assured by
the random selection process, involving genealogical indexing by
surnames appearing in official documents and the notarial record
citations by year and ship name. In addition, the nearly complete
lists of immigrants aboard ships sailing in 1659, 1660, 1662, and
1663 allow intrasample comparison to offset statistically relevant
errors occurring in the less complete lists. Hence the sample may
be handled in aggregate form for the simple computations involved
in this study.[40]

The 1,079 immigrants in the sample were a different lot from
those who had arrived before. Most notably, there were far fewer
single men in this group than in previous years—only 25 percent of
the total as compared to nearly 60 percent in the Rensselaerswyck
sample. Second, single women were present in the 1657–64 sample

39. See note 23 above. I wish to thank John Murrin for his close reading of an
earlier version of this chapter at the Conference on New York State History. His
knowledge of population estimates for New Netherland helped me correct some
important errors.

40. The voyages of the *Trouw* (1659 and 1660), the *Bontekoe* (1660 and 1663), the
Vergulde Otter (1660), the *Hoop* (1662), and the *Stettin* (1663) carried 499 immigrants
to New Netherland, constituting 46.2 percent of the total in the sample. These
ships were especially well documented in the notarial archives, and there is every
reason to believe that the passenger lists are nearly complete.

Table 6.4. New Netherland immigrants, 1657–1664

Ship[a]	Year	Total	Named passengers	Unnamed dependents	Single men	Single women[b]	Families[c]	Wife & no child
St. Jan Baptiste	1657	9	6	3	5	0	1	0
Ijsserdraadvat	1657	22	8	14	5	0	3	1
Vergulde Otter	1657	3	2	1	3	0	0	0
Moesman	1658	6	4	2	1	2	1	0
Vergulde Bever	1658	38	17	21	7	1	7	1
Bruijvis	1658	33	20	13	11	3	6	1
de Trouw	1659	98	43	55	17	9	15	2
Vergulde Otter	1659	12	6	6	4	2	2	0
Vergulde Bever	1659	21	16	5	11	2	2	1
Moesman	1659	23	14	9	9	1	4	0
de Trouw	1660	60	31	29	15	3	10	1
Moesman	1660	32	20	12	14	1	5	3
Vergulde Bever	1660	7	4	3	0	2	2	1
Bontekoe	1660	79	40	39	29	4	7	0
Vergulde Otter	1660	52	28	24	19	0	9	3
Vergulde Arent	1661	5	3	2	1	1	1	0
de Bever	1661	51	20	31	8	7	7	0
St. Jan Baptiste	1661	38	15	23	5	3	7	0
Vergulde Arent	1662	8	4	4	3	0	1	0
de Trouw	1662	27	15	12	7	1	4	1
de Hoop	1662	72	22	50	5	3	14	3
de Vos	1662	44	28	16	19	3	5	1
de Roode Rooseboom	1663	71	30	41	17	2	11	0
Bontekoe	1663	86	34	51	13	1	19	3
Stettin	1663	52	31	21	16	5	8	1
St. Pieter	1663	9	6	3	5	0	1	0
de Trouw	1664	17	8	9	2	2	4	0
Gecruijste Hart	1664	8	6	2	4	1	1	0
de Arent	1664	11	9	2	6	2	1	0
Eendracht	1664	38	16	22	7	0	9	0

[a]Five ships that appeared in O'Callaghan's list have been omitted from this table because a review of the notarial archives revealed that they either failed to reach New Netherland, as in the case of *de Lieffde*, or that they sailed as military transports or cargo ships. The five ships are *de Lieffde* (1660), *de Purmerlandkerk* (1662), *de Star* (1663), *St. Jacob* (1663), and *de Bever* (1664). Of these, only the *Purmerlandkerk* was chartered as a passenger-carrying ship for twenty-five Mennonite families bound for the colony of Nieuw Amstel on the Delaware River. Presumably these families sailed aboard her the next year. The others were primarily trading vessels. See Notarial Archives, 1516/folio 39–40 unpaginated, October 29, 1660, J. Volkertsz Oli; 2793/folio 695–97 unpaginated, October 20, 1661, Pieter van Buijtene; 1517/folio 258–59 unpaginated, June 27, 1663, J. Volkertsz Oli; 3161/48, January 24, 1664, Jacob Pondt.

[b]Only women referred to as "maidens" (*maagden*), "unmarrieds" (*ongetrouwders*), and "widows" (*widwe*) are included in this list. Many single young women were undoubtedly among the large and undifferentiated group of "servants" (*dienaaren*).

Wife & 1 child	Wife & 2	Wife & 3	Wife & 4 or more	Foreignersd	United Provinces	Farmers	Other occupationse
0	1	0	0	0	2	0	0
1	0	0	1	0	1	0	0
0	0	0	0	0	0	0	0
0	1	0	0	2	0	0	0
2	3	0	1	2	4	0	0
3	1	0	1	4	5	0	0
4	2	1	6	8	63	5	5
1	0	1	0	2	9	1	1
1	0	0	0	5	11	6	3
4	0	0	0	4	13	2	3
2	7	0	0	2	30	2	1
0	0	1	1	5	23	2	14 [12 WIC soldiers]
0	1	0	0	0	0	0	0
0	1	1	4	5	68	5	22 [18 WIC soldiers]
1	2	1	2	22	27	10	15 [15 WIC soldiers]
1	0	0	0	0	1	0	1
2	1	1	3	6	31	0	1
2	3	1	1	4	12	0	0
0	0	1	0	0	3	2	1
1	1	0	1	5	13	0	0
1	3	2	5	0	52	10	2
2	0	1	1	8	22	0	6
2	1	1	5	18	42	0	2
9	2	0	5	17	47	0	0
5	0	1	1	7	23	0	0
0	1	0	0	1	8	1	0
3	0	0	1	2	15	1	Undisclosed number of soldiers
0	1	0	0	0	0	0	0
0	1	0	0	3	3	0	0
5	1	2	1	2	14	0	0

cFamilies include all those who would normally inhabit a household with the exception of servants. Thus a man and his bride are considered a family by this reckoning.

dThose clearly indentifiable as non-Dutch by their place of origin are included in this group. The tendency of Dutch notaries to Hollandize all names makes any attempt at ethnic classification by name not only pointless but misleading. To cite one example, the famous Jacob Leisler was listed as Jacob Loestlersz van Duits, or literally Jacob, son of Loestler of Germany. Most names are not as easily deciphered.

eFor the years 1657 to 1664, listed occupations are the exception, thus this category is more a confession of the lack of data than anything else.

Sources: Edmund B. O'Callaghan, ed., *Documentary History of the State of New York*, 4 vols. (Albany, 1849–51), 3:33–42, and the notarial archives of the Gemeentelijke Archief van Amsterdam, "Hart Collection."

in a small (6 percent) but relevant proportion for the first time. These women included seventeen young women identified as "maidens" (*maagden*), four identified as "widows" (*widwe*), and forty-one listed simply as "unmarried" (*ongetrouwd*). Two of the widows brought dependent children, and fourteen of the unmarried women were servants attached to households with children.

Families made up the largest percentage of immigrants in the sample, nearly 70 percent of all those coming to the colony from the United Provinces. There were 176 families with an average size of 4.2 members in the sample, and 77 of these, or roughly 44 percent of all the families, contained two or fewer children. These figures have profound implications for the age distribution of the immigrants.

If we assume that these predominantly Dutch families were sliced piecemeal from the general fabric of Dutch life, the high proportion of small families in the sample suggests a migration of people in their early twenties with small children and infants. Recent studies of Dutch household size and age-specific fertility rates in the seventeenth century would confirm that these immigrant families were headed, on the average, by parents under twenty-five years of age. In the United Provinces, the mean size of families was generally lower than elsewhere in Europe—a low 3.72, for example, as compared to the English mean household size of 4.75 for the same period. Such considerations allow the inference that the migration to New Netherland in the period 1657–64 was approaching a nuclear family pattern that reflected the general character of Dutch domestic life.[41]

The other end of the family scale was represented by a sizable group of families with four or more children. Forty-three families were this size, representing nearly a quarter (24.4 percent) of all families in the sample. This group was considerably larger among immigrants to New Netherland than in Dutch domestic society as a whole, where such large families constituted only 14 percent of all households.[42]

This grouping of families at the ends of the size scale argues

---

41. A. M. van der Woude, "Variations in the Size and Structure of the Household in the United Provinces of the Netherlands in the Seventeenth and Eighteenth Centuries," in Peter Laslett, ed., *Household and Family in Past Time* (Cambridge, 1972), pp. 299–318.

42. Ibid., p. 311.

forcibly for the conclusion that immigrants arriving in New Netherland after 1657 were, by and large, young and vigorous. When the parents of these large families are excluded from the overall sample of family members, 659 people, or over 61 percent of all immigrants in this sample, were probably under twenty-five years of age.

New Netherland had improved its image in the eyes of prospective Dutch colonists; after 1657 it appealed to young couples in their early years of childbearing and to mature, though by no means old, couples whose large families of maturing sons and daughters ensured a labor force for the family farm. Thus the last decade of Dutch rule witnessed what must have seemed like a rebirth for the colony. Coming in the wake of the tragic Indian wars of the early 1640s, this migration of large numbers of young families promised a brighter future for New Netherland. Events occurring in the Dutch seaborne empire may help explain why New Netherland's fortunes had suddenly taken a turn for the better.

The West India Company had suffered a staggering setback in 1654, when it lost Brazil, or New Holland as it was called, to an eight-year Portuguese rebellion at Pernambuco. The checking of the sugar imports from Dutch Brazil threatened one of the only lucrative trades still nominally controlled by the once grand Company. The trafficking in slaves could still jingle guilders before the eyes of Dutch shareholders, but the fall of Holland's only colony on the mainland of South America curtailed the empire's large domestic need for slaves. It was during this time that the directors of the Amsterdam chamber considered the possibility of a slave market in New Netherland, which could serve as a supply depot for the tobacco plantations of Maryland and Virginia. As in past crises the declining fortunes of the Company in the late 1650s called for a reassessment of Company policy throughout the chartered territory.[43]

The English, too, were weighing heavily on the directors' minds in the 1650s. The first Anglo-Dutch war had dragged on from the summer of 1652 to the spring of 1654, only to end with a peace

---

43. Van Dillen, *Van Rijkdom en Regenten*, p. 168. For the best treatment of Dutch colonizing efforts in South America in these years, see Charles R. Boxer, *The Dutch in Brazil, 1624–1654* (Oxford, 1957).

treaty that avoided the main bone of contention between the two Protestant seapowers—the English Navigation Acts. Without a resolution of this issue, which was viewed by the entire Dutch merchant community as a dagger pointed straight at the heart of its prosperity, peace was impossible. The slow-to-arouse Dutch national pride had been awakened by Oliver Cromwell's blatant attempt to exclude Europe's largest merchant marine from the ports of the English empire. For many Dutchmen and Englishmen the first war came to be viewed as the opening skirmish in a struggle to determine who would rule the sealanes of world's commerce. When Charles II confirmed his royal intent to exclude Dutch vessels from the English empire with the passage of the Navigation Act of 1660, the Company and the nation began preparations for war.[44] In this decade of crisis the West India Company once more reviewed the record of New Netherland.

The threat of war with Great Britain made the colony's stock rise dramatically in the minds of Holland's statesmen and merchants. As a Dutch colony wedged between New England and Virginia, New Netherland could serve as the terminus of a commodity trade with the Indians for furs, the Virginians for tobacco, and the New Englanders for fish and barrel staves (the latter two commodities destined for the burgeoning rum, sugar, and slave trades). A permanent settlement of Dutch citizens in the colony would secure it against possible attacks from New England while the Company exploited the possibilities of circumventing the Navigation Acts with an American coastal trade.[45]

---

44. Several sources confirmed the West India Company's war preparations in the early 1660s. First, the number of soldiers was increased annually after 1659 in New Netherland. Second, instructions issued by the Admiralty College in this period cautioned skippers to avoid all contact with English vessels on the high seas until the peaceful intentions of the latter were known. And finally, a remonstrance preserved in the Royal Library at The Hague contains orders from the directors of the Company to Pieter Stuyvesant at New Amsterdam instructing him to repair the fort and set about plans for defending the colony against English attack (Gemeentelijke Archief van Amsterdam, Notarial nos. 3098, March 5, 1660, p. 55; 1450, April 14, 1660, unpaginated; 1454, May 31, 1664, unpaginated; Archief de Admiraleteijtencollege, Verzameling Van der Heim, No. 413; and *Remonstratie van de Bewinthebbers der Nederlandsche West Indische Compagnie*, No. 8755 in the Koninklijke Bibliotheek, Den Haag.

45. This was, in any case, the argument used by the New Netherland Commissioners of the Amsterdam chamber. See also Johan E. Elias, "De Tweede Engelsche

The surprising surge in immigration after 1657, therefore, may have reflected an all-out campaign by the West India Company and the Dutch government to provide New Netherland with the people it had long needed. Some hard-hitting propaganda, perhaps written at the Company's request, was effective in turning around the once poor image of New Netherland. One anonymous pamphlet of eighty-four pages titled "Short Account of New Netherland's Potential Virtues" created an idyllic Eden in the American forest, where democracy would rule supreme and every decision reached by "free living Christians" would be accepted by all. So suited was this paradise to "Dutch industry and thrift" that only riches and happiness awaited those willing to emigrate.[46] Hyperbole knew few limits in descriptions of New Netherland in the early 1660s. The resident poet at New Amsterdam added his lies to those of his countrymen when he ended a bit of doggerel with the assertion that "New Netherland has become the epitome and most noble of all climes, a maritime empire where milk and honey flowed."[47]

This combination of incentives and motivations must have had some effect, for the colony boomed in the late 1650s and early 1660s. In addition to the increase in immigrants, the volume of trade goods swelled to over 3,300 tons per annum after 1660, and plans were afoot to increase this trade when the English conquered New Netherland in 1664.

New Netherland was far from being a failed colony at the time of the English conquest. Indeed, the colony's hard luck may have just turned around at the time English warships were spotted on Long Island Sound. The abandonment of the Company monopoly at the end of the 1630s opened the door for the private merchants of Amsterdam to invest in New Netherland. Their story and their trade are as central to New Netherland's history as are the lives of the colonists.

Oorlog als het Keerpunt in onze Betrekkingen met Engeland," *Verhandelingen der Koninklijke Akademie van Wetenschappen te Amsterdam, Afdeeling Letterkunde*, n.s., 29 (1930): 26ff.

46. *Kort Verhael van Nieuw-Nederlants Gelegenheit, Deughden, Natuurlijke Voor-rechten, en bij ondere bequaemheidt* (Amsterdam, 1662), p. 61.

47. "*Nieuw Nederland is 't puijck, en 't eedelste van de Landen, een Seegenrijck, daer Melck en Honigh vloeijd,*" quoted in Albert Eekhof, *De Hervormde Kerk in Noord-Amerika, 1624–1664,* 2 vols. (The Hague, 1913), 2:68.

[7]

New Netherland and
the Amsterdam Merchants

Amsterdam chose free trade, not for theoretical reasons—for
no such theory existed at the time—but simply because its
most immediate interests were best served by continuing along
the accustomed paths. . . . The Republic may thus be said to
have by-passed mercantilism.

—Johan Huizinga, 1941

By 1640 the West India Company was faced with increasing
pressure from the merchants of Amsterdam, the shareholders in the
chambers, and the government to abandon its trade monopoly
throughout the chartered territory. With approval of the revised
Articles and Conditions by the States General in January 1639 the
last vestige of Company monopoly disappeared.[1] Amsterdam merchants benefited most from this change in policy, for they had been
largely responsible for the development of a regular shipping and
distribution system for New Netherland furs, tobacco, and timber.
They held a decided advantage as the age of free trade dawned in
the colony. Although the mighty West India Company could still
proclaim itself the largest joint-stock company operating in the
Western Hemisphere, it could no longer outfit fleets, pay its employees, or supply its colonists. The private merchants of Amsterdam were eager to take over the transatlantic trade once the cumbersome regulations governing the Company's monopoly had been
removed.

These merchants appear to have been successful in exploiting
their advantages. Figure 7.1 shows the number of sailings to New

1. See Chapter 5 above.

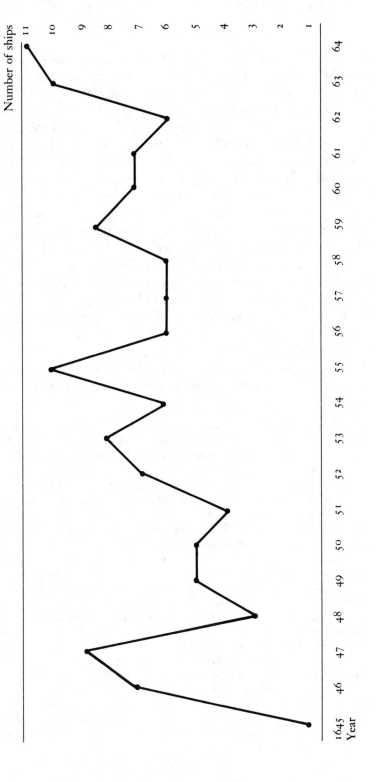

Figure 7.1. Annual sailings to New Netherland, 1645–1664

Netherland from the port of Amsterdam for the years 1645–64. If periodic disruptions of the trade caused by war between the United Provinces and Great Britain are accounted for, the trade between the fatherland and New Netherland appears to have grown steadily after 1645[2] and to have been increasing in volume in the last years before the English conquest.[3] This increase may have reflected improved market conditions for New Netherland products in Europe and a dramatic upsurge in the colony's population, largely through immigration. The latter phenomenon, which was examined in the previous chapter, is documented by the shipping records preserved in the notarial archives of the city of Amsterdam. The growth in trade volume appears to have paralleled that of immigration. Many of the ships docking at New Amsterdam in these years were filled with men, women, and children. Below decks they usually carried a bounty of liquor, guns, and cloth goods for the fur trade. A good deal can be learned from a closer examination of this movement of trade goods and people.

In Figure 7.2 the sailings are arranged to show the percentage of the total shipping controlled by the four most active Amsterdam merchants.[4] Through a variety of financial instruments, including

2. Data for this table have come from a tabulation of charter contracts, bottomry bonds, and marine insurance policies in the Gemeentelijke Archief van Amsterdam. The collection of notarial documents is the work of the late Simon Hart, director of the archives, who introduced me to this collection and supervised my use of the documents during my year stay in the Netherlands in 1973–74.

3. The unusually high number of sailings in 1655 probably reflected the movement of Company soldiers and equipment aboard privately owned vessels, whereas the large drop in annual sailings between 1647 and 1650 may have echoed higher marine insurance rates in anticipation of war with England. The amazing statistic, however, is that after 1645 no year witnessed fewer than four sailings from Amsterdam to New Netherland. If the average tonnage is computed to be 250 tons for a transatlantic freighter in the seventeenth century, the evidence for New Netherland indicates a minimum of 1,000 tons per year for the 1645–64 period. We must keep in mind, moreover, that many of these ships carried colonists on the outward voyage. For a discussion of cost factors, insurance rates, and average tonnages for Dutch shipping in this period, see Simon Hart, "The Dutch and North America in the First Half of the Seventeenth Century: Some Aspects," *Mededelingen van de Nederlandse vereniging voor zeegeschiedenis* 20 (March 1970): 5–17.

4. Various sources have served for this chart, the most important of which were the charter contracts in the Gemeentelijke Archief van Amsterdam. Much useful information also turned up in genealogical sources used for the construction of the histories of the four New Netherland–Amsterdam merchant families.

ship charters, bottomry bonds, and rental agreements for ship space, these merchants came to control many of the voyages in which they invested. The relationship between Amsterdam merchants and the colony of New Netherland has no parallel in American colonial history. This relationship, formed out of economic motives but having the qualities of an apparent collusion of self-interest, has much to tell us of the history of New Netherland. Some conclusions and speculations may be drawn from an analysis of the information provided in Figures 7.1 and 7.2.

One obvious conclusion is that during the last fifteen years of New Netherland's existence four trading firms, operating mostly out of Amsterdam, came to play an important role in the commerce between the colony and the fatherland. These firms clearly did not enjoy a monopoly or even oligopoly for every time the total number of ships increased, the percentage they controlled declined. In lean years, conversely, when war preparations drove up insurance premiums and the risks of financial ruin were on the rise, the four merchants dominated the trade, controlling 50 percent or more in twelve of the fifteen years charted. Apparently, these four Amsterdam merchant firms were the steady and reliable New Netherland trade specialists. They were not chased out when conditions deteriorated, nor did they surrender to the temptation to overexpand in boom times. Between 1640 and 1664 the merchants participating in the chartering, outfitting, and freighting of trade ships acquired the experience necessary to make the trade pay. Other merchants were less directly involved in the trade but were active in developing warehouses and hiring factors, and by 1664 many of them had become partners in the four firms operating out of Amsterdam. As partners in each other's businesses and as private entrepreneurs, the merchants of Amsterdam successfully enveloped the New Netherland trade within a web of personal obligations, ad hoc partnerships, and long-term cartel agreements.

In theory all merchants with licenses from the West India Company were free to trade with New Netherland under the regulations of 1639. In practice, however, only experienced firms could afford to cut profit margins by underselling rivals, monopolizing shipping, and buying out would-be competitors. The risks of transatlantic trade, moreover, encouraged adequately capitalized, long-term trade relationships to withstand the periodic losses resulting from shipwrecks and other disasters. The four merchant firms that came

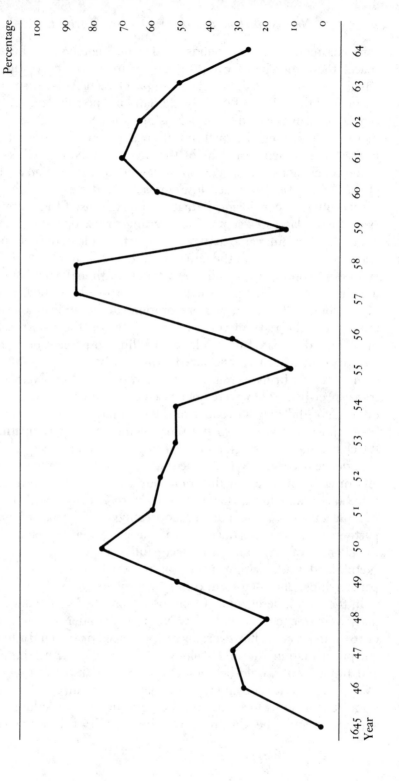

Figure 7.2. Annual percentages of shipping to New Netherland controlled by four most active trade firms

to play such an important role in New Netherland's commercial life were Gillis and Seth Verbrugge, Dirck and Abel de Wolff, Kiliaen and Jan Baptiste van Rensselaer, and Gillis van Hoornbeeck and Associates.

The Verbrugge Company, founded as a father-son partnership in the early 1640s to exploit the New Netherland and Virginia trade, was one of the first to prosper in the period of free trade following the abandonment of the West India Company monopoly. In the twenty-three years between the founding of the Verbrugge partnership in 1641 and the fall of New Netherland in 1664, Gillis and his son Seth chartered, owned, or invested heavily in some twenty-seven voyages to New Netherland and about fourteen voyages to English Virginia.[5] By the mid-1650s the Verbrugges were also sponsoring American voyages with the other important Amsterdam merchants.[6] Since none of Gillis Verbrugge's personal records have survived, what little is known of the family comes from Seth Verbrugge's wills preserved in the notarial archives of the city of Amsterdam.[7]

Seth Verbrugge had married Catharina Vermander as a young man. Living in Amsterdam, the couple soon entered into the world of the *particuliere kooplieden*, or private merchant-traders, for it appears that Seth participated in his father's enterprises from an early age. He may even have served the normal seven-year merchant apprenticeship so common at the time. Over the years, Seth drew up three wills before Amsterdam notaries. These wills and the various codicils chronicled his personal fortunes and those of his family. The first will, filed in 1650, left his sizable estate to his

5. These figures were compiled from the notarial archives of the Gemeentelijke Archief van Amsterdam, specifically from the charter contracts and bottomry bonds notarized before Amsterdam notaries. The twenty-seven Virginia voyages were documented by some thirty-nine separate entries in the protocol books of Amsterdam notaries.

6. Gemeentelijke Archief van Amsterdam, Notarial nos. 1352, October 19, 1654, p. 82; 2139, October 28, 1654, p. 87; 2197, December 18, 1654, pp. 181–83.

7. Even the place and date of birth for Gillis Verbrugge are difficult to pin down. He was not an Amsterdamer by birth, for the city's vital statistics list only Gillis's children being born in the city. A notarial document from 1656 lists his age as sixty-five, which would place his date of birth in 1591. The same document mentions Seth as being forty (b. 1616) (Gemeentelijke Archief van Amsterdam, Notarial no. 1579, November 7, 1656, p. 428).

wife, Catharina, and their four children, three sons and a daughter: Johannes, Gillis, Seth, and Anneken. Catharina was bequeathed the family townhouse in Amsterdam and all of its furnishings. In addition, Seth's profits from several voyages to New Netherland and English Virginia were included as assets in the estate. In 1654 Seth Verbrugge drew up another will. His life had undergone some wrenching changes. Catharina had died in 1653, and the thirty-eight-year-old widower had remarried within the year. His new wife was the wealthy widow Maria Wyckenburch, a native of Amsterdam and the daughter of one of the most successful merchant wholesalers in the city. Maria had two children by her previous marriage, and she brought not only wealth but political connections with her when she wed Seth Verbrugge. Seth was now connected by marriage to Maria's uncle, Edward Dill, the auctioneer for the Amsterdam Board of Admiralty. Seth may have exploited this family tie by soliciting information about confiscated vessels; several Verbrugge ships may have been purchased at auction from the Amsterdam Admiralty. The last will, drawn up in 1657, listed several other enterprises, including a number of partnerships with the de Wolff and van Hoornbeeck firms for the exploitation of New Netherland.[8]

Although little is known of the private lives of Gillis and Seth Verbrugge, much material is available about their business activities. Until the mid-1650s Gillis and Seth participated in the New Netherland and Virginia trades by chartering ships for single annual voyages. In these first years, the Verbrugges sought to keep their business dealings with North America on a cash-and-carry basis, and the notarial records suggest that they were successful in doing so. Bottomry bonds were paid on time and insurance premiums were kept up. These first contacts with New Netherland were made through trade partnerships with other Amsterdam merchants, some of whom provided short-term capital loans in return for a percentage of the return cargo.

The 1650s brought changes to the trade. The passage of the English Navigation Act in 1651 and the subsequent war with England drove up the costs of the North Atlantic trade, although

8. Gemeentelijke Archief van Amsterdam, Notarial nos. 1388, February 20, 1650, p. 10; 1393, April 18, 1654, p. 48v; 1355, June 5, 1657, p. 83v.

prices for New Netherland furs also rose when the risk of maritime trade decreased the supply. The Verbrugges were forced to seek partnerships of longer duration and to reassess the risks of the direct Amsterdam-Virginia trade.

The success of operations in New Netherland and the increasing difficulties created by the English Navigation Acts forced the Verbrugges to abandon the direct Amsterdam-Virginia trade in 1656. Relying instead on English merchants, many of them possessing dual citizenship as Virginians and New Netherlanders, the Verbrugges were able to maintain a coastal trade with Virginia which employed a small fleet of coastal sloops built especially to bring "Virginia leaves" to New Amsterdam.[9] In the late 1650s, the Verbrugges diversified their operations. At New Amsterdam they prepared to engage in the manufacture of potash on Manhattan Island.

Potash was the principal ingredient (besides fatty organic residues) in the making of soap. Under Gillis Verbrugge's plan, New Netherland's potash was to be shipped to Holland, where the tree-poor Dutch were willing to pay high prices for the scarce product. The potash project failed to turn a profit in its two years of operation, however, perhaps because it was too forward-thinking. The manufacture of potash was labor-intensive. Three to five acres of timber were required to produce one ton extract of potash and then only after the arduous process of leaching with water. In the eighteenth century potash and its refined derivative, pearl ash, would become two of the most important exports to Europe from the northern colonies.[10] By that time the colonial consumption of potash for the manufacture of soap and glass had created a market there for the raw material and the labor force to produce it. With the possible exception of raw timber, no other colonial product could so easily be assimilated into the colonial market. The Verbrugges' plan to manufacture potash in New Netherland was sound in its conception but faulty in its timing. Unfortunately for the Verbrugges, the failure of the potash enterprise was only one symptom of the family's declining fortunes.

Having concentrated the bulk of their capital on the New

---

9. Gemeentelijke Archief van Amsterdam, Notarial no. 1305, April 27, 1655, p. 65.

10. Edwin J. Perkins, *The Economy of Colonial America* (New York, 1980), p. 21.

Netherland trade, the Verbrugges suffered more than most when the Anglo-Dutch war threatened the sealanes between the fatherland and the colony. The cost of marine insurance made some merchants chance the crossing without it and others abandon the trade.[11] The notarial records suggest that the number of merchants participating in the New Netherland trade declined steadily after 1651. Charter contracts for ships and bottomry loan applications bear fewer and fewer signatures after 1651, which indicates that the increased risks may have driven out the smaller merchants or forced them into silent partnership arrangements with the four largest Amsterdam firms. The Verbrugges were especially vulnerable because their enterprises were concentrated in New Netherland and tied up in land, ships (sitting idle), and warehouse space. In 1662, when rumors of another war with England were rife, the Verbrugges were forced to sell most of their New Netherland assets to meet their creditors' demands for cash. Interestingly, but not coincidentally, the syndicate of merchants, authorized by notarized power-of-attorney to supervise the sale of the Verbrugge properties in New Netherland, included two other important New Netherland traders, Abel de Wolff and Jan Baptiste van Rensselaer, son of the patroon.[12]

Abel de Wolff had entered the New Netherland trade when his father, Dirck de Wolff, invested in a number of New Netherland voyages in the 1650s, and by the decade of the 1660s the de Wolff family enterprise was one of the four most active companies dealing with the colony.[13] Dirck de Wolff, the founder of the family business, rose from a Haarlem baker to the board of directors of the Brokers Guild in Amsterdam. His upward mobility marked him as a man of ambition, a risk taker. His first business venture involved

11. Premiums were rarely less than 10 percent after 1651, and 12 percent and more was not uncommon (Gemeentelijke Archief van Amsterdam, Notarial no. 1035, October 1648 with notarized addendum in 1664, pp. 491–493v).

12. Gemeentelijke Archief van Amsterdam, Notarial no. 1143, November 9, 1662, p. 150.

13. The following summary of de Wolff activities is drawn partly from C. H. Jansen, "Geschiedenis van de familie de Wolff: Sociale en economische facetten van de Republiek der Verenigde Nederlanden in de zeventiende eeuw," *Jaarboek van het Genootschap Amstelodamum* 56 (1964): 131–55, and from my own research in the Gemeentelijke Archive van Amsterdam.

him in a scheme to break the monopoly of the Grain Haulers Guild (*korenlichtersgild*) in the lucrative grain trade between Friesland and Amsterdam. He mortgaged everything he had to secure a loan for the building of a specially designed grain hauler, which could carry the same cargo as the standard hauler but with one-third the crew. His scheme must have been at least partially successful because within a year he was admitted into the Grain Haulers Guild. As a member of the guild, Dirck de Wolff prospered. By 1650 he owned a small fleet of grain haulers and was twice elected to the board of directors of the powerful Brokers Guild (*makerlaarsgild*). In 1659 he was made supervisor (*overman*) of grain prices.

Dirck de Wolff displayed his prosperity by building a spacious townhouse on the exclusive Heerengracht (literally, gentlemen's canal) and purchasing sixty acres of land in the countryside be-tween Haarlem and Amsterdam. For his five children by Grietje Engberts he provided the best education available. His two sons, Abel (born 1636) and Hendrick (born 1646), received generous support from their father. Abel, as heir to the family business, was to be trained as a merchant. Hendrick, the scholar of the family, received money from his father to support theological studies at the University of Utrecht, where he eventually took his degree.[14] The daughters, Geertruyd (born 1637), Trijntje (born 1639), and Judith (born 1643), received the usual high standard of education for Dutch girls, each completing primary school and some secondary school. Geertruyd was especially keen to participate in the family business, and Dirck employed her on a regular basis.

His duties as supervisor of prices included overseeing the setting of the daily exchange rates for wheat and rye and auditing the coming and going of grain ships, placing him in a position to ob-serve the fluctuations of prices for colonial commodities such as furs, timber, and tobacco. Other matters concerned him after 1650 as well, not the least of which was the need to find suitable em-ployment for his son Abel and his son-in-law, Gerrit Jansz Cuyper. Indeed, it was Geertruyd Verbrugge's marriage to Gerrit Jansz

---

14. When Hendrick died in 1700, he possessed a private library of more than one hundred volumes, mostly on subjects in theology (Gemeentelijke Archief van Amsterdam, Notarial no. 5460, undated, p. 308).

Cuyper that marked the beginning of the de Wolff involvement in New Netherland.

Gerrit Jansz Cuyper had engaged in the New Netherland trade for some years as both an agent for Amsterdam merchants and a private trader. He had worked for the Verbrugges in the late 1640s as an Indian trader and for Jan Hendricksz Sijbingh, a large textile wholesaler who supplied cloth for the fur trade, as an agent. Sijbingh was a longtime business associate of Dirck de Wolff and may have introduced Cuyper to the family.[15]

The opportunity to participate in the New Netherland trade came when Dirck, in partnership with his eldest son, Abel, and Cuyper, organized a company to trade with the colony. Dirck provided the capital and perhaps important connections in the Amsterdam merchant community, while Abel handled the management of the company in Amsterdam and Cuyper directed the operation in New Netherland. Dirck's new business interest meant the loss of his favorite daughter, Geertruyd, who sailed to the colony with her husband. The company developed a distribution system for furs, timber, and tobacco. Colonial products were assembled by Cuyper in New Netherland each year and sold for profit in Amsterdam by Abel de Wolff. By all accounts the small company was consistently profitable.

In contrast to the Verbrugges' effort in New Netherland, the de Wolff investments tended to concentrate on single projects rather than on numerous trading voyages. The chartering of ships and the outfitting of trade expeditions, for example, occupied a smaller percentage of the family's capital. Whereas the Verbrugge family had invested an average of 80 percent of their resources in ships, cargoes, and warehouses, the de Wolff investments in such enterprises never exceeded 60 percent. The family's total capital investment in New Netherland remained much more liquid, going primarily for the salaries of agents in the colony and the rental of cargo space aboard ships belonging to others.[16] Moreover, the de Wolff

15. On the account books of the textile merchant the de Wolff family stood second only to the Verbrugges as customers (Gemeentelijke Archief van Amsterdam, Notarial no. 1306, September 1, 1656, p. 162v).

16. The information on percentages of Verbrugge capital invested in the New Netherland trade comes from documents drawn up in 1667 by arbitrators for the bankrupt estate of Gillis and Seth Verbrugge. The most important document

business interests were generally more diversified than the Verbrugges'. With money invested in Baltic grain, French wine, and West African slaves, the family was protected against the financial trouble that had cost the Verbrugges their once dominant position in the New Netherland trade. This strategy paid dividends.

The de Wolffs chose to exploit New Netherland by developing the colonial market for provisions. The carrying trade continued to be the most lucrative of the family's long-term investments, but the essential thrust of the de Wolff business was the establishment of a commercial presence in New Netherland that could serve as a distribution system for manufactured goods and a conduit for furs, timber, and tobacco. One of the most interesting episodes in the history of the de Wolff operations in New Netherland was the attempt to build a large salt refinery in the colony. The venture is also illustrative of the antagonism between company officials, charged with soothing a colonial population that was becoming increasingly English, and the private merchants of Amsterdam, whose sole concern was profits.

In 1661 Dirck de Wolff, in partnership with his son and son-in-law, petitioned the directors of the New Netherland Commission within the Amsterdam chamber for permission to build a salt refinery in New Netherland. The directors approved the request after a brief discussion and ordered notaries to draw up a charter of privileges and exemptions for the de Wolff company. The charter demonstrated how far the directors of the West India Company were willing to go to attract investment in New Netherland. It granted to the de Wolff company the exclusive monopoly of salt refining in the colony for a period of ten years, during which the West India Company agreed to tax all imported salt at a rate that would make the de Wolff salt competitive in the colonial market. The salt pro-

---

arising from the arbitration is an inventory of Verbrugge assets (Gemeentelijke Archief van Amsterdam, Notarial no. 2223, February 10, 1667, pp. 258–59). The data for the de Wolff investment percentages are drawn from eleven wills and codicils prepared by Dirck de Wolff in the eight years preceding his death in 1679. These wills and codicils are in Gemeentelijke Archief van Amsterdam, Notarial nos. 2367, May 28, 1671, p. 267; 2370, December 22, 1673, p. 40; 2371, October 31, 1674, p. 60; 2371, October 31, 1674, p. 62 addendum; 2371, November 24, 1674, p. 80; 2371, July 20, 1675, p. 224; 2372, June 17, 1676, p. 214; 2372, June 17, 1676, p. 223 codicil; 2372, February 17, 1677, p. 404; 2374, June 6, 1678, p. 479v.

duced in New Netherland could not be exported to the fatherland, but no restrictions were placed on its shipment to New England, where the fishing industry promised to be its chief customer. Since the Dutch had a long-established and complicated structure for the taxing of salt, the directors of the commission decided to subsidize the de Wolff scheme during the ten-year charter period by taxing all salt produced in New Netherland at the much lower rate for "natural" salt. The location of the refinery was to be selected by de Wolff in consultation with Director-General Stuyvesant. This provision caused Dirck de Wolff some anxiety, and he protested that he and his partners should be given a free hand in selecting the site. The directors of the commission agreed and granted Dirck de Wolff the privilege of choosing his own site for a refinery, provided that the location was unoccupied and unencumbered by other deeds or grants.[17]

De Wolff hired Arent Theunisz, a blacksmith from Amsterdam, to go to New Netherland with his wife and family and serve as his agent for the selection of a site. Dirck de Wolff held promissory notes from Theunisz dating back to 1659, and he may have used the blacksmith's debts as leverage in persuading him to emigrate. In any case, Theunisz carried instructions ordering him to build the salt refinery on a suitable site near the sea. The blacksmith and his family were given the use of a house to be constructed at company expense. After the selection of the site and the completion of the house, Theunisz was to "cook salt day and night" in exchange for his expenses, drink, housing, and 15 fl. per month salary. If the salt refinery succeeded in producing profits, Theunisz was to receive a 5 fl. per month raise and one-quarter of the gross production of salt to sell for his own profit. The actual salt refining was to be the responsibility of Evert Pietersz, an Amsterdam merchant who had some experience in the "art of salt production." Pietersz was a junior partner with the de Wolffs and received for his work one-quarter of the gross production in addition to his dividends from the company. Problems arose immediately when Theunisz chose a site on Coney Island near the English settlement of Gravesande.

Shortly after the charter was amended, de Wolff had contracted

---

17. John Romeyn Brodhead, comp., Edmund B. O'Callaghan and Berthold Fernow, eds. and trans., *Documents Relative to the Colonial History of the State of New York*, 15 vols. (Albany, 1856–87), 13:99, hereafter cited as *DCHNY*.

with a certain Gijsbert op Dijck to purchase from him land on Coney Island selected by Theunisz as the location for the refinery. The land lay adjacent to the village of Gravesande on acreage used by the villagers as a common meadow for cattle and sheep. Gijsbert op Dijck claimed title to the acreage on the basis of a land patent issued by former Governor-General Willem Kieft. Ignoring the angry protest of the English villagers, Theunisz and Pietersz set about felling timber for firewood and building the house. When the people of Gravesande turned out with arms to prevent the destruction of their meadow, Stuyvesant and the West India Company found themselves in a delicate situation.

In a hearing before the governor's council at New Amsterdam, the villagers challenged the patent held by Gijsbert op Dijck on grounds that the patent Kieft had granted to op Dijck had been superseded by a patent they had received some years later from the West India Company to set up the town. Furthermore, since the land had been used for nearly six years as a common meadow, the right of effective occupation, cited in various Company documents as the sole basis for ownership of colonial land, nullified any new grants. Pieter Stuyvesant, not wishing to antagonize his English subjects, ordered an investigation of the title papers as a preliminary step in the arbitration process. The investigation revealed that the patent held by Gijsbert op Dijck was indeed fraudulent because Governor-General Kieft had never filed it with the Company in Amsterdam. Still the villagers of Gravesande could not prove to Stuyvesant's satisfaction that their West India Company patent included the disputed meadow. Hence, he authorized Theunisz and Pietersz to set up the salt refinery as planned. The people of Gravesande vowed to stop them.

The refinery was sabotaged constantly, and on one occasion the villagers threatened to throw Theunisz and Pietersz into their own salt fire. Stuyvesant received repeated complaints from both sides and angry letters from de Wolff demanding that he take some action. Finally, Dirck de Wolff took his case directly to the Amsterdam chamber of the West India Company, where he pleaded for help in protecting his property from the English. The directors of the chamber were sympathetic with de Wolff's plight and ordered Stuyvesant to station Company soldiers at the refinery to prevent further acts of sabotage and violence.

Director-General Stuyvesant, faced with countless other problems in New Netherland, not the least of which was the threat of English conquest, received the orders with astonishment. He was understandably reticent about antagonizing the English villagers at Gravesande. Furthermore, the complement of soldiers at New Amsterdam was too small to permit the stationing of troops at Gravesande to guard a half-completed salt refinery. Consequently, Stuyvesant hesitated. The report was never submitted, and in time the opposition of the English settlers proved too much for the de Wolff company. Continued difficulties with the residents of Gravesande forced de Wolff to abandon the salt refinery after two years. By 1664, Dirck de Wolff had lost faith in the New Netherland trade and turned over the family's holdings in the colony to his son.

Abel de Wolff was twenty-eight years old when he took over the management of his father's business in New Netherland. He had earned his job through years of work in Amsterdam as the broker for the family company, and he had bought a share in the business with money he earned in the New Netherland trade. His personal investment included 2,000 fl. from his own pocket and 4,000 fl. of his inheritance, pledged by his father as a wedding portion.[18]

Abel had already demonstrated an enterprising spirit in investment schemes with Gillis van Hoornbeeck and Jan Baptiste van Rensselaer. Just four years earlier, acting on his own and investing his own money, Abel de Wolff had shipped a cargo of trade goods to New Netherland aboard a large ship chartered by Gillis van Hoornbeeck. That voyage had turned out to be a financial success, contributing to Abel's private fortune and convincing the young merchant that his future lay in the development of New Netherland. In 1661 and again in 1662 Abel de Wolff joined Jan Baptiste van Rensselaer as an equal partner in the outfitting of the *Hoop* for two trading voyages to New Netherland. These voyages also turned a profit. At the close of 1662 the partnership's warehouse in Amsterdam was filled with tobacco and furs. The next year Abel de Wolff was back in partnership with his brother-in-law, Gerrit Jansz Cuyper, and Jan Baptiste van Rensselaer. This partnership, one of the last formed during the period of Dutch rule, completed one trading voyage in 1664. The voyage of the *Eendracht*,

18. Jansen, "Geschiedenis van de familie de Wolff," p. 136.

although extended by the circumnavigation of Scotland to avoid English warships, returned a profit for its investors.[19]

When Abel de Wolff took over the family business in New Netherland in 1664, more than 7,000 fl. worth of goods awaited shipment to Holland at Manhattan. In addition, the family owned a house and a few parcels of land on Manhattan Island. Under the terms of the bond signed by Abel de Wolff on the occasion of assuming direction of the trade, he was given perpetual use of the house on Manhattan and the lands surrounding it for an annual rent of 120 fl. Dirck de Wolff retained the title to the property.[20]

One of Abel's first acts was aimed at reassuring the company's employees in New Netherland that the change in management did not mean a loss of their jobs. Gerrit Baancken, Dirck de Wolff's longtime factor in New Netherland, acquired a share in the company's profits as a reward for nearly fifteen years of service. In addition to his annual salary of 500 fl., Baancken received the profits on an investment credit of 4,300 fl. personally approved by Abel de Wolff. Baancken also received a farm and house for his family on one of the parcels held by the company on Manhattan Island. Other employees received annual raises in return for notarized pledges to trade exclusively with the de Wolff company. Everything seemed in place for a major expansion of the family's enterprise in New Netherland when news of the colony's surrender reached Amsterdam.

One can only imagine the effect this news must have had on the family. Abel's dreams were shattered. Dirck's hopes for his family's fortune and his son's career were threatened. Just a year before, Dirck had invested his daughters' 8,000 fl. dowries in the New Netherland trade, perhaps as a gesture of family confidence in his son, perhaps out of enthusiasm for the trade that had lately proven lucrative.[21] In any event, Abel's two unmarried sisters, Judith and

19. Gemeentelijke Archief van Amsterdam, Notarial nos. 2224, December 1663, p. 32; 2444, February 29, 1664, pp. 134–134v; 1518, March 15, 1664, p. 115; 2768, March 26, 1664, p. 608; 3138, April 3, 1664, pp. 31, 33v–34v; 2769, April 8, 1664, pp. 54–55; 2885, April 8, 1664, p. 155; 2769, April 16, 1664, pp. 81–82; 2218, January 5, 1665, pp. 49–50; 2218, March 7, 1665, pp. 497–498v; 2223, April 27, 1667, p. 913; 2224, May 5, 1667, pp. 32–33.

20. Jansen, "Geschiedenis van de familie de Wolff," pp. 136–37.

21. Ibid., p. 136.

Trijntje, had reason to be anxious as the family awaited news from America.

The fall of New Netherland was a catastrophe for the Amsterdam merchants. It not only spelled the end of a half-century effort to make New Netherland a success, but by means of the English Navigation Acts it separated the Dutch merchant suppliers from their clients, employees, and customers. From New England to the southern boundaries of Virginia the North American seaboard was English. The Amsterdam merchants, Abel de Wolff and his anxious family among them, could only wait to see what they could salvage from the situation.

English authorities attempted to curtail Dutch trade immediately, and in their zeal to anglicize the colony's trade everyone suffered. Without the continued shipping of the private merchants of Amsterdam the commercial position of New Netherland, now New York, declined rapidly. Both the Dutch and English colonists bore the brunt of the economic collapse. In 1667, the new English governor, Colonel Francis Lovelace, ordered special passports to be drawn up, permitting Dutch merchants to send three ships a year to New York.[22] The merchants were required to pay high fees to the Duke of York's agents for these passports, and, to make matters worse, the West India Company continued to collect its licensing fees even though it had lost the colony three years before. The result was that the increased costs of the trade fell heavily on the Amsterdam merchants. Even though the de Wolffs took advantage of the passport scheme, they lost money in the New York trade. The other Amsterdam merchants lost too. The voyage of the *Oranje Boom* may serve to explain how the once profitable private trade with New Netherland had become a money-losing enterprise.

The voyage of the *Oranje Boom* was one of the last attempts by the Amsterdam merchants to maintain the trade with their former colony. All four of the Amsterdam merchant companies had a part in the enterprise. The Verbrugge Company, in receivership but participating under the management of Gerrit Zuyck as executor, was a major partner in the venture as were the van Rensselaer, van Hoornbeeck, and de Wolff companies. Abel de Wolff and his

22. Gemeentelijke Archief van Amsterdam, Notarial no. 2225, November 16, 1667, pp. 945–952v.

brother-in-law, Gerrit Jansz Cuyper, directed the outfitting of the ship and supervised the enterprise. They appear to have been the organizers of the voyage.

The *Oranje Boom* was a Dutch ship chartered and outfitted under the special passport issued by Governor Lovelace. The provisions of the passport specified that the vessel could not be manned by a Dutch crew or captained by a Dutch skipper. The trade privileges granted to the Amsterdam merchants were also limited. After loading in Amsterdam, the ship was required to sail first to England for inspection and inventory. There a commodity fee was assessed as a percentage of the total value of trade goods aboard the ship. From England the *Oranje Boom* was to sail to New York, dispose of its cargo, and return to England. This second stop in England allowed English customs officials and agents of the Duke of York to inspect the return cargo and assess fees once again. Only then was the ship permitted to return to its home port of Amsterdam.

Abel de Wolff and his partners financed the voyage of the *Oranje Boom* in the hope of returning a small profit after nearly three years of finanical loss. They were to be bitterly disappointed. When the *Oranje Boom* finally docked in Amsterdam, an accounting of the ship's expenses revealed that sale of her cargo could not cover the cost of the expedition. The long voyage, lasting nearly a year, and the increased costs of crew salaries and marine insurance rendered the enterprise a financial disaster. Less than one-third of the costs were recovered in the sale of the ship's cargo. Abel de Wolff was convinced that the trade mission had failed because the English fees levied on the cargo had been unreasonably high. In a legal suit filed before an Amsterdam notary, he testified that the English had extracted over 25,000 fl. worth of cargo as payment for the privilege of trading with New York. This exorbitant fee was more than the trade could bear. It represented ten times the rate of taxation once imposed by the West India Company in the halcyon days of the Company monopoly.[23]

The losses sustained by the Amsterdam merchants in the voyage of the *Oranje Boom* were serious but not nearly as ominous as the merchants' loss of confidence in the ability of the trade to turn a profit. In 1668, Abel de Wolff requested a four-year audit of the

23. Ibid.; and Notarial no. 2845, September 11, 1668, pp. 537–38.

accounts in New York from the company's new factor, Harmen
Vedder. The audit told a staggering tale of decline. No profits were
recorded for the four years preceding 1668. An investment of 4,400
fl. by Vedder was not recoverable, and the house and farm on
Manhattan Island had to be sold to pay debts. The company's
entire cash reserve in New York amounted to less than 3,700 fl. An
inventory of furs and tobacco was valued at less than 800 fl. From
an annual profit of 50 percent in the 1650s the New Netherland–
New York trade had become a losing proposition for Amsterdam
merchants.[24] The de Wolff family continued to trade with New
York under a series of agreements which permitted the shipment of
goods via England to America. One such agreement in 1670 involved Abel de Wolff in a syndicate of English, Dutch, and New
York merchants. The complex financial arrangements for the
chartering of the English ship *Duke of York* suggested the extreme
measures taken in these years to circumvent the Navigation Acts.

The *Duke of York* was captained by Johannes Luyck, a Hollander
by birth but a naturalized English subject living in New York. The
ship was registered as English but chartered in Amsterdam. Several
documents were notarized testifying that the trade expedition was
essentially an English undertaking in complete compliance with the
Navigation Acts; yet the sponsors of the voyage and the benefici-
aries of the marine insurance policy were all Dutch. And finally,
Abel de Wolff gave personal testimony before an Amsterdam notary which confirmed that the voyage of the *Duke of York* was "not
subject to confiscation for violations of the English Navigation
Act." Even these complicated arrangements could not make the
voyage profitable. When the *Duke of York* returned to London after
an uneventful voyage, a flurry of legal questions tied up the sale of
her cargo and forced the Dutch merchants to declare the enterprise
a loss. Abel de Wolff could no longer count on profits from the
trade with North America. He had overestimated the profits from
furs and tobacco and in anticipation of a good voyage had borrowed
heavily to pay the English fees. When his portion of the cargo was
finally sold in Amsterdam some months later, the receipts could
not begin to pay back the loans.[25]

24. Jansen, "Geschiedenis van de familie de Wolff," p. 138.
25. Gemeentelijke Archief van Amsterdam, Notarial no. 2223, May 27, 1670,
p. 34.

By 1675 Abel de Wolff was no longer seriously involved in the New York trade, but his reluctant withdrawal did not end the family's connection with the former Dutch colony. Gerrit Jansz Cuyper, husband of Geertruyd de Wolff and Abel's longtime partner, continued to participate in the New York trade until his death in 1679. As a naturalized citizen of the colony of New York, he cosponsored the voyages of the *Rebecca* in 1677 and 1678 under the command of the Englishman Thomas Williams. This partnership with English merchants was soon dissolved when Cuyper could not meet his financial obligations, but he continued to import Dutch cloth goods from Amsterdam with the Dutch textile wholesaler, Jan Hendricksz Sijbingh. Some profits must have been forthcoming in this trade because after Gerrit's death his son, Jan Gerritsz de Wolff Cuyper, took over the cloth trade; as late as 1683 he was still conducting business with former customers of the de Wolff company.[26]

In the meantime, Abel de Wolff had been quietly diversifying the family's holdings and gradually pulling his capital out of New York. In 1675 the de Wolff portfolio included charters for ships engaged in the West African slave, ivory, and gold trades. In 1670, the de Wolff profits from the African trade exceeded 50,000 fl. Whaling also attracted de Wolff capital, and in 1668 a whaling expedition to Greenland had produced the only profits the family earned that year.[27] These profits enabled de Wolff to continue in the New York trade long after it stopped bringing substantial returns. His persistence in the face of continual losses bears witness to his faith in the colony. Only the van Rensselaer family displayed a similar loyalty to New Netherland.

The van Rensselaers of Amsterdam were an old family, wealthy and genteel, steeped in tradition. They had become merchants in the late sixteenth century, and in the seventeenth they were among the most respected merchant families in the city. Their position had not always been so secure, and much of the success and wealth that distinguished them from their less fortunate fellow Amsterdamers had come the hard way. The family name was derived from an ancestral estate in the southern Netherlands dating back to the fourteenth century, when the clan lived and prospered at the Rens-

26. Jansen, "Geschiedenis van de familie de Wolff," p. 146.
27. Ibid.

selersberg. On the estate's extensive acreage the family raised dairy cattle, hogs, and crops for the local market. They supported many tenants as well. Had political events in the region remained stable, the family might have stayed close to the soil.[28]

When the Eighty Years' War began, the van Rensselaers found themselves caught between opposing armies; the Renselersberg stood on the frontier between two cultures, the Catholic-dominated Hapsburg southern Netherlands and the rebel forces of the Protestant north. Hendrik van Rensselaer, father of Kiliaen, served heroically as a captain of foot soldiers and fell in a skirmish. Hendrik's death was the second tragedy to strike the family within a year. Only months before, his brother, Johannes, had died of wounds received at the battle of Deventer. As Holland's golden century dawned the van Rensselaer family was without male leaders. At twenty-two, Kiliaen was ill prepared to assume the role of family head. He was to remember all his life the sacrifice of his father and uncle in the cause of the republic, and in later years he erected a monument to their memory at Deventer. Yet it was Kiliaen who left an indelible imprint on history, not as a soldier but as a merchant and promoter of colonization.

Kiliaen was born at Hasselt in the southern Netherlands about 1580, the only son of Hendrik van Rensselaer and Maria Pasraat. He had one sister, Maria, who married Ryckaert van Twiller, father of Wouter van Twiller, a future governor-general of New Netherland. His mother, Maria Pasraat, was the daughter of one of the owners of a famous printing firm in Deventer. The untimely death of Hendrik van Rensselaer and the uncertain conditions of war forced Maria to make an important decision about her son's future. She decided to send the young man to Amsterdam to learn the jewelry trade from his uncle, Wolfert van Bijler.

In Amsterdam Kiliaen's natural talents for business were soon evident, and van Bijler developed confidence in his nephew. As the firm's agent to the royal courts east of the Rhine, Kiliaen had the opportunity to travel throughout Europe, from Budapest to Paris

28. The van Rensselaer family has been the subject of much research. For the following summary of the family's commercial interest in New Netherland I have relied on Arnold J. F. van Laer, ed. and trans., *The Van Rensselaer–Bowier Manuscripts* (Albany, 1908), and S. G. Nissenson, *The Patroon's Domain* (New York, 1937).

and from Rome to Copenhagen. In Prague, he showed himself an acute observer of political events. In letters to his uncle, young Kiliaen commented on the nature of absolutism in eastern Europe, contrasting it with the freer attitude he found in Amsterdam. After some years as an itinerant jewel merchant, Kiliaen returned to Amsterdam to take over the management of the firm upon his uncle's retirement. He ran the business profitably for five years before selling out to a larger company in 1614.

Kiliaen merged his jewelry business with that of Jan van Wely, one of the wealthiest and most successful of Amsterdam's many jewelers. The new company began with a capitalization of 192,000 fl., one-eighth of which represented Kiliaen van Rensselaer's share. As a junior partner, Kiliaen had little say in the decisions of the company, but his talents soon found expression when Jan van Wely appointed him chief officer of the company with the responsibility of keeping the books. Kiliaen held this job for six years. It was during this period that the future patroon married Hillegond van Bijler, niece of his former patron and his own cousin.

Hillegond's dowry was just over 12,000 fl., and Kiliaen quickly found a use for the money. In 1615, he bought two lots along the recently completed Keizersgracht (emperor's canal) on which he commenced construction of a house for his bride. The new home was a stately townhouse in the most fashionable area of the city. In less than a decade after arriving in Amsterdam, Kiliaen van Rensselaer had risen from a jeweler's apprentice living in cramped quarters on the Oudezijds Voorburgswal, the old side of the city wall, to an independent merchant with a townhouse on the Keizersgracht. For a thirty-five-year-old newcomer to Amsterdam the future appeared bright indeed.

Kiliaen's marriage to Hillegond produced two sons, Hendrik and Johannes. Family life was not without tragedy, however. Young Hendrik died in childhood, and in 1627 Hillegond passed away. During these years Kiliaen's star continued to rise. After the six-year association with Jan van Wely, Kiliaen liquidated his holdings and once again entered the jewelry business as an independent broker for precious stones and metals. In Amsterdam, talk was feverish about the founding of a West India Company. For young and adventurous merchants it appeared to be an opportunity of a lifetime. Thoughts of New World treasures, far-flung colonies, exotic places, and untold profits must have occupied the jewel merchant's quiet moments as he sat in his living room along the Keizersgracht with his young son. When the waiting was finally over, he was one of the first to stake his fortune on the new company.

Kiliaen van Rensselaer's initial investment in the West India Company was at least 6,000 fl. because he was designated a principal shareholder (*hoofdparticipant*) in the Amsterdam chamber. That position gave van Rensselaer many privileges and much authority. One of the most important powers held by the principal shareholders was the right to vote for the chamber's directors. Kiliaen not only voted for the directors but became one himself when a vacancy occurred on the board in 1625. As a director he was eligible to sit on any of the chamber's commissions; he chose the one established to make policy recommendations for New Netherland.

Van Rensselaer's impassioned advocacy of the patroonship plans of 1628 and 1629 earned him many enemies on the commission and within the chamber.[29] Being a patroon put him in a difficult position. Every time he complained of Company intransigence in fulfilling the obligations undertaken in the Freedoms and Exemptions he was accused by his enemies of trying to ruin the Company for his own profit. The most persistent accusation leveled at van Rensselaer was that he planned to destroy the Company fur trade in the upper Hudson River valley by trading privately (and illegally?) in competition with it. In angry letters to his employees in New Netherland he demanded that the trade in furs be stopped. When stung by his adversaries' charges or embarrassed by the damaging testimony of former Company employees, he would dash off threatening letters to his colonists, for example: "It is . . . my express wish and desire that without my further order no one, be he free or servant in my employ, or living in my colony, shall presume to barter any peltries with the savages or seek to obtain them as a present, on forfeiture of their earnings and all their effects."[30] Such letters did little to clear the air, and van Rensselaer's position in the chamber suffered from his advocacy of his rights as a patroon. Still, he was dogged in his determination to make Rensselaerswyck succeed, and driven men seldom enjoy popularity.

Less than a year after the death of Hillegond and in the midst of

29. See Chapter 4 above.
30. Van Laer, *Van Rensselaer–Bowier Manuscripts*, p. 209.

the controversy over the drafting of the Freedoms and Exemptions, Kiliaen van Rensselaer married Anna van Wely, daughter of his former partner. Anna was rich and wise in financial affairs. Before stepping to the altar, she had a prenuptial agreement prepared before an Amsterdam notary. The agreement specified that her personal fortune could be used by her husband during his lifetime, but for all legal purposes chattel and real personal property would remain forever in her name. It was a fortunate match for van Rensselaer. Anna's wealth was now added to his own considerable fortune just at the time when his plans for establishing Rensselaerswyck demanded large capital outlays.

As Kiliaen's fortune grew so did his ambitions. In the 1620s he participated in several projects (*droogmakerijen*) which sought to recover land along the southwestern shore of the Zuider Zee just south of Amsterdam. In 1628 he purchased land near Huizen for a country home. Dutch country homes were called *lusthoeven*, literally pleasure farms, and in the seventeenth century the ownership of such a place marked the merchant family as having arrived among Amsterdam's burgher patriciate. A modern scholar has described the seventeenth-century *lusthoeven* as consisting of "modestly elegant dwellings set in grounds surrounded by waters teeming with fish."[31] They were much more, however, for they represented the attainment of social status beyond wealth. That Kiliaen van Rensselaer could contemplate the building of his *lusthoeve* when he was only thirty-eight years old is testimony to his mercantile success.

The reclamation projects and the building of his country home occupied Kiliaen throughout the 1630s. He continued to engage in the jewel trade, and his responsibilities as an officer of the West India Company increased with each passing year. But the project that consumed him from 1629 until his death in 1643 was the patroonship of Rensselaerswyck. In the wilderness of New Netherland Kiliaen found an outlet for his restless talents. There he was to risk the family fortune in his unceasing effort to carve from the forest a manorial domain, conceived in mercantile terms but ultimately resting on feudal ideas of lordship and submission. That neither his manor nor his trade succeeded in his lifetime had little

31. Audrey M. Lambert, *The Making of the Dutch Landscape: An Historical Geography of the Netherlands* (London, 1971), p. 217.

bearing on the intensity of his efforts. Like his fellow merchants and sometime partners, Kiliaen van Rensselaer refused to give up on New Netherland.

Kiliaen van Rensselaer's role as patroon of Rensselaerswyck has been explained by others, but his role as a private merchant engaged in the colonial provision, fur, timber, and tobacco trades has not been fully examined.[32] Van Rensselaer's interests in New Netherland differed markedly from those of the other Amsterdam merchants. His patroonship responsibilities were more territorial than commercial. Saddled with the problems of populating the upper Hudson River region while simultaneously jockeying with his enemies on the New Netherland Commission to acquire Company compliance with its pledges, van Rensselaer and his heirs were forced to develop a complex mercantile relationship with the colony.

As the fortunes of the West India Company waned, the Amsterdam chamber looked to private merchants for supplies and shipping. In the late 1630s the firms of Gillis and Seth Verbrugge and Dirck and Abel de Wolff were active in the New Netherland trade. By 1640, Kiliaen van Rensselaer also began to tap the provisioning trade as the first floodtide of immigration surged. He knew from his experience as the patroon of Rensselaerswyck that his colony on the Hudson River would play a key part in any scheme to provision New Netherland from America. He also considered the possibility of Rensselaerswyck becoming a grain-exporting colony to supply the Company's slaves in Brazil in exchange for sugar.[33] Kiliaen must have been aware that his colony could serve as an excellent base for a continuous transatlantic trade in furs and supplies if the Company monopoly were ever broken. Some years before, during a grain dearth in the colony, the Company had confiscated Rensselaerswyck wheat for distribution.[34] Kiliaen had considered the confiscation an outrage and had vowed never to let it happen again. Thus when the decade of the 1640s opened with the announcement

32. In English, see Nissenson, *Patroon's Domain*, and the translation of Nicolaas de Roever's monograph, "Kiliaen van Rensselaer and His Colony of Rensselaerswyck," in van Laer, *Van Rensselaer–Bowier Manuscripts*, pp. 40–85.

33. Van Laer, *Van Rensselaer–Bowier Manuscripts*, p. 482.

34. Ibid., p. 324.

of the scrapping of the Company monopoly, van Rensselaer was prepared to become a major merchant trader.

Kiliaen van Rensselaer was not a newcomer to the private shipping business. In the 1630s he had been frustrated in his efforts to supply his colonists by the West India Company's refusal to rent him space aboard its ships. In desperation, he contracted with a shipwright to build his own vessel, the sixty-ton *Rensselaerswyck*. In 1636, Kiliaen van Rensselaer and Gerrit de Forest concluded a charter agreement in which each shared equally in the estimated 25,000 fl. cost of building, rigging, and outfitting the small ship (*scheepje*) for a voyage "at first opportunity to New Netherland." The voyage had two principal goals: to carry some twenty families to the colony of Rensselaerswyck and to trade for furs and tobacco along the coast of North America. Van Rensselaer and de Forest also sought profits by selling shares of the vessel on the exchange. A one-tenth share was sold to the Varlet brothers of Amsterdam (furriers) for 1,200 fl. Other shares constituting nearly 50 percent of the ship's total insured worth were sold before she sailed to the colony.[35]

The difficulty of estimating profit margins and reasonable prices for European goods in New Netherland is revealed in a letter written by Kiliaen van Rensselaer to his chief factor in Rensselaerswyck, Jacob Albertsz Planck. The letter dates from 1636 and discusses the prices of goods shipped aboard the *Rensselaerswyck:*

> Herewith I send you in God's name goods for account of my colony, amounting to f 4,100 according to the enclosed bill and invoice, which you will employ to the best advantage; and as I bought them wholesale for cash [and as the above amount does not include] any expenses of packing, boat and lighter freight, freight across the ocean, interest, risk, insurance, damage, etc. (not even your commission)

35. Ibid., p. 323; and Gemeentelijke Archief van Amsterdam, Notarial nos. 1045, August 8, 1636, pp. 120–121v; 414, August 8, 1636, p. 173; 995, September 10, 1636, p. 578. Secondary accounts of this first van Rensselaer attempt to engage in the New Netherland trade as a private shipper have appeared in Nissenson, *Patroon's Domain*, pp. 69 and 81n, and in J. Spinoza Catella Jessurun, *Kiliaen van Rensselaer van 1623 tot 1636* (The Hague, 1917), Appendix XXI. Neither of these accounts, however, made use of the notarial documents of Amsterdam.

you must sell such goods as can stand it somewhat higher than 50%
profit, but above 60% I do not want to tax my own people, who must
earn it by hard labor. As far as others are concerned I do not have to
care, you may take as much as the market price and as you can get.[36]

This remarkable letter tersely describes the hazards of private trade
with New Netherland. The van Rensselaers could never think
solely of the market value of trade goods and provisions. Their role
as patroons forced them to subordinate their greed for quick profits
to the immediate needs of the tenants of the patroonship. The
family's ability to make money in the provisioning trade was limited by their unwillingness to fleece their own people. Outside
Rensselaerswyck, however, the van Rensselaers were as quick to
squeeze the colonists out of their furs and tobacco as any Amsterdam merchant family.

His position as a wealthy Amsterdam merchant with influential
connections gave Kiliaen access to information on ships, low-cost
loans on bottomry, and supplies. His position as patroon allowed
him to take advantage of his built-in colonial market at Rensselaerswyck, where warehouses were already built and a colonial distribution center functioned. The financial arrangements for the building
of the *Rensselaerswyck* established a pattern followed by all of the
Amsterdam merchant firms trading with New Netherland. These
arrangements encouraged cooperation among the major suppliers of
New Netherland and brought all four of the most active Amsterdam traders into contact; indeed, collusion might be a better word.

Van Rensselaer had sufficient shares in the voyages of the *Aker*
(1639 and 1641), the *Wapen van Noorwegen* (1639), the *Wapen van
Leeuwarden* (1640), and the *Coninck David* (1641 and 1642–43) to be
named the owner (*eigenaer*) on all notarial records referring to these
vessels. In other voyages during this same period his financial investment was too small to be accounted as ownership, but on at
least two large ships, the *Engel Gabriel* and the *Eijkenboom*, van
Rensselaer's portion of the operating capital entitled him to be
designated as a principal freighter (*hoofdbevrachter*). That he participated in other voyages in this period is almost certain. The notarial
records of the Verbrugge and de Wolff enterprises referred to a

36. Van Laer, *Van Rensselaer–Bowier Manuscripts*, pp. 325–26.

"notable merchant in Amsterdam, lord over vast lands in America" as one of the partners in voyages to Virginia and New Netherland. Such ventures were important undertakings for the patroon, and his son was no less enthusiastic about the profits to be made in shipping to New Netherland.[37]

Jan Baptiste van Rensselaer, eldest son of Kiliaen's marriage to Anna van Wely, was too young at his father's death in 1643 to assume leadership in the family's affairs. He had to watch instead as his half-brother, Johannes (son of Kiliaen and Hillegond van Bijler), managed the van Rensselaer fortune. Johannes was apparently not well-suited for the role of patroon. He had no love for Rensselaerswyck and certainly no commitment to make it succeed. Richaert van Rensselaer, younger brother of Jan Baptiste and half-brother to Johannes, described Johannes's attitude toward his New Netherland manor to his brother in 1658: "The patroon does not even give it [Rensselaerswyck] a thought."[38] In fact, the patroon had thought enough about the colony to turn its affairs over to his alcoholic uncle, former Governor-General Wouter van Twiller. In 1651, Jan Baptiste could no longer watch Johannes destroy his inheritance; he took ship for New Netherland to take over the affairs of Rensselaerswyck personally.

On arrival in New Netherland Jan Baptiste was astonished and dismayed to find that the patroonship was failing. Tenants were leaving or declining to work. Crops were unplanted, and the inept hand of Wouter van Twiller was everywhere to be seen. The ruinous condition of the family's inheritance in New Netherland prompted Jan Baptiste to request that his younger brother, Jeremias, come to America to assist him in bringing order out of the chaos he confronted. Jan Baptiste and his brother were to work together for four years in New Netherland. The colonial experience convinced Jan Baptiste that profits were possible in the private shipping and provi-

37. Gemeentelijke Archief van Amsterdam, Notarial nos. 1500, May 9, 1640, pp. 13–17; 1526, May 6, 1641, pp. 136–37; 1526, July 2, 1641, p. 161; 1626, July 4, 1641, unpaginated; 1626, July 6, 1641, unpaginated; 696, July 8, 1641, p. 93; 524, July 10, 1641, p. 204v; 1059, July 11, 1641, p. 116; 1501, July 20, 1641, pp. 83–84; 1501, November 26, 1641, p. 165; 1059, December 18, 1641, pp. 176–176v; 1285, April 9, 1642, p. 52; 732, May 6, 1642, p. 571; 1336, May 22, 1642, p. 27; 1569, July 24, 1642, p. 268; 732, September 13, 1642, p. 745.

38. Arnold J. F. van Laer, ed. and trans., *The Correspondence of Jeremias van Rensselaer* (Albany, 1932), p. 118.

sioning trade. When he returned to Amsterdam in 1658 he undertook to channel the family's fortune into shipping and trade.

In partnership with his uncles and brothers, Jan Baptiste chartered and outfitted no less than six ships for the New Netherland trade between 1659 and 1664. During these years the van Rensselaers also traded in partnership with the other large New Netherland merchants. With Abel de Wolff and Gerrit Zuyck, he pooled capital to purchase ships, hire crews, and obtain trade goods. In each of these enterprises he had a substantial investment and was designated an owner or a principal freighter. Even after the English conquest, he continued to invest in shipping companies organized for the New York–Amsterdam trade. Records show Jan Baptiste investing 23,000 fl. in one ship "to trade with English northern Virginia, called lately by us New Netherland," in 1676.[39]

The family remained deeply involved in the commercial affairs of the colony. Their territorial holdings alone guaranteed a continuing concern for the colony's future, but it would take another Anglo-Dutch war, a second conquest of New York, and a warrant from the Duke of York finally to legitimize the van Rensselaer claim to Rensselaerswyck. That legitimation secured the van Rensselaers within the developing English mercantile system. When they became "naturalized" citizens of His Britannic Majesty's empire, their commercial enterprises were protected by the same Navigation Acts that had rendered the continuation of the New York–Amsterdam trade too expensive for Abel de Wolff.

A frequent partner of the van Rensselaers in the last years was Gillis van Hoornbeeck. Van Hoornbeeck first appears in the notarial documents in 1656. In the eight years preceding the English conquest, however, this latecomer to the New Netherland trade exploited it as actively as did the de Wolffs and van Rensselaers. A shipowner, financier, freighter, insurance broker, and retail fur distributor, Gillis van Hoornbeeck ranked second only to Jan Baptiste van Rensselaer among the Amsterdam merchants specializing in the New Netherland trade.

Gillis van Hoornbeeck came from a family considerably less genteel than the van Rensselaers. His father, Tobias van Hoornbeeck,

---

39. Ibid., p. 342; van Laer, *Van Rensselaer–Bowier Manuscripts*, pp. 399–401, 403, 405, 670, 790, and 795.

had been a Haarlem salt refiner, vinegar distiller, and local merchant. When he died in 1637, the estate was estimated to be worth 16,260 fl. The salt refinery was assessed at 8,560 fl. and the family home and all of its furnishings at 7,700 fl.[40] This modest estate had to support his widow and four children. Johanna Baerts van Hoornbeeck refused to sell the salt refinery and vinegar distillery, even though the notarial records show that she was offered a fair price for them. She took over the business herself, and although her son constantly looked out for her interests in later life, she was always listed as an independent *keetvrouw* (salt wife) in all documents concerning the family's business affairs.[41]

Gillis was raised by his mother and half-brother, Hercules van Hoornbeeck (son of Tobias and Maria Herculesdochter Schatters of Haarlem). Gillis was to display a strong sense of familial responsibility throughout his life. When his mother finally became too old to manage the salt and vinegar works in Haarlem he arranged for her to move to Amsterdam, where she could be close to her grandchildren. His sense of responsibility extended even to his nephews and cousins. When Hercules died unexpectedly at the age of forty-four, leaving behind a seven-year-old son, Gillis adopted the boy and raised him as his own. He married Maria Wijs in 1654.[42] A poor girl without a dowry, she had lived with her widowed mother on the Achterburgwal in Amsterdam's working-class neighborhood. The marriage was a love match that lasted for twelve years, during which Maria gave birth to two children. She died a young woman as a result of complications attending her third pregnancy. Her death was a devasting blow for Gillis, who liquidated his business affairs in Amsterdam and returned with his two children to Haarlem, where he spent a year before finally shaking himself free of the grief. He never remarried.[43]

40. The van Hoornbeeck genealogy has never been extensively researched. The information for the following account of the family was drawn largely from a "working genealogy" which I compiled with the assistance of Simon Hart and the gracious staff of the Gemeentelijke Archief van Amsterdam.

41. Gemeentelijke Archief van Amstredam, Notarial no. 2295, December 11, 1667, pp. 57–58.

42. Gemeentelijke Archief van Amsterdam, Begrafnis register van de Westerkerk van Amsterdam, Jaarboek voor 1659.

43. Gemeentelijke Archief van Amsterdam, Doop, Trouw en Boedel Boeken van Amsterdam, No. 473, May 28, 1654, p. 232.

Van Hoornbeeck was an active member of the Reformed Congregation of Amsterdam. In 1661 he served as a deacon and investment counselor for the congregation. He was also a financial adviser to other congregations, notably the Flemish Baptist Congregation of Amsterdam (Vlaamse Doopsgezinde Gemeente van Amsterdam). He advised both churches to invest in the New Netherland trade.[44]

Van Hoornbeeck's first involvement in the New Netherland trade came when he formed a private shipping company with two other Amsterdam merchants. The company was chartered for four years to trade with New Netherland under license from the West India Company. It proved so successful that it was rechartered in 1660 and again in 1664 and remained in operation until 1666.[45] This was the same year the Verbrugge Company finally went bankrupt, leaving the other New Netherland trade specialists holding loans and bottomry bonds on its assets. The executors of the Verbrugge estate (both Gillis and Seth Verbrugge had died in 1663) appointed Gillis van Hoornbeeck and Gerrit Zuyck to the probate arbitration board assigned to sort out the various claims on the estate and recommend measures to return the company to solvency. Zuyck's appointment was hardly unexpected because he had taken over Verbrugge operations in the late 1650s when he offered Gillis Verbrugge a way out of his financial problems by buying out more than half of the company's shares. Van Hoornbeeck's appointment to the board after only ten years in the trade is more surprising. It appears that Gillis van Hoornbeeck obtained his seat on the arbitration board because he was the Verbrugges' largest creditor and because Jan Baptiste van Rensselaer had supported his appointment. In a notarial document concerning another matter, Jan Baptiste van Rensselaer referred to Gillis van Hoornbeeck as one of the "great traders" (*groot handelaers*)

---

44. Gemeentelijke Archief van Amsterdam, Notarial no. 2965, June 1661, unpaginated.

45. The company was formed as a shipping concern in 1656. The partners were Lambert Leyssen, merchant of Amsterdam, Simon van Apheren, "for himself and his unnamed partners," and Gillis van Hoornbeeck. The company was dissolved at Leyssen's death in 1666. Its chief agent in New Netherland was Cornelis Steenwyck (Gemeentelijke Archief van Amsterdam, Notarial no. 2895, June 11, 1666, unpaginated).

of New Netherland.[46] In 1668 van Hoornbeeck joined with the other great traders of New Netherland to form a company to trade with New York.

The new company aimed at developing a long-term market for Dutch merchants in English New York. To avoid the strictures of the English Navigation Acts the three partners, van Hoornbeeck, van Rensselaer, and de Wolff, purchased passports issued by the Duke of York. The passports were acquired through the company's two New York agents, former Director-General Pieter Stuyvesant and Cornelis Steenwyck. The operating capital, set initially at 6,000 fl., was to be increased as the needs of the trade arose. The company shares were divided into fifths with each partner receiving 20 percent of the profits in return for 20 percent of the capital. Jan Baptiste van Rensselaer was made operations officer (*hoofdbewinthebber*, literally, chief director) for the company's first voyage; van Hoornbeeck held this position for the second.[47]

The company sent three ships to New York: the *Posthoorn*, *Juffrouw Leonora*, and *Nieuw Jorck*, undoubtedly a Dutch phonetic spelling for the English ship *New York*. Only the *Juffrouw Leonora* was Dutch; the other two were chartered English ships, manned by English crews and skippered by English captains in accordance with the Navigation Acts. The three ships were loaded at Amsterdam with trade goods, passengers, and some livestock. The cargo of the *Posthoorn*, for which a number of insurance policies have survived, was assessed at 15,000 fl. Of the three, the *Juffrouw Leonora* was the smallest, listed on the charter contract as a pinnace (*pinasscheepje*) with a 120-ton displacement. She had been built by the company in the Amsterdam shipyards. There is some reason to suspect that the *Juffrouw Leonora* was designed as a slave ship to ply the waters between New York and the Dutch slave depot at Curaçao. Unfortunately, the one reference to her possible role in the slave trade is not confirmed by other documents.[48] Still, it is not

46. Gemeentelijke Archief van Amsterdam, Notarial nos. 1996, November 8, 1666, pp. 161–163v; 2223, February 10, 1667, pp. 258–59; 2232, January 11, 1670, pp. 75–76v.

47. Gemeentelijke Archief van Amsterdam, Notarial no. 2784, February 27, 1668, pp. 447–50.

48. Gemeentelijke Archief van Amsterdam, Notarial nos. 2845, March 3, 1668,

unreasonable to suppose that the company contemplated engaging in the American coastal slave trade. The demand for slaves in North America was beginning to grow in the last quarter of the seventeenth century, and the Amsterdam merchants showed little reluctance to invest in it.

Notwithstanding the careful measures taken by the partners, the company failed to live up to expectations; it was nearly bankrupt after one year of operation and was dissolved in 1669 with the mutual consent of all partners. The costs of outfitting and freighting two ships and building a third had proven more expensive than the partners had expected, but the real cause of the company's failure was the costs of trading legally as foreigners in the English navigation system. The sheer inefficiency of the administration of the system made it pointless to attempt to comply with its provisions. The passports issued to the company by representatives of the Duke of York and paid for with specie were never made official, or so His Majesty's customs agents would claim when they confiscated the return cargoes of all three vessels. The Amsterdam notarial records chronicle a long legal dispute between the Dutch merchants and the English government. The result, after years of legal wrangling, was a decision by an arbitration board, which awarded the Dutch partners less than 5 percent on their investment.[49]

By 1670 the increased costs of trading legally within the English navigation system had proved too great for the trade to bear. The four Amsterdam merchants had failed individually and collectively to maintain the profits of the pre-1664 period. Only the van Rensselaers with their unique status as patroons could continue to engage profitably in the transatlantic trade. The others were forced to abandon the trade altogether or to pursue it on a much smaller scale through London merchants. In the decade of the 1670s, for example, Gillis van Hoornbeeck restricted his investments to English chartered voyages from New York via London to Amsterdam. Aboard the *Good Fame* in 1670 he had a private consignment of tobacco, skins, and furs worth an estimated 2,558 fl. The value of

---

pp. 127v–128; 2784, March 26, 1668, pp. 642–43; 2784, March 29, 1668, pp. 669–70; 2226, April 28, 1668, pp. 994–997v.

49. Gemeentelijke Archief van Amsterdam, Notarial no. 2790, August 20, 1669, pp. 663–664v.

the entire cargo, however, was 28,000 fl.[50] Some five years later van Hoornbeeck shipped a cargo of tobacco and furs aboard the English ship the *Mayflower*. This consignment was even smaller than that aboard the *Good Fame*.[51] As the decade closed, Gillis van Hoornbeeck, Abel de Wolff, and Gerrit Zuyck (for the reorganized Verbrugge company) were hardly more than clients for London merchants. The English navigation system and the conquest of New Netherland spelled the end of the Amsterdam merchants' brief reign as colonial trade magnates. In the 1680s all but the van Rensselaers liquidated their land and property holdings in New York. Gillis van Hoornbeeck appears to have been the last one to break the tie with the colony.

The liquidation took nearly eight years, but by 1688, the year of Gillis's death, the van Hoornbeeck family had detached itself from the former Dutch colony.[52] Small cargoes on special consignment were still sent occasionally in the family's name, but they were always shipped through London. Cornelis Steenwyck, Gillis's last partner in a New York trade venture, maintained a much reduced business in Dutch goods (clogs, herring, Leiden linen, and spices) at New York City, but the business was not much more than a retail specialty trade for a select clientele of old Dutch families in the colony. Steenwyck ceased dealings with the van Hoornbeeck company in 1685, and the family closed its account ledgers with the colony.[53]

After the death of Gillis the responsibility for the family's business affairs fell to Tobias, the eldest son. Under his direction capital once invested in New Netherland was put to work in other trades. In 1694, for instance, the family was heavily involved in the slave trade, and Tobias headed a syndicate of Amsterdam merchants who concluded an agreement with the directors of the West India Company to finance the Company's slave trade to Surinam.

50. Gemeentelijke Archief van Amsterdam, Notarial nos. 4003, April 20, 1670, p. 149; 3205, November 20, 1670, pp. 311–313v.

51. Gemeentelijke Archief van Amsterdam, Notarial no. 3778, July 14, 1675, pp. 711–17.

52. Gemeentelijke Archief van Amsterdam, Notarial nos. 2315, November 14, 1680, pp. 607–9; 3252, March 8, 1681, p. 38; 3252, March 9, 1668, p. 38v.

53. Gemeentelijke Archief van Amsterdam, Notarial no. 3276, April 3, 1685, p. 151v.

The contract was renewed several times, and the van Hoornbeeck family continued to supply the money and ships for a trade that shipped a minimum of four hundred Africans to Surinam each year until 1703.[54] The slave trade proved to be more lucrative than the North American fur and tobacco trade. Like Abel de Wolff, Gerrit Zuyck, and several former directors of the West India Company, Tobias van Hoornbeeck was drawn to the slave trade after the fall of New Netherland. The rapidity with which the former New Netherland trade specialists went into the slave trade suggests that one chilling result of the fall of the colony was the release of capital and capitalists to develop the transatlantic trade in humans.

The four Amsterdam merchant families just described were not competitors. They were, instead, the constituent parts of a collective effort to exploit the free trade provisions of the revised West India Company charter after 1639. Indeed, the Amsterdam merchants were able to keep the colony's sometimes tenuous lifeline with the United Provinces open even in the face of the Company's bankruptcy, maritime war, and national indifference. That they did so with profits in mind should only serve to prove that these four families were typical of a Dutch merchant class whose profit-mindedness was legendary in the seventeenth century. How they acquired their dominant position in the New Netherland trade is revealing of the tangled world of seventeenth-century Dutch commerce, a world circumscribed by a constellation of family partnerships, kinship ties, and marriage alliances and cemented by a host of financial instruments that encouraged the pooling of capital and the limitation of liability.

One feature that appears to stand out in the Dutch mercantile relationship with New Netherland is the financial control exercised by the Amsterdam merchants. The Amsterdam-based New Netherland trade specialists were reluctant to permit control of the trade to slip from their grasp. Having vied so long with the West India Company for their rights, they were unwilling to allow their factors in the colony a free hand in setting prices or determining the percentage of European goods needed to support the trade. Bearing most of the risks of the transatlantic commerce the Amsterdam merchants expected and grasped its responsibilities. The result was

54. Gemeentelijke Archief van Amsterdam, Notarial no. 4473, August 13, 1694, unpaginated.

a form of colonialism that depended on financial power rather than government restrictions. The key to the Amsterdam merchants' success was the variety of financial instruments and institutions, as well as the inside information, available to them in the city.

A New Netherland trading voyage usually originated with the chartering of a ship.[55] In this transaction the owner of the vessel, often the skipper, agreed to make the voyage to the colony on behalf of the charterer, who bore most of the risks and paid nearly all of the expenses. The charter contracts obligated the merchant to load the ship within a specified time so the skipper could sail in the most favorable season, provide the wages and victuals for the crew and captain, replace lost or damaged equipment, arrange for marine insurance for the value of the ship (insurance on the cargo was optional), and pay for the required dock labor at each port of call. The owner of the ship bore the responsibility for the vessel's safety while at sea, but his duties ceased when it arrived in port. In the all-important business of trade the ship's captain had no role. For this purpose, the merchant usually sent along a supercargo to oversee the selling of the trade goods and the proper loading of the return cargo. His salary came directly out of the pocket of the merchant and frequently was based on a percentage of the retail value of the colonial cargo in Amsterdam.

These trade voyages tied up considerable amounts of capital for long periods. On the average, the New Netherland trade specialists could expect to receive profits from their investments within a year of the chartering of a ship. Longer periods for capital turnaround, however, were not uncommon. In fact, numerous variables, chief among them the cost of financing, played upon the profit margin in the Amsterdam–New Netherland trade.

The bottomry bond, or *bodermerijbrief*, was the origin of limited-liability, credit financing in shipping. The *bodermerijbrief* was first developed in the Netherlands as a response to the risks of maritime trade and a scheme for tapping the pool of private capital held by Dutch citizens. Its use eventually spread to other maritime nations. The Amsterdam merchants employed it as the principal means for financing the New Netherland trade.

---

55. Charter contracts are among the most numerous documents to be found in the notarial archives. More than two hundred charter contracts for the New Netherland trade appear in the collection of Simon Hart.

Bottomry bonds were loans secured by the "bottom" or keel of the ship. A merchant could borrow money to finance a trading voyage by pledging the keel of the ship he had chartered as collateral. Various laws sought to prevent unscrupulous merchants from taking more bottomry bonds on a ship than she was worth, but if the number of legal suits brought against such merchants is any indication, the laws were frequently ignored. The unique feature of the bottomry bond was that it permitted merchants to spread the risks of trade among several small investors. If the voyage was a failure and the merchant was forced to default on his bond, the lenders could attach the ship and cargo, sell them, and recover at least a percentage of their investments. Moreover, bottomry bonds were bought and sold as securities on the exchange. Purchasers of a bottomry bond considered the transaction a speculative investment, and prices fluctuated with the reputation of the skipper, his backers, and the trade. Since these bonds were transferable, they served as money, providing a key means of exchange in an age of chronic specie shortage. The interest rates for bottomry loans also provided an index of the risk factor in a given trade.[56]

The late Simon Hart, director of the Municipal Archives of Amsterdam, collected some 120 bottomry bonds drawn up by Amsterdam notaries for voyages to New Netherland in the years 1639 to 1664. These documents reveal that the risks involved in the New Netherland trade were considered high. Since the number of bonds increased dramatically after 1651, it is possible to compute average interest rates for money loaned on bottomry for the last thirteen years of New Netherland's existence as a Dutch colony (see Table 7.1).[57]

---

56. Hart, "Dutch and North America," pp. 5–17. The bottomry bonds opened up the world of Dutch private capital for the Amsterdam merchants involved in the New Netherland trade. A remarkable document from 1662 provides a glimpse of how this system worked. In that year a financier named Nicolaes Spont died leaving his heirs a handful of bottomry bonds on voyages undertaken the previous year. In the single year of 1661 Spont loaned 9,650 fl. on bottomry bonds, all at 22 percent or higher. The bonds were used to finance voyages to the Hanseatic Cities, Cadiz, West Africa, the West Indies, and New Netherland. Spont risked more than one-third of the 9,650 fl. on bottomry bonds for New Netherland. Of the 2,350 fl. invested in New Netherland voyages all but 300 fl. was loaned to purchase provisions for the colonists (Gemeentelijke Archief van Amsterdam, Notarial no. 2760, February 24, 1662, folio 392–95 unpaginated).

57. Hart, "Dutch and North America in the Seventeenth Century," pp. 14–15.

Table 7.1. Average interest rates for bottomry bonds on New Netherland voyages, 1651–1664 (percent)

1651	23.5	(calculated on a monthly 3.5%)
1652	25.0	
1653	39.0	
1654	28.0	(calculated on a monthly 4.5%)
1655	21.0	
1656	21.0	
1657	19.5	(monthly average has dropped to 3.0%)
1658	21.0	
1659	21.0	
1660	22.0	
1661	23.0	
1662	20.0	
1663	23.0	
1664	21.0	

The interest rate averages suggest that the risk factor (as a calculation of the cost of financing the New Netherland trade) fluctuated slightly between 20 and 23 percent. The degree of risk rose during the war years of 1652–54, when Protector Cromwell's Roundhead navy was wreaking havoc on Dutch merchantmen. The rates recovered quickly, however, reaching their prewar average in the first year after the conclusion of peace. In comparison to other trades such as the so-called "mother trade" (*moedercommercie*) with the Baltic, the trade with New Netherland was a high-cost and high-risk undertaking. Indeed, when one considers the plethora of investments available to the merchants of Amsterdam, including the Russian and Baltic grain trade, the wine and salt trade with southern Europe, and the highly lucrative fishing syndicates, it is a wonder that the colony found any interested merchants at all. Financing costs aside, the persistence of the four Amsterdam merchant firms in pursuing profit year after year in the New Netherland trade suggests more than philanthropy or patriotism. Enough evidence has survived to indicate that profits were made in the New Netherland trade, but the costs to the colonists were high.

In the 1630s Kiliaen van Rensselaer estimated the cost of shipping supplies to his colony to be roughly 50 percent of the original vendor price in Amsterdam.[58] Several other sources confirm van

58. Van Laer, *Van Rensselaer–Bowier Manuscripts*, pp. 325–26; Gemeentelijke Archief van Amsterdam, Notarial no. 1045, August 8, 1636, pp. 120–121v.

Rensselaer's estimate, including one from the notarial archives which noted that the West India Company store at New Amsterdam was selling shoes in the early 1660s at 140 percent above their wholesale cost in the fatherland.[59] When these estimates are added to the litany of complaints by company soldiers and returning colonists of the high cost of trade goods and commodities in New Netherland, we begin to see the classic effects of colonialism.

The population surge in the colony opened up a thriving trade in provisions after 1645, as the surviving cargo lists affirm. In New Netherland, livestock raising provided an auxiliary income to farming and fur trading for many colonists, and the Amsterdam merchants were among the first to build livestock transports and raise cattle on Manhattan Island.[60] Even former Governor-General Wouter van Twiller continued to invest in livestock through the merchant houses of van Rensselaer and van Hoornbeeck long after he had returned to Holland in disgrace.[61] Perhaps the best evidence for a thriving commodity and provisioning trade comes from March 1650, when Abel de Wolff and Jan Baptiste van Rensselaer chartered the *Valkenier* for a spring voyage to New Netherland. On board the ship when she left Amsterdam were leather boots, books, woolens and duffels, tools for husbandry, pearl-handled looking glasses, lace, and perfumed soap. In what appears to be a very complete cargo inventory, liquor and firearms, the mainstay of the Dutch fur trade, were not even mentioned.[62] It would seem that most of the cargo aboard the *Valkenier* was destined for the European settlers.

The cost of such items to the settlers had to be high because the only transportable specie they could obtain was furs and tobacco, which often made up the entire cargoes returning from New

59. Gemeentelijke Archief van Amsterdam, Notarial no. 2855, January 12, 1664, folio 361–62 unpaginated.

60. In 1639 two former West India Company farmers in New Netherland testified that livestock prices in the colony were 50 to 90 percent higher than those in Holland (Gemeentelijke Archief van Amsterdam, Notarial no. 1280, May 5, 1639, pp. 60v–61).

61. Gemeentelijke Archief van Amsterdam, Notarial no. 1332, May 7, 1639, p. 44v.

62. Gemeentelijke Archief van Amsterdam, Notarial nos. 1345, March 5, 1650, p. 21v; 2420B, March 12, 1650, p. 28; 1345, March 16, 1650, p. 26v; 1298, April 8, 1650, p. 86.

Netherland. Thus the Amsterdam merchants could receive the prized colonial products with almost no expenditures for permanent fur-trading factors in the colony. As the middlemen for the Amsterdam merchants the colonists ran all the risks involved in the fur trade, while the Amsterdam merchants benefited from a lucrative colonial secondary trade. The system was effective in driving out competition from small home-country merchants because it required access to supplies and lines of credit unavailable to newcomers. It also encouraged a collusion of capital to limit the liabilities of the trade. This system worked to bail out the Verbrugges when the failed potash factory threatened the firm's ability to meet its financial obligations to the other New Netherland trade specialists. It also explains why the de Wolff, van Rensselaer, and van Hoornbeeck interests so frequently merged in partnerships. And finally it suggests why the four Amsterdam merchant firms dominated the transatlantic trade in the years of high risk but steadily held about 50 percent of the total trade during periods of lower risk. It may be permissible at this juncture to indulge in a bit of speculation about the overall effect of the Amsterdam merchant firms and the peculiar colonialism they evolved on the economic development of the colony.

New England's better-known economic development may serve as a useful comparison with that of New Netherland.[63] The Great Migration of the 1630s had provided the fledgling New England economy with a seemingly limitless supply of specie and customers for an indigenous provision and service trade. Those who had arrived earlier found themselves in a situation calling forth skills in entrepreneurship as they struggled to provide food, shelter, and services to the thousands landing from England yearly. A decade of mass migration, therefore, created a merchant community where

63. The sources for the economic history of New England in the seventeenth century are exceedingly rich and voluminous. For the following summary of the region's economic development I have relied on Bernard Bailyn, *The New England Merchants in the Seventeenth Century* (New York, 1964), and the excellent summary of the latest scholarship on the subject provided in Perkins, *Economy of Colonial America*. It is interesting that as late as the American Revolution, artisans and merchants constituted less than 12 percent of the white colonial population in the English colonies, although higher concentrations of such occupations were found in all the port cities (ibid., pp. 81ff.).

none had existed before. When the flood of English families became a trickle and the formerly lucrative provisioning trade dried up as quickly as the supply of new specie, New England merchants faced the realities of their predicament as competitors with the mother country. The fur trade might have saved them, but it posed as many problems as it solved.

In the first instance, New England had a poor supply of otter and beaver—the furs most highly prized. Second, the strategically important waterways were controlled or at least claimed by rival French and Dutch traders. Of course, the exception was the Connecticut River valley, for which the New England colonists demonstrated a willingness to go to war. But even there, the ultimate attraction was the land, not the furs. To be sure, these obstacles did not prevent the development of a New England fur trade, but they did serve to restrict its size and profitability to such an extent that it could not withstand a large influx of new traders after 1640. Out of necessity New England merchants developed the profitable West Indies trade in which they were to prosper for two centuries.

By 1700 New England's merchant community, forced to strike out in new trades, had developed as an independent economic class. The class-consciousness of these men aroused a sense of dignity and pride, and they vied successfully with the Puritan establishment for control of the society. The astonishing success and rapid sophistication of New England's colonial culture must be attributed at least partially to the success with which her merchants turned necessity to profit. New Netherland presents a different scenario.

Blessed (perhaps cursed) from the beginning with an abundant fur supply and the Hudson River to carry the furs to market, New Netherland offered lucrative rewards to private traders who could master the intricacies of the transatlantic trade. The numerous attempts by the West India Company to impose monopoly conditions on the trade failed ultimately because the private merchants of Amsterdam were able blatantly to circumvent the company regulations in the 1620s, operate under license from the patroons in the 1630s, or participate as free traders under the provisions of the 1639 Articles and Conditions. Unlike New England, the individuals largely responsible for exploiting New Netherland's resources were merchants of the home country. Secure in their Amsterdam countinghouses, the merchants grasped control of the colony's lifeline to

Holland and held fast. Profits from their enterprises flowed into coffers in Amsterdam, thus depriving New Netherland of capital and the opportunity to develop a viable, colony-based merchant community. The results of this private colonialism were evident in the 1660s. When the English conquered New Netherland they acquired a colony that had long suffered under a colonial system no less debilitating than that exercised by the much maligned West India Company. Yet it was a peculiar colonialism. Nurtured by the free trade policies of the bankrupt West India Company, the private merchants of Amsterdam had succeeded all too well. Their success may have been New Netherland's undoing.

[8]

Triumphs and Tragedies:
New Netherland's Last Years

As to the natives of this country, I find them entirely savage and wild, strangers to all decency, yea, uncivil and stupid as garden poles, proficient to all wickedness and godlessness; devilish men, who serve nobody but the Devil, that is, the spirit which in their language they call Menetto; under which title they comprehend everything that is subtle and crafty and beyond human skill and power. They have so much witchcraft, divination, sorcery and wicked acts, that they can hardly be held in by any bands or locks. They are as thievish and treacherous as they are tall; and in cruelty they are altogether inhuman, more than barbarous, far exceeding the Africans.
—Rev. Jonas Michaëlius, 1628

New Netherland's last years were filled with triumphs and tragedies. As the tide of immigration finally solved the colony's chronic population shortage and the colonists attained institutions of local government, the firm if autocratic hand of Pieter Stuyvesant gradually brought political stability. These years also witnessed the success of Dutch arms, when, under company instructions, a combined force of militia and West India Company soldiers expelled the Swedes from the colony of New Sweden on the Delaware River. In diplomacy, the Dutch finally achieved at least the promise of peaceful coexistence with New England in the Hartford Treaty of 1650. The tragedies were no less dramatic. Bloody Indian wars threatened to wipe out Dutch and English settlements from Esopus to the Delaware in the 1640s and again in the 1650s and 1660s. And, of course, in 1664 the ultimate tragedy befell the colony when a squadron of English warships conquered New Netherland. The era began ominously with an Indian war.

Along the waterways, where the fur trade brought Indian and European into murderous contact, and on the fringes of settlement, where farmers from both cultures competed for the best agricultural land, the two worlds collided. The confrontation was inevitable, given the different views of each culture with regard to land and its ownership. The Dutch had always tried to be evenhanded with the Indians of New Netherland, but as the savage quotation above shows, this attitude was not motivated by thoughts of equality or even by a desire to treat the original occupiers of the land fairly. Rather, it derived from a healthy sense of self-preservation. Unlike their neighbors in New England and Virginia, the Europeans of New Netherland never gained superiority of numbers over the Indians in their colony. Consequently, their relationship with the Indians was one of cautious and calculated appeasement. A more belligerent policy, especially in the upper reaches of the Hudson Valley, where the Five Iroquois Nations held sway, would have been suicidal. The Dutch never fought a war with the Iroquois, for they were too powerful and too necessary for the profitable continuance of the fur trade. The Algonkian tribes of the lower Hudson and Delaware regions and the western tip of Long Island were another matter. In the 1640s, the spread of firearms among the Algonkian hunters dramatically accelerated the annual peltry take, resulting in the eradication of fur-bearing animals in these regions and the increase in antagonisms between Indians and Europeans.[1] The issue of landownership lay at the heart of the terrible troubles that would beset the colony in these years.

The Indians conceived land as an element within nature's patchwork. Like water, air, fire, clouds, and wind, land was not to be possessed as one would possess a tomahawk or a quiver of arrows. Indian "ownership" of a tract of land merely indicated ability to master or dominate a given area with strength and presence. Possession was tied to the concept of use: the loss of possession occurred whenever the "owner" ceased or failed to use the land.

---

1. Calvin Martin, "The European Impact on the Culture of a Northeastern Algonquian Tribe: An Ecological Interpretation," *William and Mary Quarterly*, 3rd. ser., 31 (1974): 3–26.

Moreover, the Indians of New Netherland had institutionalized the ownership of land within the collective of the tribe; individuals never owned land apart from the tribe to which they belonged. Ultimately it was the ability of the tribe to dominate and make use of the land which conferred ownership rights to the individual members.[2] Thus land was connected socially, religiously, and mystically to the identity of a tribe. The Dutch concept of land-ownership with its attendant right of perpetual disposal was wholly foreign to the Indians of New Netherland. The concepts of contract, title transfer, and legality burst like thunderclouds over the heads of the Algonkian tribes. The loss of the southern fur trade had turned the once necessary Algonkians into an obstacle to Dutch agricultural expansion. Contracts signed and agreed to by sachems as far back as the 1620s became the basis for Dutch expansion in the 1640s and 1650s. As the Algonkian tribes felt the pressure of increased European immigration, the competition for the best agricultural land threw white man and red man into a series of bloody and tragic wars.

The first of these wars broke out in 1639, caused by the foolhardy act of Willem Kieft. Of all the Dutch governor-generals, Kieft had the best contemporary knowledge of the Indians and an understanding of the critical situation that would face the colony should a sustained Indian attack be waged against the European settlers. Most people, including the commissioners of New Netherland, had been impressed with Kieft's learning. Even Roger Williams, who had a unique opportunity to talk with Kieft about New Netherland's Indians while passing through New Amsterdam in 1643, was sufficiently impressed with Kieft's views to record a summary of their conversations: "At my now taking ship at the Dutch Plantation, it pleased the Dutch governor [in some discourse with me about the natives] to draw their line from Iceland, because the name Sackmackan (the name for an Indian Prince, about the Dutch) is the name for a Prince in Iceland."[3] Kieft's theories on the origins of the North American Indians suggest that he was familiar with the work

2. George S. Snyderman, *Concepts of Landownership among the Iroquois and Their Neighbors* (Washington, D.C., 1951), pp. 15–16.
3. Quoted in E. L. Raesly, *Portrait of New Netherland* (New York, 1945), p. 75.

of Hugo Grotius, whose *De origine gentium Americanorum* had appeared in Holland some years earlier.[4]

Kieft's learning, however, did not elicit a kind or even sympathetic view of the culture of the Indians. He remained a man of singular vision in his dealings with the Indians of the colony. The Iroquois were to be appeased and coddled, even when it required swallowing Dutch pride and accepting the unequal power balance that existed between the two cultures in the upper Hudson Valley. The Algonkians, however, had ceased to be of importance to the Dutch fur trade and were, in fact, a dangerous obstacle to the peopling of Manhattan, Long Island, and the Delaware Valley with Europeans. Kieft held that the Algonkians ought to be removed and exterminated, a view that was later to be roundly condemned by company officials in a report that described the ensuing war as "unnatural, barbarous, unnecessary, unjust, and disgraceful."[5]

The war erupted when Kieft attempted to levy a tax or *contributie* on the Algonkian tribes. In 1639 he ordered the yacht *Vreede* to collect the year's *contributie* from the Indian summer settlements along the colony's waterways, where the Algonkians usually lived from May to August while they fished, gathered wild fruits, and dried fish for the winter season. Kieft ordered the *contributie* to be paid in pelts, which were to be loaded aboard the yacht and brought back to New Amsterdam for recording before shipment to the fatherland. The skipper of the yacht, Cornelis Pietersen, was clearly overzealous in carrying out his orders, for when he came upon a village in which stacks of pelts could be seen from the ship, he assumed that the furs were for payment of the tax and ordered his men to load them aboard. When Pietersen accompanied his men ashore to pick up the furs he was attacked by the village sachem and slashed severely across the face with a hunting knife. The village warriors then attacked the crew and tried to storm the ship while at anchor. Pietersen and his men barely escaped with their lives. Pietersen's report after the safe return of the yacht to New Amster-

---

4. J. W. Schulte-Nordholt, "Nederlanders in Nieuw Nederland, de oorlog van Kieft," *Bijdragen en Mededelingen van het Historische Genootschap* 80 (1966): 44.

5. Report submitted to the States General in 1650, Algemeen Rijksarchief, Archief van de Staten-Generaal, Locketkas: West Indische Compagnie, No. 30.

dam accused the Indians of treachery. No sooner had Kieft received the report than news reached Manhattan that Indians had destroyed some hogs on a Dutch farm on Staten Island. Kieft believed the two incidents were related, although no proof has ever surfaced to support that contention. In any event, he ordered the organization of a punitive expedition against the Indians on Staten Island.[6]

The result was a tactical victory for the Dutch. A few Indians were slain, some villages burned, and livestock scattered. Kieft prided himself on having taught the Algonkians a lesson. He was convinced that his actions, however barbarous, had restored peace to the colony. One of these actions included the first bounty placed on Indians with the expressed intent of exterminating an entire tribe. In 1640, at the height of the war, Kieft issued a proclamation offering a bounty of ten belts of wampum for every head of a Raritan Indian delivered to the fort at New Amsterdam. Double bounty would be given for the head of an accused murderer.[7] Such barbarity did not pacify the Indians; rather the opposite, for Keift's willingness to resort to arms eliminated the possibility of reaching a mutual understanding about land boundaries and the rights of Indians within the borders of New Netherland. This diplomatic failure was to prove especially tragic because the Dutch practice of fencing their crops and allowing their livestock to forage until the fall slaughter or the winter lockup became the source of much friction between the Europeans and the Indians. Indian farmers, who had never fenced their fields, were forever complaining that their crops were trampled and devoured by the cattle, hogs, and sheep of the European intruders. Finding no justice at New Amsterdam, angry Indian farmers had taken to killing the livestock of Europeans as retribution for damage done to crops. An anonymous chronicler described the situation: "As the cattle and hogs [of the Dutch settlers] usually roamed through the woods without a herdsman, they frequently came into the corn of the Indians which was unfenced on all sides, committing great damage there; this led to frequent

6. John Romeyn Brodhead, comp., Edmund B. O'Callaghan and Berthold Fernow, eds. and trans., *Documents Relative to the Colonial History of the State of New York*, 15 vols. (Albany, 1856–87), 13:22–23; hereafter cited as *DCHNY*.

7. Schulte-Nordholt, "Nederlanders in Nieuw Nederland," p. 60.

complaints on their part and finally to revenge on the cattle without sparing even the horses, which were valuable in this country."[8]

Nearly a year passed before the next confrontation. In the interim, the governor-general sought advice and support from the leading citizens of New Amsterdam. To this end he called an assembly of the freedmen of the town from whose number twelve men were chosen to assist him in dealing with the Indian crisis. Kieft's autocratic views had not undergone a transformation, but he did demonstrate a surprising willingness to hear the views of the Board of Twelve Men. The next year found the governor-general agreeing to requests from them for such mundane and routine ordinances as a prohibition against the selling of English livestock on Manhattan Island, the establishment of annual musters for a colonial militia, and measures to deflate the colony's currency (a combination of Company scrip, pelts, hides, and tobacco). The inflation had been caused by a number of factors, not the least of which was the high costs of provisions (already largely in the hands of a few Amsterdam merchant firms) and a corresponding drop in the on-station prices of furs and tobacco.[9] The main function of the Board of Twelve Men, however, was to advise Kieft on the best course to take against the Indians. Kieft made no effort to hear Indian complaints much less to redress their grievances against European colonists. On the northeast coast of Manhattan Island, a reclusive, elderly wheelwright named Claes Smits paid for Kieft's incompetence with his life.

One day in 1641 an Indian came to the home of Claes Smits. The young warrior requested supplies for a hunting expedition. Smits invited the Indian to eat with him while they settled the deal for supplies. While at the table with the old wheelwright the Indian asked whether Smits had a blanket he wished to sell. Smits thought

8. J. Franklin Jameson, ed., *Narratives of New Netherland, 1609–1664* (New York, 1909), p. 273.

9. *DCHNY*, 1:201–3. For a discussion of how Kieft's use of the Board of Twelve Men (1641) and the Board of Eight Men (1643) fits into a developing pattern of political tension in the colony, see Langdon G. Wright, "Local Government and Central Authority in New Netherland," *New-York Historical Society Quarterly* 57 (1973): 17–19. New Netherland's struggle with inflation in prices of provisions is documented in several notarial documents; see Chapter 6, nn. 12 and 13.

for a moment and walked over to a large chest to look. When he bent over the chest the Indian picked up the wheelwright's ax and cut off the old man's head. After plundering the house, he fled into the woods.[10]

The murder of the old wheelwright sent a shudder through the colony. Governor-General Kieft ordered the sachem of a local band of Indians to assist him in finding the murderer and bringing him to trial. The sachem not only refused but expressed disappointment that only one Christian had been killed instead of twenty. The sachem's obstinacy and sarcasm only confirmed Kieft's conspiracy theories. The governor-general called together a war council to prepare for an all-out military effort.[11]

The rest of the sorrowful tale is one too familiar in American history. The Dutch superiority in weaponry and the willingness of some Indians to side with the Europeans in conflicts with other tribes rendered the resistance of the Algonkian-speaking bands brave but futile. After a series of broken truces and a number of bloody raids on the women and children of both sides, the war was ended when a platoon-sized contingent of Company soldiers and settlers stormed a village of Delaware Indians. A witness to the carnage at the Battle of Pavonia described the grisly scene:

> The moon was then at the full, and threw a strong light against the hills. . . . The Indians were wide awake, and on their guard, so that our people determined to charge and surround the houses, sword in hand. The Indians were so hard pressed that it was impossible for one to escape. In a brief space of time there were counted one hundred and eighty dead outside the houses. Presently none durst come forth, keeping within the houses. . . . The general perceived that nothing else was to be done, and resolved . . . to set the huts on fire, whereupon the Indians tried every means of escape, not succeeding in which they returned back to the flames preferring to perish by the fire than to die by our hands.[12]

Even the spectacle of human beings being consumed by fire failed to touch the heart of the witness. He admired the Indians' courage

10. Jameson, *Narratives*, pp. 274–75.
11. Ibid., p. 275.
12. Ibid., p. 283.

but felt little compassion for them. He wrote of their suffering in almost clinical terms: "What was most wonderful is, that among this vast collection of men, women, and children not one was heard to cry or scream."[13]

By 1645 the war was over. Along the coast of Long Island and deep into the interior, settlements lay wasted and survivors trekked toward New Amsterdam. Among the dead were Anne Hutchinson and her children. She had fled the intolerance of New England only to meet death at the hands of Indians incited to war by a reckless Dutch governor. Everywhere farms were abandoned and fields lay fallow. Food was an immediate concern, as was the hope for a new colonial administration. Ships docking at New Amsterdam were returning to the fatherland with former settlers who had given up the struggle. The Company directors received a letter from some of the leading citizens of New Amsterdam describing the desperate scene on Manhattan Island:

> Our fields lie fallow and waste; our dwellings and other buildings are burnt; not a handful can be planted or sown this fall on the deserted places; the crops which God the Lord permitted to come forth during the past summer, remain on the field standing and rotting in diverse places, in the same way as the hay, for the preservation of which we, poor people, cannot obtain one man. We are burdened with heavy families; we have no means to provide necessaries for wife and children; and we sit here amidst thousands of Indians and barbarians, from whom we find neither peace nor mercy.[14]

In Amsterdam, only the private merchants, secure in their countinghouses and in front of their hearths, continued to have faith in the colony. They actually benefited from the devastation brought on by Kieft's Indian wars because prices for provisions increased, and on-station prices of furs decreased. Only the colony's fur trade was relatively untouched by the devastation, for peace with the Iroquois in the Hudson Valley ensured its continuation. The highly prized varieties of beaver and otter had piled up in warehouses at

13. Ibid.
14. Quoted in George L. Smith, *Religion and Trade in New Netherland: Dutch Origins and American Development* (Ithaca, 1973), p. 156.

Fort Orange during the war years, driving down prices for pelts in the colony while simultaneously driving up prices in Amsterdam.

The peace that had proven so elusive elsewhere in New Netherland had been maintained at Fort Orange by Arent van Curler, a Company agent charged with administering the trade at the fort. His success in keeping the trade going during the war years may be attributed to self-interest on the part of both the Dutch and the Iroquois. Both sides had too much to lose in a war: the Dutch stood to lose their entire colony, or at least the most profitable source of furs; the Iroquois, their source of firearms, which they were already using to expand their hunting grounds to the north and west. Van Curler's policy centered around the Dutch-Mohawk alliance, which had sealed the fate of the nonaligned tribes such as the Susquehannocks. Dutch firearms helped the Five Nations, led by the warlike Mohawks, to push into the territories once dominated by other tribes. As long as the fur trade could supply the Mohawks with guns, cloth, and liquor, they were content to do the Dutch bidding. This meant peace in the Hudson Valley but war almost everywhere else.[15]

The directors of the Amsterdam chamber pondered possible solutions for the colony. The Indian wars had been costly. Salaries for Company soldiers, munitions shipments, and other war expenses had forced the chamber to borrow money on bottomry bonds. By 1645 the directors were beginning to hear a barrage of reports about the conditions in the colony. These reports were riddled with complaints about the incompetent leadership of Willem Kieft. One angry letter concluded its tale of woe with a warning to the Company directors that New Netherland would remain unpopulated "until a different system be introduced here, and a new governor be sent out with more people, who shall settle themselves in suitable places, one near the other, in the form of villages and hamlets."[16]

15. Lawrence M. Hauptman and Ronald G. Knapp, "Dutch-Aboriginal Interaction in New Netherland and Formosa: An Historical Geography of Empire," *Proceedings of the American Philosophical Society* 121 (April 1977): 171.

16. Quoted in Smith, *Religion and Trade*, p. 156. As late as the 1640s the Europeans of New Netherland had not developed institutionalized town and village forms. Doubtless prompted by the sorry state of the colony's defense, the directors ordered the colonists to settle in towns in 1645. This late emergence of

In May 1645, the Nineteen, on the recommendation of the Amsterdam chamber, approved the commission of Pieter Stuyvesant as director-general of New Netherland. It took nearly a year to receive final approval from the States General, but finally in July 1646, at the West India House in Amsterdam, Stuyvesant took the oath of office and swore his loyalty to the Honorable West India Company and their High Mightinesses of the States General. Five months later, on Christmas day, the new director-general sailed out of the Zuider Zee, bound for New Netherland.[17]

Stuyvesant was thirty-seven years old in May 1647 when he stepped from the gangplank at New Amsterdam, his peg leg sporting a silver tip and a broadsword secured in a scabbard at his waist. A soldier by profession and temperament, Stuyvesant was fiercely patriotic, fearless in battle, capable of towering rages, and an autocratic leader with a reputation for discipline and work. He had lost his leg while leading the assault on the Spanish fort on the island of St. Martin in 1644. Legend had it that he had stayed at his station giving orders to his troops while bleeding from the shattered stump until relieved by another officer. Refusing to retire on his pension, he had stayed on in the West Indies, serving the Company as the post commander of the Curaçao garrison. He left Curaçao in the summer of 1644 because the surgeons felt that the humid climate was preventing his leg from healing properly. He spent a little over two years recuperating in the fatherland before taking ship for New Netherland. He would live out the rest of his life in America.[18]

---

town life among the non-English settlers of New Netherland has been noted by several scholars, including Albert S. McKinley, "English and Dutch Towns of New Netherland," *American Historical Review* 6 (1900): 1–18; Wright, "Local Government and Central Authority," p. 15; and, David Cohen, "How Dutch Were the Dutch of New Netherland?" *New York History* 62 (1981): 45. A recent study of Dutch town life in New Netherland, however, has argued that the Dutch settlers brought with them an elaborate heritage and commitment to various "Dutch forms" of town design and government. See Donna Merwick, "Dutch Townsmen and Land Use: A Spatial Perspective on Seventeenth-Century Albany, New York," *William and Mary Quarterly*, 3d ser., 37 (1980): 53–78.

17. Alexander C. Flick, ed., *History of the State of New York*, 10 vols. (New York, 1933), 1:297.

18. Recent scholarship has shed light on Stuyvesant's earlier career. For example, the birth date on his burial vault at St. Mark's in the Bowery is incorrect.

Pieter Stuyvesant, painted from life, ca. 1660. Courtesy of the New-York Historical Society, New York City.

His commission as director-general was the reward of a lifetime for a Company man, and Pieter Stuyvesant was determined to justify the trust and honor he had received. He must have been aware of the reputations of his predecessors. The record had become all too public over the years—Minuit had deserted the Company with secret maps and information that enabled him to help found the Swedish West India Company, Wouter van Twiller had been fired amid rumors of alcoholism and fraud, and the man Stuyvesant was replacing had recklessly plunged the colony into an Indian war. He arrived in New Netherland at the colony's darkest hour, and he must have fancied himself something of a savior because from the moment he stepped ashore he became a whirlwind of activity, issuing proclamations, closing down brothels and taverns, and setting a new tone of optimism.

Stuyvesant's would be the longest reign by a colonial governor of New Netherland, or New York for that matter. His seventeen years as director-general would close out the colony's brief history and leave an impression on contemporaries of an arrogant but capable man, given to authoritarian flurries but tempered with an understanding of the possible. He was more feared than loved, respected than revered, but he was, without a doubt, the most capable man the Company had ever sent to New Netherland. He was a loyal Company man, to be sure, but he was not above using delaying tactics and even disobeying the spirit of his orders from the Amsterdam chamber when it appeared that the directors were seriously out of touch with the situation in the colony. He was a proud man who demanded that the rituals of his office be observed scrupulously. For example, he insisted on the correct forms of

---

Dutch scholar J. H. P. Kemperink has proved that Stuyvesant was born around 1610, making him a relatively young thirty-seven when he arrived in New Netherland rather than a worn and bedraggled fifty-one as tradition has held. See Kemperink, "Pieter Stuyvesant, waar en wanneer werd hij geboren?" *De Navorscher*, 98 te Jaargang, nr. 3 (1959): 49–59. I am indebted to Charles Gehring, director of the New Netherland Project, for alerting me to the new findings on Stuyvesant and for sharing with me information about Stuyvesant's last months in Curaçao which he has recently uncovered in his translation and editing of the Curaçao Papers.

address from his subjects. One of his harshest critics summed up the director-general's attitude by noting that until Stuyvesant's arrival "the word *Mijn Heer Generael* and such like titles, were never known here."[19]

Stuyvesant's most immediate concern was the sorry state of provincial government at New Amsterdam. Years of angry exchanges between Willem Kieft and his Board of Twelve Men, then eight, had poisoned the atmosphere with charge and countercharge and rendered all but ineffectual the attempts by the provincial government to enforce its policies on the inhabitants of the colony. Shortly after his arrival in New Netherland, Stuyvesant reorganized the council, expanding the older institution, which had included usually, but not always, the governor-general, *kommis* (store and record keeper), the *schout* (equivalent to a prosecuting attorney and sheriff), and the *fiscal* (colonial secretary) to include nine men drawn from the leading citizens and Company employees. Stuyvesant was merely extending a policy begun by Kieft to meet the crisis of the Indian wars. What the new director-general had not bargained for, however, was the depth and intensity of the animosity still felt toward his predecessor. He was, therefore, angered and dismayed when two members of the new council requested him to join with them in an investigation of Kieft's conduct of the late Indian war.

To Stuyvesant the request smacked of treason and offended his highly sensitive view of the rights of magistrates. Not only did he deny the request for an investigation, but he imprisoned the two council members who had had the temerity to suggest that subjects of the West India Company could question the actions of a governor-general. An indictment was forced through a rump council at Stuyvesant's urging, and a trial convicted the two men. They were fined heavily and banished from the colony. As a final statement, Stuyvesant exceeded his authority by denying the defendants even the civil right of appeal to the States General, which had been granted to every group of colonists who settled New Netherland from the Walloons of 1624–25 to the latest groups who had come out

19. Adriaen Van der Donck, *Remonstrance of New Netherland*, ed. and trans. Edmund B. O'Callaghan (Albany, 1856), p. 42.

under the expanded privileges of the Articles and Conditions and the subsequent new Freedoms and Exemptions issued to various groups from 1640 until 1664.[20]

Stuyvesant's autocratic attitude may have been necessary. The colony was in a desperate condition, and the Company expected its new commander to bring the situation to hand quickly. In repeated letters to Stuyvesant, the directors of the Amsterdam chamber stressed the need for discipline and firmness in dealing with opposition to Company rule. Although company directors were to condemn Kieft's actions severely, they were doubtless relieved that Stuyvesant successfully prevented the establishment of the precedent of popular review of Company policy. Stuyvesant may have been correct in perceiving the request for an investigation as a grave threat to the orderly administration of the colony. He was cautious not to give his newly founded Board of Nine Men any substantive power. They were forbidden to meet independently of the director-general, and even the three arbitrators, who were to serve by rotation as a sitting court of the nine men, were expressly limited to deciding cases of small consequence.[21]

One of the most persistent problems facing Stuyvesant as he settled into his new job was the lack of government institutions to communicate and enforce Company policy. The West India Company, as we have seen, was ill-prepared to assume the role of governing New Netherland. Moreover, it had no experience and little inclination to permit public participation in an enterprise still considered a business venture by its directors and stockholders. Furthermore, the colonists were a heterogeneous lot sharing no common political tradition. The English towns on western Long Island chafed under the authoritarianism they perceived in company directives and in Stuyvesant's less than amiable attitude toward their demands for self-government. The English wanted town charters and self-government such as the New England townships enjoyed, whereas the predominantly Dutch villages along the Hudson were generally more content with shared governance. They demanded nothing like the grass-roots democracy of the New England town

20. Flick, *History of the State of New York*, 1:297.
21. Wright, "Local Government and Central Authority," p. 18.

meeting and were most familiar with the limited popular participation found in the closed-corporate *dorpjes* (hamlets) of the United Provinces. Since the Dutch were usually slower to organize themselves into towns and villages, they displayed little of the fervent commitment to participatory governance seen among the town-conscious English immigrants. This situation was not to remain static. As the English villages on Long Island scored success after success in their efforts to acquire self-government, the other Europeans in New Netherland came to take the English system of town governance as the model for their aspirations.[22] Stuyvesant's quarrels with the colonists over local government were made more difficult by a series of religious disputes which threatened what one scholar has aptly called the "undefined and unstable balance between central authority and local autonomy."[23]

The religious history of New Netherland reflects a tension between the needs of commerce, which dictated a lighthanded policy of toleration, and the needs of the Reformed clergy, whose very presence in the colony involved the Company in efforts to enforce religious conformity. It was a tension long familiar to most Dutchmen. In the fatherland the solution had been compromise—outward conformity to the Reformed church, including the payment of taxes for its support—and freedom of conscience and toleration for private worship, as long as such worship remained secret. In practice, the compromise was even more lenient toward nonconfor-

---

22. Ibid., p. 21. The success of the English towns in acquiring self-government in New Netherland was in part the result of their homogeneity. In stark contrast to the rest of New Netherland's population, the English settlers were culturally, religiously, and linguistically connected. Moreover, as "foreigners" in a Dutch colony they relentlessly sought to maintain the familiar forms of English local government. The Dutch authorities, desperate for colonists after 1645, conceded to their demands. Beginning with Newtown in 1642, charters were issued to several English towns—Hempstead (1644), Gravesend (1645), and Flushing (1645). Somewhat later, Dutch towns received similar privileges—Breuckelen (1646), Beverwyck (Albany, 1652), and Midwout (Flatbush, 1653). Differences persisted, however, and generally speaking the charters (usually called *Vryheden en Exemptien*—Freedoms and Exemptions) granted the Dutch towns contained fewer concessions to local autonomy. See ibid., pp. 13–14, and Wright's "Local Government in Colonial New York, 1640–1710" (Ph.D. dissertation, Cornell University, 1974).

23. Wright, "Local Government and Central Authority," p. 29.

mity, as the famous *schuilkerken* or "hidden churches" of Amsterdam proved. It was possible, for example, in this Protestant city to attend mass in the Onze Lieve Heer op Zolder (Our Blessed Lord in the Attic), a large *schuilkerk* on the Oudezijds Voorburgwal just a few doors down from the apartment where young Kiliaen van Rensselaer had spent his apprenticeship years and less than five modern city blocks from the Nieuwe Kerk, the centerpiece of Dutch Calvinism on the great Dam Plein.[24]

Although the West India Company had assumed the responsibility of providing *predikanten* (ordained preachers) for its colonists, the directors had never shown much enthusiasm for supporting a colonial ministry and in fact looked to the Classis of Amsterdam, the ruling body of the national church, to provide volunteers to serve in the chartered territories. Generally speaking, the *predikanten* who were willing to serve in New Netherland were not among the best qualified, and in some cases they were clearly incompetent.[25] Others were qualified by education and training but not by personality. Sent to the antipodes to do God's work, they came to see themselves as the defenders of the Hervormde Kerk and the last bulwark against what appeared to be a floodtide of nonconformity and heresy.[26] The polyglot character of New

24. The best treatment of the role of religion in the United Provinces and New Netherland is Smith, *Religion and Trade*, esp. pp. 93–113. Smith's analysis of the struggle for toleration in the United Provinces (based for the most part on Dutch-language sources) is one of the best in any language.

25. The chronic shortage of *predikanten* meant that many pastors stayed on past their prime. One such case became something of a public scandal when the parishioners of Breuckelen refused to pay taxes to support the aged Dominie Johannes Polhemius. The local magistrates complained to Stuyvesant that his services were so short that the sermon could not be distinguished from the opening and ending prayers. It was not his fault, for "his great age is the cause of all and . . . his faculties are evidently not, what they were formerly" (Wright, "Local Government and Central Authority," p. 27n).

26. There were exceptions to the generally poor quality of *predikanten* who served in the colony. One of these was Dominie Hendrik Selijns, who replaced Wilhelmus Nieuwenhuysen as the pastor of the New York Reformed Church in the 1680s. His intervention stopped the bloodletting in the Salem witch trials. Selijns had acquired his post on the recommendation of Gillis van Hoornbeeck, who not only pushed his candidacy before the Classis, but also loaned the young minister money for his passage. In New York, Selijns married Margareta de Reimer, widow of van Hoornbeeck's former agent, Cornelis Steenwyck. It seems

Netherland's population made the jobs of the *predikanten* more difficult. In no other colony was there such a diversity of religious
beliefs. The Dutch Reformed clergy were hard-pressed during the
years of demographic expansion to root out heresy and nonconformity. Everywhere there appeared challenges to the catechism of the
Synod of Dordrecht; everywhere the heretic threatened God's
flock. The two eager watchdogs of conformity during New
Netherland's last years were Dominie Johannes Megapolënis and
Dominie Samuel Drisius, copastors of the New Amsterdam
Church.

In October 1653, a group of petitioners requested Director-
General Stuyvesant to grant them permission to organize a congregation and conduct public services according to the Augsburg
Confession. These Lutherans probably represented the largest non-
Calvinist body in the colony. The Company's liberal land and trade
policies after 1639 had encouraged large numbers of people from
predominantly Lutheran regions of Europe to immigrate to New
Netherland. Germans, Swedes, and Finns were already present in
significant numbers by 1650, and the colony of New Sweden on
the Delaware River would add still more Lutherans to the colony's
population when Stuyvesant incorporated that colony by conquest
into New Netherland. Stuyvesant's reply to the petition was reflec-
tive of the difficult situation facing the colony. He could not cate-
gorically deny the petition without arousing the fears of every religious minority in New Netherland. To grant the petition, however, would have been a violation of his oath of office and an open
invitation to other groups to seek similar concessions. Stuyvesant
did what any good bureaucrat would have done in such a situation:
he passed the petition on to his superiors in Amsterdam and pa-
tiently waited for their decision.[27]

The directors of the Amsterdam chamber were not only unwill-

---

that even in matters of religion, the Amsterdam merchant wielded considerable
influence. The entire story of the Selijns-van Hoornbeeck-Steenwyck relationship
is detailed in a long notarial document of 1693 (Gemeentelijke Archief van Amsterdam, Notarial no. 2342, May 19, 1693, pp. 51–69v).

27. Smith, *Religion and Trade*, p. 192; H. J. Kreider, *Lutheranism in Colonial New
York* (Ann Arbor, 1942), pp. 14–15; and John W. Pratt, *Religion, Politics, and
Diversity: The Church-State Theme in New York History* (Ithaca, 1967), p. 16.

ing to concede the request of the petitioners, they were upset at Stuyvesant for bringing the problem to them. Such matters were no-win situations for the Company. Dutch officials could not hope to attract large numbers of Europeans to their colony if strict religious conformity was enforced. Hence the directors instructed Stuyvesant "not to receive any similar petitions, but rather to turn them off in the most civil and least offensive way."[28] The directors had already received advice from the Classis, whose members had been informed of the "project of our Lutheran friends" by Megapolënsis and Drisius.

The two *predikanten* had reacted predictably, if somewhat hysterically, to the threat posed by the Lutheran petition. In a letter dated just two days after the receipt of the petition by Stuyvesant, Megapolënsis and Drisius warned their superiors that an affirmative response would "tend to the injury of our church, the diminutions of hearers of the Word of God, and the increase of dissensions." They went on to suggest that delegates of the Classis should meet with the "Hon. Directors, in whom we have the greatest confidence, . . . to refresh their memories, lest through want of proper attention to the subject, the requested permission should be given."[29]

Nearly two years were to pass before the next challenge to orthodoxy appeared. Once again it involved Lutherans on Long Island. In the last months of 1655 rumors reached Megapolënsis and Drisius that a group of Lutherans in the village of Middleburg were holding church services without an approved *predikant*. The copastors quickly informed Stuyvesant of the situation and requested his assistance in stopping the activities at Middleburg. In February 1656, the director-general issued an ordinance forbidding all religious conventicles not expressly approved by the Reformed clergy. The ordinance imposed stiff fines for violators: one hundred pounds Flemish for those who "presume to exercise . . . the duties of preacher" and twenty-five pounds Flemish for "each man or woman, married or unmarried who is found at such a meeting."[30]

The ordinance was only a partial victory for orthodoxy, howev-

28. Quoted in Smith, *Religion and Trade*, p. 192.
29. Quoted in ibid., p. 193.
30. Quoted in ibid., p. 195.

er, because the fines and punishments applied to formal, nonconformist worship. The unmistakable Dutch aversion to enforcing private orthodoxy was seen in the ordinance's last paragraph: "The Director General and Council, however, do not hereby intend to force the consciences of any, to the prejudice of formerly given patents, or to forbid the preaching of God's Holy Word, the use of Family Prayers, and divine services in the family; but only all public and private conventicles and gatherings, be they in public or private houses, except the already mentioned usual, and authorized religious services of the Reformed Church."[31] Even these words were not enough to convince the directors of the Amsterdam chamber that Stuyvesant had not once again gone too far in his role as the civil arm of the Hervormde Kerk. Furthermore, when word reached Amsterdam that the director-general had imprisoned some colonists for violations of the ordinance, the directors fired off an angry letter to Stuyvesant, in which they fumed against the inflexible position he had taken and warned him in no uncertain terms "not [to] publish such or similar placats without our knowledge."[32]

The dispute would drag on for years until the Company hit upon a solution that permitted the Lutherans to worship publicly in the Reformed church through a slight adjustment in the catechism.[33] The compromise thrust the Company into a theological controversy with the *predikanten* of New Netherland and the Classis of Amsterdam. The *predikanten* accepted the compromise only when the directors informed Stuyvesant that the Company was planning to replace the New Amsterdam copastors with two or three young ministers "not . . . infected with scruples about unnecessary forms, which cause more division, than edification."[34] The Classis of Amsterdam was forced to accept the compromise because the

31. Quoted in ibid.
32. Quoted in ibid., p. 196.
33. The change in the catechism involved the deletion of the Dutch word "*alhier*" (here) from the second article of the baptismal formula, which asked parents to affirm that "the doctrine which is expounded in the Old and New Testaments and in the articles of Christian faith, and which is taught in the Christian church *here* [italics mine], is true and sufficient for salvation." The directors of the Amsterdam chamber even went so far as to ship out obsolete copies of liturgy books that did not contain the offensive *alhier*. See Smith, *Religion and Trade*, pp. 206, 210; Albert Eekhof, *De Hervormde Kerk in Noord-Amerika, 1624–1664*, 2 vols. (The Hague, 1913), 2:25.
34. Quoted in Smith, *Religion and Trade*, p. 209.

Seal of the township of New Amsterdam. Courtesy of the New Netherland Project, New York State Library, Albany.

formula whereby Lutherans were admitted to church service had a long history in the fatherland and was likely to find many formidable defenders among the Lutheran directors of the Amsterdam chamber. Other religious groups would prove more difficult to accommodate.

In September 1654 twenty-three Jews arrived in New Netherland. They were war refugees from Brazil, forced to flee the colony of New Holland when it fell to the Portuguese. They landed penniless with little more than the clothes on their backs. The wave of bigotry their arrival precipitated was far out of proportion to the threat their presence posed to the Reformed church. It was in part motivated by economic concerns. Some colonists complained that the Jews would become public charges, which they did during the winter of the first year. The main source of the antisemitism, however, came from the director-general and the *predikanten*, who together mounted a campaign with the company to ban Jews from settling in New Netherland.[35]

35. Samuel Oppenheim, *The Early History of the Jews in New York, 1654–1664* (New York, 1909), pp. 4–5; see also A. V. Goodman, *American Overture: Jewish Rights in Colonial Times* (Philadelphia, 1947), pp. 76–77.

Pieter Stuyvesant was a committed antisemite who referred to the recently arrived refugees as members of a "deceitful race" and "blasphemers of the name of Christ." He requested the directors to give him authority to ban the Jews so that they would "be not allowed further to infect and trouble this new colony."[36] Stuyvesant's request fell on deaf ears in Amsterdam, and for good reason, for as the directors' carefully worded reply pointed out, "To effectuate and fulfill your wishes . . . would be somewhat unreasonable and unfair, . . . because of the large amount of capital which they [Jews] still have invested in the shares of this company."[37]

Stuyvesant's rebuke did not prevent the colony's *predikanten* from pursuing the matter with the Classis of Amsterdam. Dominie Megapolensis wrote the Classis in March 1655 requesting assistance in ridding New Netherland of "these godless rascals." Furthermore, he added, "These people have no other God than the unrighteous Mammon, and no other aim than to get possession of christian property, and to win all other merchants by drawing all trade towards themselves."[38] The Classis did not need much convincing, and within days after Megapolensis's letter was received, a delegation arrived at the West India House to confer with the directors of the Company. The delegation received a bureaucratic cold shoulder. The reverend brethren were simply told that these Jews had suffered "considerable loss, with others, in the taking of Brazil" and were thus to be allowed to "travel and trade to and in New Netherland and live and remain there."[39]

In 1656, in reply to a request from Stuyvesant concerning the rights of Jews to practice their religion, the directors recommended that the colony's Jews be segregated in their own community and permitted to worship as a group in private. They were specifically forbidden to build a synagogue, but they continued to enjoy more personal freedom in New Netherland than in any other colony in North America.[40] This grudging toleration was granted because the West India Company could ill afford to anger its Jewish stockholders. Ironically, Mammon had triumphed on the side of the

36. Quoted in Oppenheim, *Early History of the Jews*, p. 5.
37. Quoted in Pratt, *Religion, Politics, and Diversity*, p. 23.
38. Quoted in Smith, *Religion and Trade*, p. 213.
39. Quoted in ibid., p. 214, and Pratt, *Religion, Politics, and Diversity*, p. 23.
40. Pratt, *Religion, Politics, and Diversity*, p. 24.

Gentiles. The Quakers would find an even less hospitable welcome in New Netherland.

The humble members of the Society of Friends were the religious lepers of the seventeenth and early eighteenth centuries. They were tolerated nowhere in colonial America until the founding of Pennsylvania. Their appearance in New Netherland evoked a vile torrent of intolerance and persecution and threatened a political crisis as well. The first Quakers arrived secretly in New Netherland in August 1657, when several of them came ashore from an English ship. On the streets of New Amsterdam the intruders might have gone unnoticed had they been content to bear the Inner Light in silence, but such was not the temperament of a Quaker. Two women from the landing party had the misfortune to be seized by the Spirit on the streets of New Amsterdam. Quaking violently in spasms on the ground, they excited a large crowd of spectators. When news reached the government compound, the women were arrested and banished from the colony. Three men from the party managed to cross the East River to Long Island. One of these, Robert Hodgson, took refuge in the English village of Hempstead.[41]

Hempstead had been founded by English Calvinists some years before and was one of the more orthodox villages on the island. Thus when Hodgson attempted to preach in public, the selectmen (*schepens*) ordered his arrest. He was tied with ropes and taken to New Amsterdam. Stuyvesant questioned the Quaker personally before convicting him of insolence. During the interview, Hodgson had offended the director-general by his refusal to remove his hat and his insistence on addressing Stuyvesant in the familiar pronoun. Hodgson refused to pay the fine and was repeatedly beaten and tortured for his failure to labor in the work gangs around the fort. Finally released after public opinion had turned to sympathy, he was banished forever from the colony.[42]

Hodgson's arrest and punishment did not quiet the English villagers on Long Island, many of whom held antinomian beliefs,

41. Ibid., pp. 19–20.
42. Eekhof, *Hervormde Kerk*, 2:78–81; Henry Onderdonck, "The Rise and Growth of the Society of Friends on Long Island and in New York, 1657–1826," *Annals of Hempstead, 1643–1832* (Hempstead, N.Y., 1878), pp. 4–8. The best summary in English is Smith, *Religion and Trade*, pp. 222–23.

which were compatible with the free will doctrine of the Quakers. In Gravesend (Gravesande), Jamaica, and Flushing (Vlissingen) secret Quaker meetings were held, and the enthusiasm for the new religion spread.rapidly. In the fall of 1657 Stuyvesant, at the insistence of Johannes Megapolënsis and Samuel Drisius, issued a proclamation subjecting any ship bringing Quakers to New Netherland to seizure. Furthermore, any colonists receiving Quakers in their homes or attending a Quaker meeting were to be fined fifty Flemish pounds, with half the sum going to the informer.[43]

Stuyvesant's ordinance was received with some grumbling throughout New Netherland, but in the Long Island hamlet of Flushing the response was defiance. Flushing had had a rocky religious history in New Netherland. Founded in 1645 under a charter of Freedoms and Exemptions issued by Willem Kieft, Flushing had for some time maintained a running dispute with Dutch authorities over the appointment of a minister. Stuyvesant had been forced to impose the services of the Reverend Francis Doughty on the recalcitrant villagers, only to discover that the inhabitants refused to attend church services and to pay the pastor's salary. Facing bankruptcy, Doughty had taken ship for Virginia in 1655, and the village had been without a spiritual leader until the arrival of the Quakers in 1657.[44] The anti-Quaker ordinance aroused the people of Flushing to sign a remonstrance drawn up by the town clerk, Edward Hart, at the urging of the town's *schout* (sheriff), Tobias Feake. This remarkable document, usually referred to as the Flushing Remonstrance, signed by thirty-one of the townspeople, is one of the clearest statements on religious toleration to come out of seventeenth-century America. It states the justification for religious toleration and freedom of worship simply: "God is a consuming fire, and it is a fearful thing to fall into the handes of the liveing God; wee desire therefore in this case not to judge least wee be judged, neither to Condem least wee bee Condemed, but rather let every man stand and fall to his own . . . our desire is not to offend one of his little ones in whatsoever forme, name or title hee appeares in, whether Presbyterian, Independent, Baptist or Quaker; but shall be glad to see anything of God in any of them."[45]

43. *DCHNY*, 14:402–3.
44. Smith, *Religion and Trade*, pp. 224–25.
45. Quoted in ibid., pp. 225–26.

Stuyvesant ordered the *schepens,* who signed the Flushing Remonstrance with *schout* Feake, placed under arrest and made to stand trial in New Amsterdam. The defendants were charged with a violation of the director-general's orders and the various charters of Freedoms and Exemptions, which had outlawed all public worship except the Reformed church. Three of the defendants recanted and were released. Tobias Feake refused to admit his error or to ask for a pardon and subsequently became a test case for the colony. Removed from office and fined heavily, he was banished from New Netherland forever.

Stuyvesant and the *predikanten* would spend the next four years trying to root out Quakerism in the English towns on Long Island. Arrests were made, trials showcased, and former colonists exiled. By 1663 Stuyvesant's zeal in hunting down Quakers had come to the attention of the Company directors in the form of a long written protest by the former colonist and notorious Quaker John Bowne. Stuyvesant's harsh treatment of Bowne convinced the directors that he was once again overreacting without judging the consequences for the colony as a whole. In a letter of mild rebuke, the directors admitted that "we heartily desire that these and other sectarians remained away from there, yet as they do not, we doubt very much, whether we can proceed against them rigorously without diminishing the population and stopping immigration, which must be favored at so tender a stage of the country's existence." The directors implied that Stuyvesant had been too zealous in his search for nonconformists and sectarians. They suggested that he shut his eyes to nonconformity, or "at least not force people's consciences, but allow every one to have his own belief, as long as he behaves quietly and legally, gives no offence to his neighbors and does not oppose the government."[46] By 1663 religious problems were becoming the least of Stuyvesant's worries. Across Long Island Sound the ominous din of war could be heard as English axes slowly cleared the primeval forest in the Connecticut Valley.

The Anglo-Dutch rivalry in North America was nearly four decades old when Stuyvesant arrived in New Netherland. From the moment of his commission in Amsterdam he must have known that the success of New Netherland, indeed its continued existence, depended on his ability to compromise with the New En-

46. Quoted in ibid., p. 230.

gland colonies about boundaries. Thus one of his first official acts as director-general was to send a letter of greeting to Governor Winthrop of Massachusetts in which he appealed to the common cause of Protestants against the hated papists and reminded the English Puritan that Holland had been a home to many Englishmen in times of persecution. The director-general attempted to establish a bargaining position early in the negotiations by asserting the "indubiate right" of the West India Company and the Dutch nation "to all that land betwixt that River called Connecticut, and that by the English named Delaware." He ended the letter with a request for a meeting to discuss the boundary issue.[47]

When the letter reached Governor Winthrop, he laid it before the commissioners of the United Colonies of New England, a mutual defense league established after the disastrous Pequot War to provide coordinated action in the event of hostilities. That Winthrop felt compelled to bring the letter to the attention of the representatives of the other colonies suggests that he might have already been considering the Dutch a military threat requiring a united approach. The reaction among the commissioners was mixed. Some, including Winthrop, recommended accepting the Dutch governor's offer to meet for the purpose of ironing out differences. The majority, however, cautioned against conceding to a meeting too soon. Accordingly, Winthrop wrote Stuyvesant thanking him for his letter and agreeing to meet "in proper time and place" sometime during the coming winter. Before the meeting could be set up, however, an incident involving a Dutch ship illegally trading in New Haven brought the Dutch and English to the brink of hostilities on the issues of boundaries and trade regulations.

In late August 1647, news reached New Amsterdam that a ship named the *St. Beninio* was engaged in trade with the English at New Haven. The ship was known to Stuyvesant because shortly after her arrival in New Haven, where she had been tossed by a storm, her skipper, Cornelis Claesz Snoij from Edam, sent word to Stuyvesant of his arrival and the circumstances that prevented him from sailing directly to New Amsterdam to apply for the required Company license to trade in the chartered territories.[48] Thus when

47. Quoted in Edmund B. O'Callaghan, *History of New Netherland, or New York under the Dutch*, 2 vols. (New York, 1845–48), 2:44.

48. The *St. Beninio* incident is described in several sources. The notarial archives contain the notarized testimony of Captain Snoij taken for insurance purposes

Stuyvesant heard that the *St. Beninio* was trading in New Haven rather than seeking repairs he determined to seize the ship as an example of the Company's serious intent to enforce its charter regulations. Word had also reached Manhattan that the next stop on the ship's trade mission was English Virginia, a clear violation of the West India Company's charter and a challenge to Stuyvesant's ability to enforce the law. The director-general laid plans for the seizure of the *St. Beninio* before she could make sail for Virginia.

A Dutch ship, the *Swoll*, had recently been sold by Stuyvesant to the deputy governor of New Haven in an effort to raise revenue for the repair of the colony's defenses on Manhattan Island. The agreement of sale had specified delivery of the vessel to New Haven sometime in October. Stuyvesant decided to use that occasion to seize the *St. Beninio* as she lay at anchor in the English port. On October 11, the *Swoll* sailed from the East River toward New Haven with seventy Company marines aboard. When she arrived in New Haven harbor the soldiers forcibly boarded the *St. Beninio*, cut her loose from her moorings, and sailed her to New Amsterdam. There, Stuyvesant proclaimed the ship to be in violation of the company charter. He confiscated the ship, her cargo, and her rigging. The crew was released almost immediately, but Captain Snoij spent eight months in the stockade before being released to return to the fatherland. The seizure of the *St. Beninio* was to unleash a torrent of legal suits in Amsterdam.[49] In New Netherland the incident nearly brought the English and Dutch to blows.

The seizure of the *St. Beninio* and the receipt in New Haven a few days later of a letter from Stuyvesant citing Dutch claims to all the lands bordering Long Island Sound outraged public opinion in the English colony and prompted Governor Theophilius Eaton to dispatch a blistering letter to New Amsterdam. After a terse opening, he came to the point quickly:

---

after his return to Amsterdam, which confirms that the ship had been damaged in a storm: "Because of bad weather he fell into the coast along New England. There, having had their water barrels broken they ran in at New Haven" (Gemeentelijke Archief van Amsterdam, Notarial no. 1080, June 11, 1649, pp. 12v–13). For a full account of the incident see O'Callaghan, *History of New Netherland*, 2:47–50.

49. Gemeentelijke Archief van Amsterdam, Notarial nos. 1080, June 11, 1649, pp. 12v–13; 1574, April 18, 1648, p. 173.

Without grounds you pretend to land in these parts, one while from Delaware to Connecticut River, and another while you extend your limits further even to Cape Cod. . . . And now, lately, in a ship belonging to New Haven, as bought by Mr. Goodyear, you have sent armed men, and without license, not so much as first acquainting any of the magistrates of this jurisdiction with the cause or ground thereof, seized a ship within our harbor. . . . Wherefore we have protested, and by these presents do protest against you, Peter Stuyvesant, Governor of the Dutch at Manhattan, for disturbing the peace between the English and Dutch . . . we hereby protest that whatever inconveniences may hereafter grow, you are the cause and author of it.[50]

Governor Eaton's angry letter surprised Stuyvesant, perhaps its tone even frightened him, for he replied with a conciliatory letter that sought to smooth over the differences between the two colonies, while avoiding any attempt at justifying the seizure of the *St. Beninio.* Diplomacy was not one of Stuyvesant's strong suits, but he was a pragmatic man who realized that continued confrontations with the English could be catastrophic for the colony. The irascible director-general may have been able to put the *St. Beninio* incident behind him had not a new episode complicated Anglo-Dutch relations once again.

As Dutch luck would have it, a few "miscontents" had escaped the authorities on Manhattan Island and shortly afterward showed up in New Haven seeking asylum. Hence Stuyvesant asked Governor Eaton for his assistance in extraditing the criminals in the same letter that had carried his message of conciliation. Eaton's reply was nearly as hostile as the initial letter. He refused to extradite the fugitives until the Dutch adopted a more civil attitude toward English sovereignty. What angered him most was not the request for extradition but Stuyvesant's claim to land rightfully belonging to the English government.

When news of the dispute between Stuyvesant and Eaton reached the commissioners of New England, John Winthrop recommended that a letter be sent immediately to Stuyvesant expressing regret that such differences had been allowed to arise between two Protestant allies. The letter, which also promised to intercede

50. Quoted in O'Callaghan, *History of New Netherland,* 2:49–50.

on Stuyvesant's behalf with Governor Eaton in the negotiations for the extradition of the fugitives, was sent first to New Haven, where it was to serve as a warning to Eaton that the rest of the New England colonies were unwilling to condone his militant posturing with the Dutch. The plan failed when Governor Eaton refused to forward the letter to New Amsterdam or to discuss the extradition of the fugitives.

Meanwhile, ignorant of the attempts by the Confederation of New England to intervene in the dispute, Stuyvesant decided to retaliate by issuing a proclamation granting refuge to any fugitive of New Haven. This time the citizens of New Amsterdam thought the director-general had gone a bit too far in his squabble with Governor Eaton. They complained that the proclamation would attract the most unsavory and vile elements to the Dutch colony. Notwithstanding their objections, Stuyvesant went forward with his plan. Fortunately, the Dutch governor was able to outwit Eaton. By writing secretly to the fugitives and granting them amnesty, Stuyvesant was able to obtain their return without challenging the English sanctuary. Shortly thereafter Stuyvesant rescinded the proclamation and Anglo-Dutch relations returned to normal.

In spring 1648 complaints began to reach English authorities in New Haven and Boston that Dutch traders were arming the Indians of the Connecticut Valley with the intent of launching a war against the English colonists there. Stuyvesant received several dispatches from the English and a few from his own subjects which suggested that there was some truth to the English charges. In an effort to clear the air, the director-general hoped to send his assistant, Cornelis van Tienhoven, to New Haven to investigate possible Dutch involvement in the firearms trade with the Indians. In a letter to Eaton, Stuyvesant expressed his determination to stamp out the trade in firearms. Although he doubted that Dutch traders were involved in the trade, he assured Eaton that if they were they would be punished accordingly. He concluded by repeating his request for a summit meeting of the governors of all the colonies to determine territorial claims.

Two years were to pass before the long-hoped-for summit meeting could take place. In the meantime, Anglo-Dutch relations were strained once again by a boundary dispute, this time involving the Delaware River valley. On August 2, 1649, the commissioners of

New England heard a proposal by a group of promoters for the establishment of a permanent colony along the Delaware. The promoters were members of the Delaware Company of New Haven and included in their number nearly every important merchant in the colony of New Haven.[51] Their intention was to establish a settlement on Delaware Bay for the purpose of pursuing the fur trade and engaging in other farming and trade activities. The proposal was really only a request for the official sanction of a colonization that had begun in 1642.

Under the unauthorized and illegal charter of the Delaware Company of New Haven, English families had been settled in two locations in the region: at Varkens Kill (Pigs' Creek) and on the Schuylkill River. The settlement had been challenged officially by former Governor-General Willem Kieft in a letter he delivered to Robert Cogswell, the commander of the vanguard party of English settlers. In the same words he had used to warn Pieter Minuit that his colony of New Sweden was illegally situated on land belonging to New Netherland, Kieft informed Cogswell that he was not "to build or plant on the South river, lying within the limits of New Netherland, nor in the lands extending along it."[52] Kieft had been assured by Cogswell that he did not propose to settle in an area within the jurisdiction of New Netherland but hoped instead to "select a place over which the States General have no authority." Kieft was later to learn that Cogswell did not keep his pledge, and by the end of 1642 some twenty families from New Haven were settled in the region.

The Delaware Valley, like the Connecticut, was a jurisdictional nightmare of competing colonial claims, patents, and charters. In addition to the claims of the New Haven promoters, the 1632 patent issued to the second Lord Baltimore for his colony of Maryland had extended the northeastern border of the proprietary to the western bank of the Delaware River and as far north as the fortieth parallel. Thus the Calverts could claim all of the western side of the

51. Various documents examined by C. A. Weslager suggest that Governor Theophilius Eaton was the principal shareholder in this company together with Stephen Goodyear, John Dane, Thomas Grigson (Gregson), Richard Malban, Matthes Gilbert, and John Turner. See Weslager, *The English on the Delaware, 1610–1682* (New Brunswick, N.J., 1967), p. 94.

52. *DCHNY*, 2:144; also quoted in Weslager, *English on the Delaware*, p. 100.

Delaware Valley. The eastern bank of the river had first been settled by the Dutch in the 1620s, when they constructed Fort Nassau on the present site of Gloucester, New Jersey. The Calvert patent included only land as yet uncultivated by Europeans, and for this reason the Dutch settlement at Fort Nassau legally cut off English claims to the area that would eventually become the colony of New Jersey.[53]

Legal niceties notwithstanding, Charles I continued to use the Delaware Valley as a means of consolidating his support among England's Catholic noblemen. Within a month of the issuance of the Calvert patent, Charles I granted the eastern half of the valley to Sir Edmund Plowden, "a contentious Roman Catholic nobleman . . . in whose soul burned great aspirations."[54] Plowden's colony of New Albion was to prove abortive, but the patent continued to be a difficult obstacle to boundary disputes in the area as late as the 1690s.

And finally, the most formidable threat to Dutch rights along the Delaware came from the Swedes, who in 1637 sponsored an expedition to the Delaware River under the auspices of the newly formed Swedish West India Company. The expedition was commanded by Pieter Minuit, former commander of the New Netherland garrison and one of the three cofounders (with Willem Usselinx and Samuel Blommaert) of the Swedish West India Company. A settlement was established near present-day Wilmington, Delaware, named Fort Christina after Queen Christina of Sweden. The colony was called New Sweden. Between 1643 and 1653 the expansionist policies of Governor Johan Printz resulted in the extension of Swedish authority over the other European settlements in the valley.[55] Only the Dutch continued to resist the Swedes by

53. Weslager, *English on the Delaware*, pp. 74–75.

54. Ibid., p. 76; see also Appendix: "Document Relating to New Albion Sent by Charles I to Jamestown, c. 1642," pp. 255–57.

55. Johan Bjornssen Printz was a Swedish soldier of fortune. Sent out to New Sweden by the crown shortly after the original Dutch founders of the company had been bought out, he immediately sought to engulf the entire Delaware Valley fur trade with a series of fortifications at Varkens Kill (present-day Salem Creek, New Jersey), New Gothenburg on Tinicum Island, and Fort Krisholm near the mouth of the Schuylkill River. He was succeeded in 1653 by Johan Classon Rising, whose continuation of Printz's policies finally resulted in Stuyvesant's

building Fort Beversrede in 1648 on the Schuylkill River at the
present site of Philadelphia and Fort Casimir in 1651 (Newcastle,
Delaware). The Swedes attacked and captured Fort Casimir in
1654, thereby cutting off Fort Nassau from the sea. With an increasing percentage of the area's fur trade going to the Swedes at
Fort Christina, Stuyvesant was forced to turn to a military solution. He led an assault on the colony in 1655, forcing its surrender.
New Sweden was then annexed to New Netherland, but the debts
incurred by the Company to the city of Amsterdam (which loaned
sums to finance Stuyvesant's military expedition and occupation)
forced the directors to give over a portion of the west bank of the
Delaware to the city. The Company kept the area north of Christina Creek and south of Boompeties Hoeck (Bombay Hook). The
city of Amsterdam underwrote a colonizing expedition in 1657.
Under the leadership of Jacob Alrichs, 167 colonists were settled at
Fort Casimir, which was rechristened New Amstel. The Dutch
were to maintain their domination of the Delaware Valley until
their ouster by the English in 1664. In the meantime, however, the
conflicting claims of Holland, Sweden, and England to the Delaware region complicated the negotiations for boundaries elsewhere
in New Netherland.

When Stuyvesant received reports that the commissioners of
New England were considering giving official sanction to the activities of the Delaware Company of New Haven, he hurriedly
wrote to Governors Endicott and Bradford outlining the complexities of the claims to the Delaware Valley and recommending that
they not condone further settlement there until each of the claims
could be discussed and verified. He had no doubt that Dutch
claims, which antedated all others by at least a decade, would
eventually prevail, but his approach was clearly conciliatory and
flexible. Whether Stuyvesant's letters had any influence on the

---

punitive expedition. It is clear that Printz's activities were sanctioned by the
Swedish crown. See, for example, Amandus Johnson, trans., *The Instruction for
Johan Printz* (Philadelphia, 1930). The exhaustive treatment of the history of New
Sweden remains Amandus Johnson, *Swedish Settlements on the Delaware*, 2 vols.
(Philadelphia, 1911). A critical appraisal of Johnson's work and a succinct survey
of New Sweden's history is found in Weslager, *English on the Delaware*, pp. 54–71,
107–32.

decision of the commissioners not to sanction the activities of the Delaware Company is unknown, but it is certain that English claims were foremost in their minds when a few days later they informed the Dutch director-general that a resolution had passed the commission forbidding any subject of a foreign prince to carry on trade with the Indians from the Delaware to Cape Cod. The resolution was the result of a desperate effort to stop the trade in firearms with the Indians, but the fact of the extension of authority over areas already settled by other European nations suggests that the English colonial claim to the entire North American seaboard was being touted once again. Since the English were convinced that Dutch traders were the main culprits in the gun trade, the resolution may have been meant as a warning. Whatever its intentions, it constituted one of the boldest and least justified claims of territory yet made by the English colonies. The resolution was totally unenforceable, of course, but it excited near panic in New Amsterdam and compelled Stuyvesant to defend his policies against an angry wave of complaints that had arrived at the West India House in Amsterdam.[56]

The troubles with the English over boundaries and the continued problems plaguing New Netherland in the aftermath of the Kieft wars, not to mention the various religious squabbles Stuyvesant had involved himself in, had created a falling out on the Board of Nine Men. In 1649, in defiance of Stuyvesant's expressed orders, a delegation of the nine men drew up three documents for submission to the directors of the West India Company and Their High Mightinesses, the States General.[57] The three documents, among other things, blamed Director-General Stuyvesant for provoking the English resolution by his militancy. The directorship may have been swayed by the petitions, for shortly after their receipt in 1649, the Company informed Stuyvesant that war with the English was to be avoided at all costs. In no uncertain terms the directors made it clear that the States General would hold him personally responsible for any breach of the peace between New Netherland and the

---

56. O'Callaghan, *History of New Netherland*, 2:106–8.

57. The three documents were the "Remonstrance," "Petition," and "Additional Observations." The Remonstrance is printed in English in Jameson, *Narratives*, pp. 285–354. The Petition and Additional Observations are in *DCHNY*, 13:322–28.

colonies of New England: "If we . . . are compelled to a rupture with the English, we question not but the deputies of their High Mightinesses will take it amiss, especially as the delegates have left nothing untried to persuade that college that you will be the cause of such a war."[58] The directors need not have cautioned Stuyvesant. He was well aware of the dangers of war and had already adopted a less militant posture before the letter of reprimand arrived in New Netherland. He chose to ignore the resolution, as doubtless did every Dutch, Swedish, and French trader in North America. It was a wise policy because less than a year later the beheading of Charles I made the Cromwellian Rump Parliament an international pariah. England needed her old Protestant ally again, and the Dutch were anxious to use the opportunity to settle some of the issues that divided the two Protestant republics.

When England erupted in the Puritan revolution, the States General had tried to remain neutral, but the execution of Charles I horrified the Dutch and nearly threw the United Provinces into the arms of the absolutist governments of the Continent. Later, however, both sides demonstrated a willingness for conciliation. An English delegation was dispatched to The Hague in the early months of 1651 to conclude a treaty with the States General, and on January 28 the left-wing Calvinist independents in the States General succeeded in gaining recognition of the Republic of England. Unfortunately, in the negotiations for a possible Protestant alliance, arguments broke out over political and commercial matters. In October of that year the English Parliament passed a Navigation Act aimed specifically at excluding the Dutch from the English carrying trade.[59] Before the Navigation Act had been proclaimed, however, an atmosphere of renewed trust returned to Anglo-Dutch relations, and during the brief thaw the proposal for a North American conference to decide boundary disputes was accepted. The convention was planned for Hartford in September 1650.

Director-General Stuyvesant arrived in Hartford on September 23 with his secretary and enough Company soldiers and retainers to make a grand impression on the inhabitants of the village. The New England commissioners were already in attendance and had

58. Quoted in O'Callaghan, *History of New Netherland*, 2:107–8.
59. Maurice Ashley, *England in the Seventeenth Century* (Baltimore, 1961), p. 97.

received a list of grievances from New Haven that they were later to brandish before the Dutch delegation as proof of hostile and injurious actions taken by the Dutch against English colonists. Stuyvesant had also come prepared. When the time approached for him to address the conference, he began by complaining of English incursions in the Connecticut, Delaware, and Hudson river valleys. He noted that several misunderstandings had arisen over the years because the boundaries between the English and Dutch colonies had never been formally established. Thus he proposed that the conference take up the issue of boundaries immediately and that appropriate maps and other documents be prepared to submit to the respective home countries for final approval. In a written brief, which Stuyvesant had prepared before his arrival, he addressed his remarks to the "governors now meeting in New Netherland," implying that the settlement of Hartford was one of the misunderstandings. The commissioners demanded that Stuyvesant cease referring to the disputed territory as "New Netherland." Stuyvesant answered that he would refrain from calling the area New Netherland if his worthy colleagues would likewise not refer to it as New England. The commissioners reluctantly agreed, and the negotiations began.

The conference decided to appoint an arbitration board to examine the various claims and make recommendations about boundaries. The board was composed of Simon Bradstreet of Massachusetts, Thomas Prince and Thomas Willet, both of New Plymouth, and George Baxter of New Netherland. The last named was an English resident of Long Island who served Stuyvesant as an assistant during the conference. All members of the arbitration board were English, and the discussions were conducted in English. Still, there is no reason to suppose that Dutch rights were not defended adequately by Baxter, who despite his later defection was a loyal assistant to Stuyvesant at Hartford. The three men conferred for one day and retired to prepare a document entitled "Articles of Agreement" which was then signed by all participants.[60]

The text of the Articles of Agreement skirted or ignored the issues of most concern for the establishment of permanent claims

60. The complete text of the "Articles of Agreement" is printed in O'Callaghan, *History of New Netherland,* 2:151–55.

and boundaries. Instead, it dealt with practical matters, the most important of which was the setting of provisional boundaries for the Dutch and English colonies:

> Firstly, that upon Long Island a line run from the westernmost part of Oyster Bay, so, and in a straight and direct line, to the sea, shall be the bounds betwixt the English and Dutch there; the easterly part to belong to the English, the westernmost part to the Dutch. Secondly, the bounds upon the main[land] to begin at the west side of Greenwich Bay, being about four miles from Stamford, and so to run a northerly line twenty miles up into the country, and after as it shall be agreed by the two governments of the Dutch and of New Haven, provided the said line come not within ten miles of the Hudson River; and it is agreed that the Dutch shall not at any time hereafter build any house or habitation within six miles of the said line.[61]

The Dutch had clearly lost territory once claimed for New Netherland. Some of the more important concessions included the loss of the Connecticut Valley, the reduction by almost two-thirds of Dutch claims on Long Island, the loss of all claims to the area around Hartford, and the reduction of Dutch territory on the eastern side of the Hudson Valley to a ten-mile corridor, six miles of which were to remain unsettled as a demilitarized zone. Yet Pieter Stuyvesant found the terms acceptable and much preferable to the instability that had existed hitherto. Moreover, the provisional boundaries merely reflected the realities of demography. The English were already well into the colonization of eastern Long Island, and the Connecticut Valley had ceased to be Dutch the moment the first English farmers arrived to set up their towns. The Hudson Valley was more prized by the Dutch as a highway for the fur trade than as a place for large-scale agricultural development. Hence the eastern corridor was more than adequate to protect the fur trade, and the provisional nature of the boundaries did not rule out adjustments in the future. Indeed, this may have been the English commissioners' attitude as well, for they had clearly not pressed the Dutch as hard as some, particularly the New Haven settlers, might have wished. Although the Articles of Agreement were never to be

61. Ibid., pp. 153–54.

approved by the respective home governments, both sides honored the provisional boundaries established at the Hartford conference until the fall of New Netherland. Had peace continued to reign in Europe, the Hartford Articles of Agreement might have had a long life in American colonial history. Regardless, the document constituted a significant achievement in colonial diplomacy. Stuyvesant had accomplished what no other Dutch governor had—he had persuaded the English settlers of New England to accept boundaries and limits on their claims to colonial territory. Optimism would have to wait, however, because the outbreak of the first Anglo-Dutch war made the fate of New Netherland once again uncertain.

New Netherland's fate was sealed by the intensification of the maritime rivalry between England and the United Provinces in the last half of the seventeenth century, a rivalry destined to cause three wars. In the first war only the fortunate arrival of news of a truce prevented the conquest of New Netherland by a combined land and naval force launched from New England. Months before the second war was officially declared, the colony fell to the English. In the third war the colony was recaptured by a Dutch expedition only to be turned back to England in the peace negotiations. Thus New Netherland's last years were spent conducting and preparing for war. Nevertheless, it must have come as a surprise when a report reached New Amsterdam that a savage naval battle had been fought by the English and Dutch in the Dover Strait on May 28, 1652. By the time word reached New Netherland the war was two months old. The immediate cause of the collapse of peace had been the October 1651 passage of the Navigation Act.

Few acts of the English Parliament were to have as profound a historical impact as the Navigation Act of 1651. Passed by a Rump Parliament largely composed of regicides, hard-line religious zealots, and practical-minded merchants, it came to embody the system of mercantilism which would evolve in its wake for the next century and a half. The law simply and directly attempted to exclude all foreign ships from the English maritime trade by prohibiting "the introduction into any territory of the Commonwealth of produce of any country in Asia, Africa, or America, except in vessels owned by Englishmen or by the inhabitants of English colonies, and manned by crews of which more than one half were of English nationality."[62]

There was little doubt against whom the Navigation Act was aimed. Commercial competition between the two Protestant seapowers had been keen for years, and a number of bloody confrontations "beyond the line" had aroused nationalistic sentiment on both sides. War hysteria, fed by rumors of atrocities in the Indies and elsewhere, created a market for jingoistic publications that kept the public of both countries stirred up if not well informed.[63] Nowhere were the rumors more apocalyptic or the war hysteria more rampant than in the American colonies of both nations.

When news reached New Amsterdam of the outbreak of war with England, it excited a near panic. Stuyvesant had been expecting war and had even begun a review of the colony's defenses in the expectation of a naval and land attack from the English colonies. Such an eventuality had been the recurrent nightmare of every governor who ever served in New Netherland. Stuyvesant, however, was the only one who had to face a serious threat of attack. His response was what one might have expected of an old soldier: he turned every means at hand to the effort to make New Netherland impregnable. But first he tried diplomacy.

In the Connecticut Valley English settlers became convinced of a Dutch conspiracy to arm the Indians of the area in preparation for an all-out attack on the English towns. The rumors took many forms but the most persistent told of the Dutch arming the Indians daily at New Amsterdam while plans were being formulated for an attack. The commissioners of New England took the rumors seriously and in April 1653 called a special meeting of the confederation at Boston to investigate the Dutch threat. After several futile attempts to uncover evidence of a conspiracy, the commissioners contented themselves with drawing up a long document which accused the New Netherlanders of being in "bloody colours" with the Indians of New England. Although no facts were cited to prove the existence of the conspiracy, the document addressed to Stuyvesant was deadly serious in its tone. When the director-general received the document, he immediately penned a reply denying the

62. George M. Trevelyan, *History of England*, 3 vols. (Garden City, N.Y., 1926; rpt. 1953), 2:211–12n.

63. See note 77 below.

conspiracy and inviting delegates from New England to come to New Amsterdam and investigate for themselves. The commissioners accepted Stuyvesant's offer and dispatched three men to New Amsterdam. As a precautionary measure, they approved the recruitment of a five-hundred-man militia.[64]

The delegation arrived in New Amsterdam in the early summer of 1653 determined to ferret out evidence of the Dutch contraband trade in firearms. Shortly after arriving on Manhattan, the delegation exchanged angry words with Stuyvesant. In the days to follow several heated quarrels broke out between the members of the delegation and Stuyvesant's staff. Most of the time was spent in issuing new lists of grievances against the Dutch. When the investigators finally took their leave, they were as firmly convinced of the conspiracy as before they arrived. One member of the delegation used his time in New Amsterdam for a more practical purpose. Captain John Leverett, who would command the militia force soon to be assembled in New England, used the opportunity to observe the defenses of the colony. His was essentially a reconnaissance mission, and he spent his time in New Amsterdam noting the town's weak state of preparedness and calculating the most likely avenues of attack on the fortress at the island's tip. Diplomacy having failed, Stuyvesant turned his attention east, where an English fifth column appeared to be rising among the towns on Long Island.[65]

Not content to wait for the results of the investigation, the leaders of the New Haven colony had begun a correspondence with John Underhill, an Englishman living in New Netherland and the commander of Kieft's militia during the Indian wars. Underhill appears to have been a born adventurer. A militant defender of English rights on Long Island, he had long been a problem for Dutch authorities at New Amsterdam. The letters from New Haven asked Underhill's assistance in uncovering evidence of the Dutch-Indian conspiracy, which he agreed to do. When word reached Stuyvesant that Underhill was openly flaunting his mission, the director-general had him arrested. Released a short time later, he began to campaign openly against Dutch authority on Long Island. In one carefully staged provocation he raised the flag

64. O'Callaghan, *History of New Netherland*, 2:254–55.
65. Ibid., pp. 257–58.

of Parliament at Hempstead (Heemsteade in Dutch) and Flushing and proceeded to preach revolution against the Dutch. He was forced to flee to New England after this last boisterous episode. There he offered his services to the people of Rhode Island.[66]

Even after Underhill's departure, the English towns of Hempstead and Flushing continued to be centers of insurgency. They were a constant worry to Stuyvesant and a source of friction between the director-general and his superiors in Amsterdam. The directors of the Company, convinced that the liberal terms offered to the English settlers by Kieft and Stuyvesant were responsible for this outbreak of disloyalty, wished Stuyvesant to move vigorously against the English traitors. They warned him to be more cautious in granting privileges to the English in New Netherland, "that we may not nourish serpents in our bosom, who finally might devour our hearts."[67] In all fairness to Stuyvesant, any action he took against the English on Long Island was sure to provoke an attack from New England. Caught between the need to establish Dutch authority over the English towns and the realization that to do so might endanger the entire colony of New Netherland, he chose to make New Amsterdam secure from a possible attack.

On the morning of March 13, 1653, nearly a month before the meeting of the commissioners of the Confederation of New England, Stuyvesant had called an emergency meeting of the Council of New Netherland, together with the Burgomasters and Schepens of the City of New Amsterdam. He opened the meeting by reading some recent letters from the directors of the Company which told of reports they had received confirming war preparations in New England. Although the directors were unclear about the nature of

66. The colorful Captain John Underhill has had several biographers. Whether he was New Netherland's most celebrated traitor or New England's most famous spy depends on one's perspective. John Fiske labeled him "a combination of swashbuckler, heretic, and gay Lothario." His decisive role in the Indian wars is well documented, but his later relation with Stuyvesant has been less objectively assessed. See Henry C. Shelley, *John Underhill: Captain of New England and New Netherland* (New York, 1932), pp. 360–63. Shelley gives credence to the Dutch-Indian conspiracy and believes that Underhill's actions were justified by Stuyvesant's autocracy, but I have been unable to confirm the presence of a conspiracy. See also L. Effingham De Forest and Anne Lawrence De Forest, *Captain John Underhill: Gentleman Soldier of Fortune* (New York, 1934).

67. *DCHNY*, 14:216.

the preparations or whether they were defensive or offensive, they commanded Stuyvesant to move swiftly to repair and expand the defense works around New Amsterdam. At Stuyvesant's urging the delegates adopted several resolutions for the defense of the colony.[68] One resolution established a citizens' guard to police the town after dark. The fear of English spies and saboteurs may have prompted this action, for the guard was allowed to lapse after the war. New Amsterdam would not get a permanent police force until 1658, when Stuyvesant established the Rattle Watch.[69] Other resolutions pledged to repair the fort and raise revenue to pay for the defense of the colony. A final resolution established a defense strategy for the colony and created a civil defense system for the town of New Amsterdam:

> Considering said Fort Amsterdam [sic] cannot hold all the inhabitants nor defend all the houses and dwellings in the City, it is deemed necessary to surround the greater part of the City with a high stockade and a small breastwork, to draw in time of need all inhabitants behind it and defend as much as possible their persons and goods against attacks. For the present it is impossible to protect by stockades the villages, where the people live at great distances from each other and thus carry out the good intentions and orders of our Masters. It is also not possible, to protect and defend them in such manner against attacks; therefore it has been decided to concentrate the forces of New Netherland for the better protection of one place.[70]

At the time, an armed merchant ship, the *Visscher*, was in the harbor, and the delegates issued a directive to her captain, Jan Jansen, "to bend his sails, to load his pieces of artillery and to keep his ship constantly clear for every emergency."[71] Stuyvesant then suspended the meeting until afternoon, while he conferred with his council and the leading citizens of New Amsterdam on the creation of a defense fund.

68. Court Minutes of the Burgomasters and Schepens of New Amsterdam, March 13, 1653, in Berthold Fernow, ed., *The Records of New Amsterdam*, 7 vols. (New York, 1897), 1:65–66.

69. John E. O'Connor, "The Rattle Watch of New Amsterdam," *De Halve Maen* 43 (1968): 11ff.

70. Court Minutes, March 13, 1653, pp. 65–66.

71. Ibid., p. 66.

When the meeting resumed, the first item of business was the announcement of a defense assessment on the leading citizens of the city. The defense fund was set at 5,000 fl., with assessments ranging from 50 fl. to 200 fl. spread somewhat unevenly among forty-four individuals.[72] The burgomasters and *schepens* then met separately to consider the defense of the town and their contribution to it. Their meeting must have been heated because the representatives returned with a resolution that clearly demonstrated that the citizens of New Amsterdam were still anxious to try diplomacy before resigning themselves to war with the New England colonies. A resolution was sent to the director-general requesting him to dispatch "some delegates to the respective Colonies of New England, our neighbors, deputies of which, as is learned, are going to meet on the first of April next." It was hoped that the delegation could offer "good and binding conditions for the continuation of our former intercourse and commerce, besides learning how far they are affected by the differences and the war in Europe, broken out between their High Mightinesses and the present government of England."[73] Stuyvesant reluctantly agreed to send a diplomatic mission to New England, but he must have known that the moment was not right to approach the commissioners directly, for he delayed the selection of envoys until after the April meeting of the commissioners. Meanwhile, war hysteria had spread across New England, bringing with it renewed calls for a military expedition against New Netherland. The smaller New England colonies appeared to have been the more demanding in their requests for military action against the Dutch.

Meetings of the commissioners of New England were becoming increasingly heated as the colonies of New Haven and Connecticut clamored for war and Massachusetts and New Plymouth sought a more reasonable course of action. The hawks were led by the New Haven men, who doubtless viewed a war with the Dutch as an excellent opportunity to secure their hold on the Delaware Valley. Disgusted with Massachusetts's pacifism, the leaders of the New Haven colony wrote Oliver Cromwell personally, requesting an expedition against the Dutch. In the letter, they denounced the

72. Ibid., pp. 66–67.
73. Ibid., p. 68.

cowardly behavior of their fellow New Englanders who they said feared "their own swords." They concluded by requesting three frigates and an order from Parliament commanding Massachusetts to support her countrymen in the war against the Dutch.[74]

In June 1653 the people of Rhode Island became aware that they had been excluded from the war preparations of the other New England colonies, and panic set in. Rumors circulated that a Dutch attack was expected at any time along the coast of Long Island Sound. Turning to Captain John Underhill, whose activities in Rhode Island had undoubtedly added considerable credence to the rumors, the citizens of the colony authorized the equipping of a force of men under his command for an expedition against Fort Good Hope, the Dutch trading post on the Connecticut River. In July the expedition moved against the trading post and took it without opposition.[75]

By the time Stuyvesant heard about the capture of Fort Good Hope it was too late. Bracing himself for a war with New England, he moved to secure his southern flank by sending two envoys to Virginia. Acting governor Richard Bennett received the envoys cordially but declined the offer of a nonaggression pact. Dominie Samuel Drisius was sent to Virginia at the close of the year, and his mission was a success. The Virginia governor agreed to a commercial treaty between the two colonies, and although no mention was made of the ongoing Anglo-Dutch war, the treaty secured New Netherland's southern border against English attack. Stuyvesant's worst fears were to be realized, however, when Cromwell's republic sent four warships to New England in February 1654.[76]

The lord protector may have been encouraged to undertake an expedition against New Netherland as a way of silencing the public outcry over atrocities attributed to the Dutch by an anonymous pamphlet entitled *The Second Amboyna Tragedy; or a Faithful Account of a Bloody, Treacherous and Cruel Plot of the Dutch in America, Purporting the Total Ruin and Murder of all the English Colonists of New England.*[77] This pamphlet had aroused the friends of the New En-

74. O'Callaghan, *History of New Netherland*, 2:259.
75. Shelley, *John Underhill*, pp. 365–83.
76. O'Callaghan, *History of New Netherland*, 2:235–36.
77. The pamphlet appeared in London in early 1654. Actually the Amboyna Tragedy took place in 1623 on the island of Amboyna in the Dutch Moluccas. A

gland theocracy (who were legion in this period) to call for an assault on the Dutch colony. The letters from the New Haven colony may also have convinced Cromwell that a quick end to the unpleasant war could be attained with a victory on the Hudson. Whatever the motivations, the intentions were clear. New Netherland was to be captured.

Owing to poor sailing conditions, the small fleet did not arrive in New England until June 1654. Notwithstanding, steps had already been taken to raise troops in Hartford and New Haven. Massachusetts remained officially aloof from these activities, but nearly five hundred militiamen were reported to have been recruited in the Bay Colony. At the end of June, the fleet had been revictualed and the troops assembled for the expedition. Nine hundred foot soldiers were to take part in the assault, accompanied by a company of cavalry with their steeds.

In New Amsterdam things were going badly for Stuyvesant as he frantically tried to prepare the colony for war. At Gravesande, his former assistant, George Baxter, had initiated a correspondence with New England authorities and was attempting to organize a Long Island militia. At Middleburg, site of the recent dispute with the Lutherans, the inhabitants proposed to "open the ball" with an attack on their fellow New Netherlanders. Stuyvesant reacted to these internal threats with a proclamation aimed at the English conspirators. The proclamation forbade suspicious persons from moving their belongings to safer areas and imposed summary trials for those convicted of "stirring to mutiny" the citizens of the colony.[78]

On the eve of the fleet's departure a merchant vessel arrived bringing news of a truce. A day of general thanksgiving was pro-

---

small contingent of English settlers had colonized Amboyna and were actively engaged in growing cloves for the spice trade. The Dutch sent a Captain Towerson with a company of soldiers to the island to dislodge the intruders. The Dutch troops began to run amuck shortly after stepping ashore. The colonists were tortured and mutilated until a few confessed to crimes against the VOC (East India Company). After receiving the confessions, the English were put to the sword. Only a few escaped. See D. W. Davies, *A Primer of Dutch Seventeenth-Century Trade* (The Hague, 1961), p. 52.

78. O'Callaghan, *History of New Netherland*, 2:263–65.

claimed throughout New England. On Manhattan, Director-General Stuyvesant received the good news with a sigh of relief. When he announced the peace in New Amsterdam, there were celebrations in the streets. New Netherland had been saved.

New Netherland had been lucky; she would not be so fortunate in the next war. Still, the last ten years were prosperous ones for the colony. Immigration increased annually after 1654, and the fur trade reached its greatest volume during the entire colonial period—forty-six thousand pelts per year from Fort Orange alone.[79] Stuyvesant continued to have problems with his colonists over religious conformity and the rights of local government, but the last years saw an expansion of local rights throughout most of New Netherland. Dutch towns requested and received charters in the 1660s similar to those granted the English towns on Long Island in the late 1640s and early 1650s, and the burgher rights granted to New Amsterdam in 1653 and to New Amstel in 1656 testified to the increasing sophistication of New Netherland's political culture.[80] Linguistic, religious, ethnic, and racial pluralism would continue to characterize the colony's population, but the restless single men who had once constituted the majority of the European population were gradually becoming a minority as large numbers of families took advantage of the generous incentives offered by the 1640 Freedoms and Exemptions (and subsequent revisions) to settle permanently in New Netherland. The new colonists came to earn their fortunes in the fur

79. For immigration see Chapter 6 above. The figure for the fur trade at Fort Orange comes from Allen W. Trelease, *Indian Affairs in Colonial New York: The Seventeenth Century* (Ithaca, 1960), p. 131.

80. Langdon Wright argues correctly that the charters granted to the Dutch towns contained fewer privileges than those given the English. Still, throughout New Netherland local government appeared to be gaining at the expense of centralized company administration. See Wright, "Local Government and Central Authority," pp. 12–13, 28–29. New Amsterdam's fight for municipal government began with the struggle of the Board of Nine Men in 1649. Submitting a Remonstrance and Petition to their High Mightinesses complaining of the lack of "suitable government," they touched off a heated controversy that pitted Stuyvesant as the defender of executive government against the leading citizens of New Amsterdam. After years of delay, the States General finally granted a charter to New Amsterdam in 1653 which, among other things, established the right of the citizens to select a *schout* (sheriff) two burgomasters (city managers), and five *schepens* (aldermen). See Philip L. White, "Municipal Government Comes to Manhattan," *New-York Historical Society Quarterly* 37 (1953): 146–57.

trade and by farming, and the interests of the white farmer and trader clashed with those of the Indian farmer and trader. The result was another series of tragic Indian wars.

The wars of Governor-General Kieft had exhausted both white and red societies, but the devastation they wrought on European settlements in the interior had been so catastrophic that large areas of New Netherland remained devoid of Europeans for several years. Villages had disappeared as the bedraggled colonists made their way to the relative safety of Manhattan Island and Fort New Amsterdam. Entire Indian settlements had been wiped out as well. It has been estimated, for example, that the Wappingers tribes along the western bank of the lower Hudson had lost over 50 percent of their population of three thousand.[81] Moreover, disease had taken a terrible toll of Indian life. In one particularly virulent outbreak of smallpox in 1656 the epidemic spread throughout the entire population of Indians in the Hudson Valley, killing by Adriaen Van der Donck's unscientific estimation almost 90 percent of the settled Indian village population.[82] All of these factors had played a part in maintaining the peace between Europeans and

81. Shelburne F. Cook, "Interracial Warfare and Population Decline among the New England Indians," *Ethnohistory* 20 (1973): 11.

82. Adriaen Van der Donck, *A Description of New Netherland*, ed. Thomas F. O'Donnell (Syracuse, 1968), p. 64, and Hauptman and Lawrence, "Dutch-Aboriginal Interaction," p. 174. Even though smallpox continued to break out occasionally among New Netherland's European population, the Dutch colony may have had the most "disease-experienced" European population in North America. An examination of the origins of the colonists who came to New Netherland shows that, for the most part, New Netherlanders came from central and western Europe (Holland, Germanies, and France-Belgium) with a large percentage from the Scandinavian countries of Sweden and Finland. These areas had literally been "burned over" with smallpox during and after the Thirty Years' War. Immigrants from such areas carried with them not only the bacillus but also a formidable population-level resistance to its scourges. The disease became an unconscious biological weapon for the Europeans. Thus New Netherland's Europeans probably survived the ravages of 1656 and 1662 in significantly larger numbers than did the Indians. For the origins of New Netherland's colonists see Chapter 6 above and Cohen, "How Dutch Were the Dutch of New Netherland?" For an explanation of how disease resistance works, see William H. McNeill, *Plagues and Peoples* (Garden City, N.Y., 1976), pp. 1–13, 176–207. For a somewhat dated survey of the impact of smallpox on the American Indians, see Esther Wagner Stearn and Allen E. Stearn, *The Effect of Smallpox on the Destiny of the Amerindian* (Boston, 1945).

Indians for almost fifteen years. Demographic change came rapidly to New Netherland in this period, however. The pressure of expanding populations, both of the Europeans who arrived in large numbers after 1657 and of the Indians who were beginning to recover from the twin scourges of war and disease, accelerated the frequency of contact between white and red culture and consequently the possibility for misunderstanding and violence.

Stuyvesant's first Indian war broke out while he was dislodging the Swedes from the Delaware Valley in 1655. While most of the soldiers and a large number of the men were absent with Stuyvesant, a combined force of Mahicans, Pachamis, Esopus, and Hackensack Indians launched an assault on Manhattan Island. Avoiding New Amsterdam itself, they concentrated their depredations on the farms and orchards surrounding the fort. Before Stuyvesant could return, the Peach Tree War, as it came to be called by the colonists (because it had supposedly begun in a peach orchard), had spread beyond the confines of Manhattan to villages on Long Island and in the Hudson Valley. Stuyvesant was finally able to crush the Indians in a series of attacks on their farms and villages. The costs had been high: fifty colonists dead, sixty Indians slain, twenty-eight farms destroyed, five hundred cattle lost, and an entire crop of corn burned to the stalks.[83]

The colony's next Indian war erupted in September 1659, when a dozen or so colonists and company soldiers attacked a handful of Indians while they drank themselves into a stupor around a campfire near the Hudson River settlement of Esopus (present Kingston). The cause of the incident has remained hidden, but its consequences were soon evident. From fall 1659 until July 1660 the war raged on. In the Hudson Valley several attacks on European farms and villages took place, and the savage character of the warfare struck terror and excited panic among Europeans from Fort Orange to New Amstel. The war ended in the summer of 1660, when Stuyvesant relieved the village of Esopus after a twenty-three-day siege. In the peace negotiations Stuyvesant agreed to return a band of Indians he had sold into slavery in Curaçao and to pay gifts to the Esopus and Wappingers as a gesture of peace and friendship. During the treaty discussions the sachems of the Esopus tribe warned

83. Michael Kammen, *Colonial New York: A History* (New York, 1975), p. 68.

Stuyvesant that the location of the new settlement of Nieuwe Dorp (literally, "new village," present Hurley) was unacceptable because it occupied land used by the tribe for farming. The warning was not to be heeded. Three years later, on June 7, 1663, after a Dutch land cession had expanded the Nieuwe Dorp grant to include the disputed farm land, the Esopus Indians threw themselves into a series of brutal attacks on the villages of Nieuwe Dorp and Wilt-wyck (the new name given Esopus in the charter of 1661).[84]

The so-called Second Esopus War did not end until May 1664, and then only because the Indians were bled white and exhausted by repeated savage attacks on their farms, villages, and families. The peace treaty imposed upon the tribes of the lower Hudson estuary ended their dominance of the region. The river Indians (Delawares, Raritans, and Mahicans) were compelled to cede most of their ancestral tribal lands around the European settlements. They ceased to be a major obstacle to European expansion in the colonial period.[85] When Stuyvesant returned to New Amsterdam in May 1664, he proclaimed a day of thanksgiving to mark the end of the long and bloody Indian war. Three months later, the Dutch themselves had fallen to conquerors.

In the summer of 1663, James, Duke of York and Albany, broth-er to Charles II, became the proprietor of the territory that would soon become New York. In the first month of the new year an invasion plan had been drawn up at the Council of Foreign Planta-tions by James himself and a few members of his household. The plan followed closely that devised by Samuel Maverick of Mas-sachusetts, who had petitioned the Council of Foreign Plantations in 1661 urging an immediate attack on New Netherland. He be-lieved that a force consisting of three frigates and several hundred soldiers would be required, but the effort would be worthwhile because the revenue from the fur trade alone would more than compensate for the expense. The plan had been rejected in 1661 because only a war with the United Provinces could possibly justi-fy an attack on the Dutch colony. Thus matters stood until the spring of 1664.[86]

84. Hauptman and Lawrence, "Dutch-Aboriginal Interaction," p. 173.
85. Ibid.; Kammen, *Colonial New York*, p. 69.
86. Robert C. Ritchie, *The Duke's Province: A Study of New York Politics and Society* (Chapel Hill, 1977), pp. 12–14.

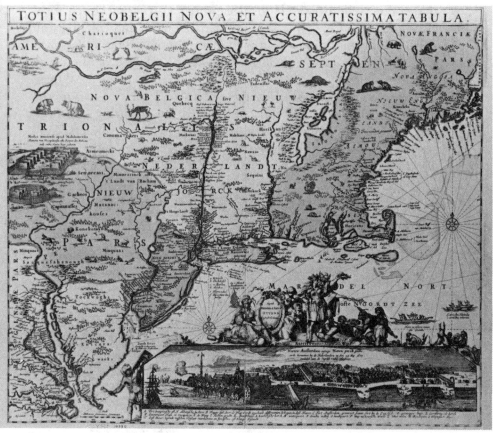

Map of New Netherland commemorating the recapture of the colony in the third Anglo-Dutch war, August 24, 1673, with inset view of New York City, from Carolus Allardt, *Totius Neobelgii nova et accuratissima tabula* (Amsterdam, 1673). Courtesy of the New York State Library, Albany.

The second Anglo-Dutch war was precipitated by events along the slave coasts of West Africa, where the Dutch West India Company and the recently chartered Royal African Company were locked in a deadly competition to acquire control of the best slaving posts. When Sir Robert Holmes captured a string of Dutch forts along the Gold Coast in 1663, an unofficial naval and colonial war engulfed the maritime empires of both nations. The undeclared war was only months old when the Duke of York received his royal patent on March 12, 1664. The patent gave the duke control over an area presently occupied by three states and parts of two more. To secure his colony the duke authorized the outfitting of a fleet and the recruitment of an army of three hundred soldiers. Assembled in Portsmouth during the spring, the fleet departed England on May 15, 1664.[87]

The expedition had planned to rendezvous on eastern Long Island, but rough weather in the crossing scattered the ships, so that they straggled into Long Island Sound separately in the last weeks of July. On July 29 the expedition assembled at Nantucket Island, while Colonel Richard Nicolls, its commander, completed his final preparations for the attack. Sailing west into the sound, the invasion fleet bore down on New Amsterdam. Meanwhile, Stuyvesant had received reports of the fleet from several sources, including Sir John Scott, an English rogue who had informed the director-general in January 1664 that New Netherland was to be conquered by an English fleet after the region had been officially ceded to James, Duke of York. Stuyvesant had corresponded with the directors of the Company asking them what they knew of an invasion fleet poised to fall on New Netherland. The directors responded by reassuring Stuyvesant that the fleet was being prepared to attack the wayward Puritans of New England.[88]

When the sails of the English ships were first sighted at New Amsterdam, Stuyvesant must have known the game was over. With fewer than 150 professional soldiers at his command and a panic-stricken civilian population imploring him to surrender, the old soldier gave in to reason and the humanitarian arguments of Dominie Drisius. In a tavern along the Strand, the irascible old Dutch governor and New Amsterdam's two burgomasters met

87. Ibid., pp. 15, 17–18, 20.
88. Ibid., p. 20.

with Governor John Winthrop, Jr., of Connecticut. Winthrop sought to negotiate a surrender by assuring the Dutch that their commercial interests would be protected. He also told them that immigration from the United Provinces could continue unabated under English rule. As evidence of his goodwill the English governor revealed a letter from Colonel Nicolls guaranteeing the rights of Dutch trade and continued immigration. Apparently this was enough to convince the burgomasters, for they offered to read the terms immediately to the people of the city. Stuyvesant could stomach the proceedings no longer. Rising to leave, he snatched up the letter, tearing it in two before he stormed out the door.[89]

By the end of the day the contents of the letter had been discussed by every burgher in the city. A large crowd gathered before the Stadhuys demanding to see the letter. Stuyvesant showed up within minutes and attempted to whip the crowd into a war fever. He implored them to fight for their honor, their country, and their colony, but the stunned people refused to listen. Finally, Stuyvesant agreed to reveal the contents of the letter. Sometime later a delegation of ninety-three citizens signed a document calling for the immediate surrender of the colony. Finding no one to stand with him in defiance of the English, the director-general agreed to terms for the surrender of New Netherland in a meeting held at his *bouwerij* on August 27, 1664.[90]

Within the week the other Dutch garrisons fell. Six days of war had resulted in the loss of the entire colony. New Netherland had become New York. The achievements of a half-century could not change the final outcome. Surrounded by English colonists, occupying a vast territory that attracted the greed of even the best men, decimated by Indian war, wracked by internal divisions that reflected the pluralism of the colony's polyglot population, New Netherland had succumbed to the pressures that had rendered its entire history precarious. The great merchant families of Amsterdam would continue their operations for two more decades, and several generations of New Yorkers would jealously guard their Dutch culture, trying to preserve it in rituals, architecture, and song, but in the end, they too would be forced to adopt English ways or find themselves outcasts in an English society.

89. *DCHNY*, 2:248–50.
90. Ritchie, *Duke's Province*, p. 22.

Conclusion

It should be evident that the particular historical method used in this study is capable of illuminating only some portions of the history of New Netherland. The perspective has been imperial and Dutch, focusing more on the eastern than the western side of the Atlantic and more on the economic relationship between the colony and the fatherland than internal events in New Netherland. I believe this approach offers a new perspective on the first half-century of New York's history.

New Netherland was a unique colony in many respects. As the best North American source of furs for at least the first half of the seventeenth century, it pandered to Dutch merchants' hopes for riches. The trade, however, was risky and expensive. With the establishment of the West India Company in 1621 the trade was lost to all but a few Amsterdam merchants who held shares in the Company and exploited their privileges with ruthless cunning. The Company began its long decline almost immediately after the brief excitement of Admiral Piet Heyn's capture of the Spanish treasure fleet. Various plans were formulated to attract colonists to New Netherland; but nothing succeeded like the lure of profits in the fur trade and the hope of acquiring free land. The latter phenomenon suggests interesting parallels with the history of Virginia. By 1639 the West India Company was forced by an impatient States General to relinquish its stranglehold on the colony's trade, and except for population losses incurred in a series of bloody Indian wars, New Netherland grew by stops and starts to nearly nine thousand inhabitants by the time of the English conquest.

The last twenty years witnessed a growing population and a rising trade with the fatherland. These two phenomena were related, and much of the profits in these years came from the provisioning trade. In both the provisioning trade and the transoeanic exchange of furs, hides, tobacco, timber, and slaves the trump cards were held by the Amsterdam merchants, a relatively small group of whom were specializing in the New Netherland trade as early as the 1630s. Their relationship with the colony was complex, reflecting the intricate nature of Dutch commercial life and an amazing penchant for deriving profit from an enterprise that virtually bankrupted the mighty West India Company.

The financial clout wielded by the Amsterdam merchants allowed little room for the emergence of an indigenous colonial merchant community. One might have grown up in time, but the risks involved with trading with the more populous English colonies after the first Anglo-Dutch war closed off, or at least made less accessible, the one sure avenue for the development of a colony-based merchant community. For the colonists of New Netherland the hold of the Amsterdam merchants could be felt in the persistently high costs of provisions, trade goods, and European consumer items. Yet the evidence remains suggestive rather than conclusive. That the Amsterdam merchants influenced on-station prices for furs and trade goods seems evident, but how much control they exercised over the internal economic development of the colony remains unclear. Certainly, their reign was brief. Their ruin was brought about by Anglo-Dutch commercial rivalry in the last half of the seventeenth century. Just the threat of maritime war imposed crushing burdens on the transoceanic trade between Amsterdam and New Netherland. Although several scholars have argued that the English Navigation Acts were not very effective in eliminating Dutch competition in the carrying trade, the evidence to be found in the notarial records of Amsterdam suggests otherwise.

Because the North Atlantic trade was largely based on credit obtained through volatile bottomry bonds and complex financial instruments, it could ill afford any sustained disruption. The cost of marine insurance alone could rise by 50 percent during times of war, and most of the Amsterdam merchants were cautious in their enterprises. When New Netherland became a victim of the commercial rivalry between England and the United Provinces, they were quick to leave the trade, particularly when the obstacles became too difficult in the aftermath of the English conquest.

New York underwent a painful and (by at least one interpretation) politically violent anglicization in the two decades following the surrender of New Netherland. Nonetheless, the anglicization of New York was surprisingly rapid, particularly in commerce and trade; in less than one generation the ethnic Dutch merchant establishment was supplanted. Hence New Netherland passed on to New York a verdant wilderness served by a magnificent river, an ethnically and culturally diverse population, and a Dutch merchant community not much older than the English one that would replace it. The new conquerors could gaze upon a landscape that bore a few marks of European habitation on the surface but was poised to enter into the Atlantic economy as a grain- and staple-producing colony with the second generation of English farmers. To those thousands who came after the Dutch the land still stood in its virginal state, awaiting the ax and the plow.

Bibliography

PRIMARY SOURCES

Manuscripts

Algemeen Rijksarchief (National Archives). The Hague, Netherlands.

Staten-Generaal bijlagen (States General Collections)
Several important documents relating to New Netherland were found in these monumental collections. Many of these were first extracted by John R. Brodhead; a large number, however, are used for the first time in this book.

De ordinaris resolutiën (Official Resolutions):
Minuten van de notulen van de vergaderingen, 1576–1684. 257 vols.
De eerste serie registers van net-resolutiën, 1576–1671. 148 vols.
De tweede serie registers van net-resolutiën, 1637–1795. 437 vols.
De secrete resolutiën (Secret Resolutions):
De minuten van de secrete notulen van de Staten-Generaal, 1592–1670. 656 vols.
Registers van secrete net-resolutiën van de Staten-Generaal, 1592–1796. 238 vols.
De ordinaris en secrete resolutiën over speciale onderwerpen. (Official and Secret Resolutions Concerning Special Projects):
Registers van minuut- en net-resolutiën, alsmede extract-resolutiën van de Staten-Generaal over speciale onderwerpen, 17e en 18e eeuw. 61 vols. Only the following volumes contain information relating to New Netherland:
> Copie-resoluties der Staten-Generaal rakende octrooien en exploicten, 1614–1768. 1 vol.
> Registers van resolutiën betreffende de Oost-Indische Compagnie, 1602–70. 3 vols.

Registers van resolutiën betreffende de West-Indische Compagnie, 1638–70. 3 vols.

Archief van de Staten-Generaal, locketkas: West-Indische Compagnie, No. 30.

Staten-Generaal liassen (States General Files)
This remarkable collection contains the incoming letters and documents from the provinces and the chartered companies as well as miscellaneous minutes of committee meetings and several volumes of extracts from documents long since lost. Only a few of these files were examined for this study. A complete review of the materials on file would take a lifetime and is not to be attempted by a foreigner. My work in the liassen was largely superficial, although several important documents were turned up, thanks mostly to the expert staff of the Algemeen Rijksarchief, who demonstrated much patience in showing an *uitlander* through this collection. The following packets of documents were used:
De liassen West-Indische Compagnie, 1623–77. Numbered packets, nos. 5751–5815.
De liassen Admiraliteijten, 1613–1795. 245 packets cataloged by year.

Resolutiën van de Staten van Holland en West Friesland (Resolutions of the States of Holland and West Friesland):
Only volume 55, which contained the request of the Walloons to settle in New Netherland, was used.

Aanwinsten (Acquisitions)
This miscellaneous collection contains materials donated to the national archives by families, government agencies, and the like. The documents are cataloged in "yearbooks" corresponding to the date the archives cataloged the donations. One very important item was discovered in this collection, the extant copy of the Freedoms and Exemptions for 1628.

Archief de Admiraleteijtencollege, Verzameling Van der Heim. Packet 413.

Gemeentelijke Archief van Amsterdam (Municipal Archives of Amsterdam). Amsterdam, Netherlands.

This is one of the finest city archives in the world, thanks largely to the work of the late Simon Hart. Scholars familiar with the history of Dutch trade and commerce in the seventeenth century revere the work of Hart, and much of what is known of the intricacies of Dutch economic history in the golden age is the product in one fashion or another of his lifelong work in cataloging the massive notarial archives of Amsterdam. His collection of notarial records for New Netherland is the basis for many of the findings in this study.

Notarial Archieven (Notarial Archives)
"Hart Collection" of Notarial Records. Approximately 5,000 separate entries on "Nieuw Nederland" used for this book. Cataloged by the "protocols" of the separate notaries and numbered consecutively by date. The work on the index system to this collection continues under the senior archivist of the Gemeentelijke Archief, Hans Ernst. In 1985 there were more than 7000 cards containing brief summaries of approximately 2200 notarial minutes. This remains a tiny fraction of the Amsterdam notarial archives, which is estimated to contain two million notarial minutes just for the period 1624–1664.

Begrafenis register van de Westerkerk van Amsterdam, Jaarboek voor 1659.
Doop, trouw en boedel boeken van Amsterdam. No. 473, May 28, 1654.

Published Sources

Asher, G. M., ed. *Henry Hudson the Navigator.* London: Hakluyt Society, 1860.
Bloch, Julius M.; Herschkowitz, Leo; Scott, Kenneth; and Sherman, Constance D., eds. *An Account of Her Majesty's Revenue in the Province of New York, 1701–09: The Customs Records of Early Colonial New York.* Ridgewood, N.J.: Gregg Press, 1966.
Bradford, William. "Correspondence of William Bradford." *New York Historical Society Collections*, 2d ser., 1 (1841):365–68.
_____. *The History of Plymouth Plantation, 1608–1650.* Ed. Harold Paget. New York: E. P. Dutton, 1920.
Brodhead, John Romeyn, comp.; O'Callaghan, Edmund B., and Fernow, Berthold, eds. and trans. *Documents Relative to the Colonial History of the State of New York.* 15 vols. New York: Weed, Parsons, 1856–87.
Fernow, Berthold, ed. *The Records of New Amsterdam.* 7 vols. New York: Knickerbocker Press, 1897.
Fz, S. Muller, ed. *De reis van Jan Cornelisz May naar de IJszee en de Amer-*

ikaansche kust, 1611–1612. The Hague: Werken Linschoten Vereeniging, 1909.

Gehring, Charles T., ed. *A Guide to Dutch Manuscripts Relating to New Netherland in United States Repositories*. Albany: State University of New York Press, 1978.

———, ed. and trans. *Land Papers*. Baltimore: Genealogical Publishing Company, 1980.

Jameson, J. Franklin, ed. *Narratives of New Netherland, 1609–1664*. New York: Charles Scribner's Sons, 1909.

Johnson, Amandus, trans. *The Instruction for Johan Printz*. Philadelphia: Swedish Colonial Society, 1930.

Kort Verhael van Nieuw-Nederlants Gelegenheit, Deughden, Natuurlijke Voorrechten en bijzondere bequaemheidt. Amsterdam, 1662.

Laer, Arnold J. F. van, ed. and trans. *The Correspondence of Jeremias van Rensselaer*. Albany: University of the State of New York Press, 1932.

———. *Documents Relating to New Netherland, 1624–1626, in the Henry E. Huntington Library*. San Marino, Calif.: Henry E. Huntington Library and Art Gallery Press, 1924.

———. *New York Historical Manuscripts: Dutch*. 4 vols. Baltimore: Genealogical Publishing Company, 1974.

———. *The Van Rensselaer–Bowier Manuscripts*. Albany: University of the State of New York Press, 1908.

Laet, Johannes de. *Iaerlijk Verhael van de verrichtinghen der Geoctroyeerde West-Indische Compagnie, in derthien boecken*. Ed. S. P. L'Honore Naber. 4 vols. The Hague: Martinus Nijhoff, 1931–37.

O'Callaghan, Edmund B. *Documentary History of the State of New York*. 4 vols. Albany: Weed, Parsons, 1849–51.

Purple, Samuel, ed. *Index to the Marriage Records of the Dutch Reformed Church in New Amsterdam and New York*. New York: Privately printed, 1890.

Stokes, Isaac Newton Phelps. *The Iconography of Manhattan Island, 1498–1909*. 6 vols. New York: R. H. Dodd, 1915–28.

Van der Donck, Adriaen. *A Description of New Netherland*. Ed. Thomas F. O'Donnell. Syracuse, N.Y.: Syracuse University Press, 1968.

———. *Remonstrance of New Netherland*. Ed. and trans. Edmund B. O'Callaghan. Albany: Weed, Parsons, 1856.

Versteeg, Dingman. *Manhattan in 1628 as Described in the Recently Discovered Autograph Letter of Jonas Michaëlius Written from the Settlement on the 18th of August of That Year, and Now First Published; with a Review of the Letter and an Historical Sketch of New Netherland to 1628*. New York: Dodd, Mead, 1904.

Bibliography

Wassenaer, Nicolaes van. *Historisch verhael alder ghedenck-weerdichste geschiedenissen die hier en daer in Europa, als in Duijtschlant, Vranckrijck, Enghelant, (Denemarcken) Hungarijen, Polen, (Sweden, Moscovien) Sevenbergen, Wallachien, Moldavien, Turckijen, (Zwitserland) en Nederlant, (in Asia . . .; in Africa . . .) van den beginne des jaers 1621: (tot Octobri 1629), voorgevallen sijn.* 17 vols. Amsterdam: Jan Evertsz Cloppenburgh en Ian Iansz., 1622–30.

West Indische Compagnie. *Remonstratie Van de Bewinthebbers der Nederlandsche West Indische Compagnie.* The Hague, 1660? Catalog No. 8755 of the Koninklijke Bibliotheek.

Winthrop, John. *Winthrop's Journal: "History of New England, 1630–1649."* Ed. James K. Hosmer. 2 vols. New York: Charles Scribner's Sons, 1908.

SECONDARY WORKS

Books

Archdeacon, Thomas. *New York City, 1664–1710: Conquest and Change.* Ithaca: Cornell University Press, 1975.

Ashley, Maurice. *England in the Seventeenth Century.* Baltimore: Penguin Books, 1961.

Bachman, Van Cleaf. *Peltries or Plantations: The Economic Policies of the Dutch West India Company in New Netherland, 1623–1639.* Baltimore: Johns Hopkins University Press, 1969.

Bailyn, Bernard. *The New England Merchants in the Seventeenth Century.* New York: Harper & Row, 1964.

Barbour, Violet. *Capitalism in Amsterdam in the 17th Century.* Ann Arbor: University of Michigan Press, 1966.

Boxer, Charles R. *The Dutch in Brazil, 1624–1654.* Oxford: Oxford University Press, 1957.

――――. *The Dutch Seaborne Empire: 1600–1800.* New York: Knopf, 1965.

Brodhead, John Romeyn. *History of the State of New York.* 2 vols. New York: Harper & Brothers, 1853–71.

Condon, Thomas J. *New York Beginnings: The Commercial Origins of New Netherland.* New York: New York University Press, 1968.

Davies, D. W. *A Primer of Dutch Seventeenth-Century Trade.* The Hague: Martinus Nijhoff, 1961.

De Forest, L. Effingham, and De Forest, Anne Lawrence. *Captain John Underhill: Gentleman Soldier of Fortune.* New York: De Forest Private Printing, 1934.

Dening, Dorothy. *The Settlement of the Connecticut Towns.* New Haven: Yale University Press, 1933.

Dillen, J. G. van. *Bronnen tot de Geschiedenis van het Bedrijfsleven en het Gildewesen van Amsterdam, 1512–1611.* 2 vols. The Hague: Martinus Nijhoff—Rijks Geschiedkundige Publicatien, 1929–33.

———. *Van Rijkdom en Regenten: Handboek tot de Economische en Sociale Geschiedenis van Nederland tijdens de Republiek.* The Hague: Martinus Nijhoff, 1970.

Eekhof, Albert. *De Hervormde Kerk in Noord-Amerika, 1624–1664.* 2 vols. The Hague: Martinus Nijhoff, 1913.

Fiske, John. *The Dutch and Quaker Colonies in America.* 2 vols. Boston: Houghton Mifflin, 1899.

Flick, Alexander C., ed. *History of the State of New York.* 10 vols. New York: Columbia University Press, 1933.

Forest, Mrs. Robert de. *A Walloon Family in America: Lockwood de Forest and His Forebears, 1500–1848; together with A Voyage to Guiana, Being the Journal of Jesse de Forest and His Colonists, 1623–1625.* 2 vols. Boston: Houghton Mifflin, 1914.

Geyl, Pieter. *The Netherlands in the Seventeenth Century: Part One, 1609–1648.* New York: Barnes and Noble, 1961.

———. *The Revolt of the Netherlands, 1555–1609.* London: Ernest Benn, 1958.

Goodman, A. V. *American Overture: Jewish Rights in Colonial Times.* Philadelphia: Jewish Publication Society of America, 1947.

Goslinga, Cornelis Ch. *The Dutch in the Caribbean and on the Wild Coast, 1580–1680.* Gainesville: University of Florida Press, 1971.

Grol, G. J. van. *De grondpolitiek in het West-Indische domein der generaliteit; een historische studie.* 3 vols. The Hague: Algemeen Landsdrukkerij, 1934–47.

Harrison, A. W. *The Beginnings of Arminianism to the Synod of Dort.* London: University of London Press, 1926.

Hart, Simon. *The Prehistory of the New Netherland Company: Amsterdam Notarial Records of the First Dutch Voyages to the Hudson.* Amsterdam: City of Amsterdam Press, 1959.

Huizinga, Johan. *Dutch Civilisation in the Seventeenth Century and Other Essays.* New York: Harper & Row, 1969.

Jessurun, J. Spinoza Catella. *Kiliaen van Rensselaer van 1623 tot 1636.* The Hague: Martinus Nijhoff, 1917.

Johnson, Amandus. *Swedish Settlements on the Delaware.* 2 vols. Philadelphia: Swedish Colonial Society, 1911.

Kammen, Michael. *Colonial New York: A History.* New York: Charles Scribner's Sons, 1975.

Kreider, H. J. *Lutheranism in Colonial New York*. Ann Arbor: Edwards, 1942.

Lambert, Audrey M. *The Making of the Dutch Landscape: An Historical Geography of the Netherlands*. London: Seminar Press, 1971.

Lemon, James T. *The Best Poor Man's Country: A Geographical Study of Early Southeastern Pennsylvania*. Baltimore: Johns Hopkins University Press, 1972.

Ligtenberg, Catharina. *Willem Usselinx*. Utrecht: A. Osterhoek Uitgeverij, 1914.

McNeill, William H. *Plagues and Peoples*. Garden City, N.Y.: Doubleday Anchor Books, 1976.

Motley, John Lothrop. *The Life and Death of John of Barneveld*. 2 vols. New York: Harper & Brothers, 1874.

Nissenson, S. G. *The Patroon's Domain*. New York: Columbia University Press, 1937.

Norton, Thomas Elliot. *The Fur Trade in Colonial New York, 1686–1776*. Madison: University of Wisconsin Press, 1974.

O'Callaghan, Edmund B. *The History of New Netherland; or, New York under the Dutch*. 2 vols. New York: D. Appleton, 1845–48.

Oppenheim, Samuel. *The Early History of the Jews in New York, 1654–1664*. New York: American Jewish Historical Society, 1909.

Parr, Charles McKew. *The Voyages of David de Vries*. New York: Crowell, 1969.

Penrose, Boies. *Travel and Discovery in the Renaissance, 1420–1620*. New York: Antheneum, 1962.

Perkins, Edwin J. *The Economy of Colonial America*. New York: Columbia University Press, 1980.

Pratt, John W. *Religion, Politics, and Diversity: The Church-State Theme in New York History*. Ithaca: Cornell University Press, 1967.

Raesly, E. L. *Portrait of New Netherland*. New York: Columbia University Press, 1945.

Rees, O. van. *Geschiedenis der staathuishoudkunde in Nederland tot het einde der achttiende eeuw*. 2 vols. Utrecht: Kemink en Zoon, 1868.

Ritchie, Robert C. *The Dukes's Province: A Study of New York Politics and Society*. Chapel Hill: University of North Carolina Press, 1977.

Shelley, Henry C. *John Underhill: Captain of New England and New Netherland*. New York: D. Appleton, 1932.

Smith, George L. *Religion and Trade in New Netherland: Dutch Origins and American Development*. Ithaca: Cornell University Press, 1973.

Snyderman, George S. *Concepts of Landownership among the Iroquois and Their Neighbors*. Washington, D.C.: Bureau of American Ethnography, 1951.

Sprunger, Keith L. *Dutch Puritanism: A History of English and Scottish Churches of the Netherlands in the Sixteenth and Seventeenth Centuries.* Leiden: E. J. Brill Uitgeverij, 1982.

Stearn, Esther Wagner, and Stearn, Allen E. *The Effect of Smallpox on the Destiny of the Amerindian.* Boston: B. Humphries, 1945.

Tex, Jan den. *Oldenbarnevelt.* 2 vols. Cambridge: Cambridge University Press, 1973.

Trelease, Allen W. *Indian Affairs in Colonial New York: The Seventeenth Century.* Ithaca: Cornell University Press, 1960.

Trevelyan, George M. *History of England.* 3 vols. Garden City, N.Y.: Doubleday, 1926. Reprint 1953.

Weslager, C. A. *The English on the Delaware, 1610–1682.* New Brunswick, N.J.: Rutgers University Press, 1967.

Wieder, F. C. *Het stichting van New York in Juli 1625: reconstructies en nieuwe gegevens ontleend aan de van Rappard documenten.* The Hague: Martinus Nijhoff, 1925.

———. *Onderzoek naar de oudste kaarten van de omgeving van New York.* Leiden: E. J. Brill, 1918.

Articles

Breen, Timothy H., and Foster, Stephen. "Moving to the New World: The Character of Early Massachusetts Immigration." *William and Mary Quarterly,* 3d ser., 30 (1973):189–222.

Campbell, Mildred. "Social Origins of Some Early Americans." In *Seventeenth-Century America: Essays in Colonial History,* ed. James Morton Smith, pp. 63–89. Chapel Hill: University of North Carolina Press, 1959.

Cohen, David. "How Dutch Were the Dutch of New Netherland?" *New York History* 62 (1981):43–60.

Cook, Shelburne, F. "Interracial Warfare and Population Decline among the New England Indians." *Ethnohistory* 20 (1973):1–24.

Diamond, Sigmund. "From Organization to Society: Virginia in the Seventeenth Century." *American Journal of Sociology* 63 (1958):457–75.

Dunn, Richard S. "Barbados Census of 1680." *William and Mary Quarterly,* 3d ser., 26 (1969):3–30.

Elias, Johan E. "De Tweede Engelsche Oorlog als het Keerpunt in onze Betrekkingen met Engeland." *Verhandelingen der Koninklijke Akademie van Wetenschappen te Amsterdam, Afdeeling Letterkunde,* N. S., 29 (1930):26–44.

Emmer, P. C. "De slavenhandel van en naar Nieuw Nederland." *Economische- en Sociaal-Historisch Jaarboek* 34 (1974):94–147.

Bibliography

Ernst, Hans. "Het Amsterdamse notarieel archief als bron voor de geschiedenis van Nieuw-Nederland." *Tijdschrift van de Koninklijke Nederlandse Oudheidkundige Bond* 84 (1985):142–50.

Friis, Henry R. "A Series of Population Maps of the Colonies and the United States, 1625–1790." *Geographical Review* 30 (1949):463–70.

Galenson, David W. "'Middling People' or 'Common Sort?': The Social Origins of Some Early Americans Reexamined." *William and Mary Quarterly*, 3d ser., 35 (1978):499–524.

Gehring, Charles. "Peter Minuit's Purchase of Manhattan Island—New Evidence." *De Halve Maen* 55 (Spring 1980):6ff.

Goodwin, Maud Wilder. "Fort Amsterdam in the Days of the Dutch." In *Historic New York: The Half Moon Papers*, ed. Alice Carrington Royce, Goodwin, and Ruth Putnam. 1:1–37. 4 vols. Port Washington, N.Y.: Ira J. Friedman, 1897. Reprint 1969.

Hart, Simon. "The Dutch and North America in the First Half of the Seventeenth Century: Some Aspects." *Mededelingen van de Nederlandse vereniging voor zeegeschiedenis* 20 (March 1970):5–17.

Hauptman, Lawrence M., and Knapp, Ronald G. "Dutch-Aboriginal Interaction in New Netherland and Formosa: An Historical Geography of Empire." *Proceedings of the American Philosophical Society* 121 (1977):166–82.

Houtte, J. A. van. "Het economisch verval van het Zuiden." *Algemeen Geschiedenis der Nederlanden* 5 (1952):193–200.

Jameson, J. Franklin. "Willem Usselinx, Founder of the Dutch and Swedish West India Companies." *Papers of the American Historical Association* 2 (1887).

Jansen, C. H. "Geschiedenis van de familie de Wolff: Sociale en economische facetten van de Republiek der Verenigde Nederlanden in de zeventiende eeuw." *Jaarboek van het Genootschap Amstelodamum* 56 (1964):131–55.

Kemperink, J. H. P. "Pieter Stuyvesant, waar en wanneer werd hij geboren?" *De Navorscher*, 98 te Jaargang, nr. 3 (1959):49–59.

McKinley, Albert S. "English and Dutch Towns of New Netherland." *American Historical Review* 6 (1900):1–18.

Martin, Calvin. "The European Impact on the Culture of a Northeastern Algonquian Tribe: An Ecological Interpretation." *William and Mary Quarterly*, 3d ser., 31 (1974):3–26.

Menard, Russell R. "From Servant to Freeholder: Status Mobility and Property Accumulation in Seventeenth-Century Maryland." *William and Mary Quarterly*, 3d ser., 30 (1973):37–64.

Menkman, W. R. "De Nederlanders in West-Africa en de Nieuwe Wereld." *Algemeen Geschiedenis der Nederlanden* 6 (1953):110–25.

Merwick, Donna. "Dutch Townsmen and Land Use: A Spatial Perspective on Seventeenth-Century Albany, New York." *William and Mary Quarterly*, 3d ser., 37 (1980):53–78.

O'Conner, John E. "The Rattle Watch of New Amsterdam." *De Halve Maen* 43 (1968):11ff.

Onderdonck, Henry. "The Rise and Growth of the Society of Friends on Long Island and in New York, 1657–1826." *Annals of Hempstead, 1643–1832.* (Hempstead, N.Y.: Lott van der Water, 1878).

Rink, Oliver A. "Company Management or Private Trade: The Two Patroonship Plans for New Netherland." *New York History* 59 (1978):5–26.

――――. "The People of New Netherland: Notes on Non-English Immigration to New York in the Seventeenth Century." *New York History* 62 (1981):5–42.

Schulte-Nordholt, J. W. "Nederlanders in Nieuw Nederland, de oorlog van Kieft." *Bijdragen en Mededelingen van het Historisch Genootschap* 80 (1966):38–94.

Weslager, C. A. "Did Minuit Buy Manhattan Island from the Indians?" *De Halve Maen* 43 (October 1968):5–6.

White, Philip L. "Municipal Government Comes to Manhattan." *New-York Historical Society Quarterly* 37 (1953):146–57.

Woude, A. M. van der. "Variations in the Size and Structure of the Household in the United Provinces of the Netherlands in the Seventeenth and Eighteenth Centuries." In *Household and Family in Past Time*, ed. Peter Laslett, pp. 299–318. Cambridge: Cambridge University Press, 1972.

Wright, Langdon G. "Local Government and Central Authority in New Netherland." *New-York Historical Society Quarterly* 57 (1973):7–29.

Index

I have adopted the Dutch convention of alphabetizing family names according to their principal capitalization. Kiliaen van Rensselaer is thus listed as Rensselaer, Kiliaen van, but Adriaen Van der Donck is listed as Van der Donck, Adriaen.

Index

Index

Index

Library of Congress Cataloging-in-Publication Data

Rink, Oliver A., 1947–
   Holland on the Hudson.

   Bibliography: p.
   Includes index.
   1. New York (State)—History—Colonial period, ca. 1600–1775. 2. Dutch—
New York (State)—History—17th century. I. Title.
F122.1.R56   1986   974.7'02   86-2317
ISBN 0-8014-1866-6 (alk. paper)